Hierarchical structures and social value

Hierarchical structures and social value

The creation of Black and Irish identities in the United States

RICHARD WILLIAMS
Department of Sociology
SUNY Stony Brook

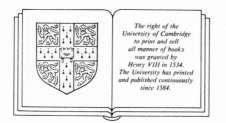

The right of the
University of Cambridge
to print and sell
all manner of books
was granted by
Henry VIII in 1534.
The University has printed
and published continuously
since 1584.

CAMBRIDGE UNIVERSITY PRESS

Cambridge

New York   Port Chester   Melbourne   Sydney

Published by the Press Syndicate of the University of Cambridge
The Pitt Building, Trumpington Street, Cambridge CB2 1RP
40 West 20th Street, New York, NY 10011, USA
10 Stamford Road, Oakleigh, Melbourne 3166, Australia

First published 1990

Printed in the United States of America

Library of Congress Cataloging-in-Publication Data
Williams, Richard E., 1947–
Hierarchical structures and social value: the creation of Black
and Irish identities in the United States / Richard Williams.
p.   cm.
Includes bibliographical references.
ISBN 0-521-35147-2
1. Ethnicity – United States.   2. Afro-Americans – Social
conditions.   3. Irish Americans – Social conditions.   4. Social
structure – United States.   5. Social values.   I. Title.
E184.A1W48   1990
305.8'96073 – dc20   90–33316
                                                                   CIP

British Library Cataloguing in Publication Data
Williams, Richard
Hierarchical structures and social value: the creation of
Black and Irish identities in the United States.
1. United States. Black persons. Social conditions,
history
2. United States. Irish immigrants. Social conditions,
history
I. Title
305.89162073

ISBN 0-521-35147-2 hardback

To my mother
Albertha Smalls-Williams
and in memory of my brother
Dan Williams (1934–1990)

Contents

Preface

In this book I investigate the historical processes that created the marks of *race* and *ethnicity* in the United States. I concentrate upon two situations, the processes through which those who became the *Black* race and those who became the *Irish* ethnic group were incorporated into the United States with specific social values. (I have italicized these terms to emphasize the fact that they are social constructs, rather than primordial or ahistorical categories.)

I intend to establish a relationship between social structures and the social value of what are characterized as racial and ethnic groups by starting with the assumption that the Black race and Irish ethnic group are sociohistorical creations. Thus, their identities can be established in a more general manner than if race and ethnicity are taken as given presocial groups that are merely contained by social systems. In so doing we can relate what has been characterized as race and ethnicity in the abstract to the existence of hierarchically stratified social systems.

My point of departure therefore is the notion that race and ethnicity are social designations rather than natural categories. However, I am not as concerned with proving their social basis as I am with clarifying the macrophenomena that provided the context in which these constructs have been transformed into *natural* phenomena.

My conscious choice of categories for this analysis are the Blacks and the Irish. Within the logic of the argument, *White* and *American* also of necessity enter the discussion. The choice of the Blacks and the Irish however, is not arbitrary. In keeping with my reliance on Durkheim's insistence upon "the importance of frameworks of knowledge being built at the inception of a society," the Black/White dichotomy repre·sents the fundamental racial distinction that eventually became embodied through law in the early stages of the development of the United States (Durkheim and Mauss, 1963; Schwartz, 1981).

Similarly, the Irish/American dichotomy represents the association of one of the largest groups (composed of sectors of the Irish population) with an ethnic distinction that migrated to the United States during the nineteenth century. Of equal importance is the fact that the population that became characterized as the Irish consisted of the first mass migration of a population to the United States primarily as wage laborers. The cases of the Blacks and the Irish are therefore of sufficient historical importance tc help us understand how race and ethnicity became social realities in the society while taking the form of mystified natural categories in our minds.

My objective is thus to describe and analyze the processes that merged structural and moral inequality within hierarchically stratified societies, rather than to make comparisons between Blacks and the Irish in the United States. I have chosen *ethnicity* and *race* as the specific forms of classification that represent those inequalities, while the dichotomies Black/White and Irish/American are the real world embodiments of those instances.

Although the theoretical implications of this work are clearly intended to apply to ethnicity and race, that is by no means its sole focus. My larger intention is to give further insights into the manifestation of marks of vertical classification as a means of understanding how inequality generally impacts upon human beings in social systems. To do so, I rely primarily upon secondary historical sources as illustrations rather than as proof of these ideas. This enterprise, therefore, consists of descriptions and analyses of social processes that fundamentally affect our identities, attitudes, and, most important, our life chances.

In Chapter 1 I introduce the notion of vertical classification and discuss how it generally functions within stratified social systems. Race and ethnicity are introduced as specific instances of marks of vertical classification. I also discuss some differences between viewing race and ethnicity within this theoretical framework as opposed to how these phenomena are viewed within the sociological tradition. Chapter 2 discusses the European world system, England, West Africa, and Ireland in relationship to vertical classification. In addition, seventeenth- through nineteenth-century England, Africa, Ireland, and the United States are located within the context of the world system. These social systems are the contexts for the racial and ethnic categories that concern us.

In Chapter 3 I analyze the English search for an empire and its eventual impact upon the settlement of the Virginia colony. This analysis provides information about the hierarchical context within which the United States was born. In Chapter 4 I discuss how the social structure of the United States was initially created. There I show that, contrary to popular belief, the United States was from its inception a hierarchically structured social system. In Chapter 5 I discuss West African social structures to demonstrate that there were hierarchically stratified societies in West Africa prior to European contact. This provides an arena in which to discuss possible group conflicts within some of those societies. In Chapter 6 I analyze the internal features of those societies. Within the context of hierarchically stratified social systems, I discuss the logic of sectors of the elite in West Africa engaging in the trading of surplus nonelite members of their social system. Having laid out the context that provided the conditions for the supply of a labor force from Africa, I move back to the United States during the seventeenth century in Chapter 7. There I discuss the creation of the slave labor slot in Virginia and demonstrate that the colony's unfree labor needs were structural rather than inherently attached to Africans.

In Chapter 8 I turn to the Irish case, first discussing the social structure of the United States prior to the mass migration from Ireland during the nineteenth century. I then show how the need for cheap unskilled labor in the United States made mass migration a social necessity during that period. In Chapter 9 I turn to the counterpart of this historical process by analyzing the historical circumstances through which Ireland became a peripheral sector of the seventeenth-century European world economy. During that period, the stage was set for fundamental transformations in the relations between Ireland and England as well as between social groups within those societies. In Chapter 10 I look at the specific details of the political and economic responses to the potato blight in nineteenth-century Ireland. There I view the resulting emigration as a structural conflict rather than a religious conflict or a response to natural phenomena. Finally, in Chapter 11 I present a theoretical review and a further historical discussion of how race and ethnicity have been transformed in the collective consciousness of the people of the United States. This discussion centers around the significance of the insights gained from the analysis of the creation of ethnicity and race as specific forms of vertical classification within our general understanding of hierarchically stratified social structures.

Without the intellectual and general help of Eviatar Zerubavel and my wife Sonia Ospina, this project would never have been accomplished. Their support can never be repaid. Philip McMichael has been an intellectual supporter for many years. Despite some differences, his sense of the world is also expressed in this final product. Terence K. Hopkins provided his time at critical moments. My thanks also to Phil Alkana, whose copyediting made this a more polished product.

List of figures and tables

1 Race and ethnicity: forms of vertical classification

This book is a study of one form through which social values become attached to individuals, resulting in the development of a group identity. The text will explain the existence of inequality within social systems and will focus specifically on the historical conditions that allowed social values to become attached to two particular sectors of the population, Blacks and the Irish within the United States. The conceptual context of these processes is the European world system (with Ireland, England, West Africa, and the United States as interconnected units), whereas the United States, including its formation and development, is the specific state structure within which the development of group identities is analyzed.

By extension, this work is premised upon questioning the sociological usefulness of *race* and *ethnic* categories as they are presently conceived. Such is the case because, as this book attempts to demonstrate, they distort historical and social realities. To the extent that they distort, they are dysfunctional as conceptual guides for sociological work. The concern here, however, is not with replacing those terms. I will in fact utilize them as indicators of social value and structural place. Rather my concern is simply to call into question their use in an unreflexive manner.

Social value is here used in the Durkheimian sense in which value is socially attached to groups as well as to structural positions via status duality (good or bad) and spatial duality (high or low). In this sense the sacred (good status, high structure) and the profane (bad status, low structure) are the two levels of value duality within a system of vertical classification. All individuals and groups are then placed in either the sacred or the profane position. Theoretically, they are mutually exclusive categories. From this perspective, vertical classification is conceived of as the rigid segregation of human beings into categories of good or bad and high or low (Durkheim and Mauss, 1963; Schwartz, 1981).[1]

My formulation of the issue takes the rigid segregation, suggested by Schwartz (1981) in the sacred/profane split, as one historical moment in the attachment of social value. It is a critical moment, but not the totality of the process of social value. If vertical classification is perceived as reflecting a strict demarcation between the sacred and the profane, however, it then only provides us with a single moment of

1

human interaction. At that moment divisions are absolute and each entity can be in only one category, hence that absolute perception of vertical classification abstracts people from the flux of their history. Such an abstraction is a frozen moment, however, whereas life is fluid. This point is important because it provides us with another reason to move away from the assumption that racial and ethnic attitudes are reflections of human values that are fixed. At the same time it allows for the possibility of assuming that there are links between changes in attitudes and changes in social systems.

Within the context of this study, skin pigmentation (a natural feature of humans) is one embodiment of the sacred/profane split in the U.S. system of vertical classification.[2] The combination of skin pigmentation, which is a natural mark, with culture, a social mark, is another embodiment of this split within the vertically classified system of the United States.

In the case of ethnicity the absolute split in a system of rigid vertical classification is replaced by a more ambiguous system of classification. This occurs when one of the segregated entitites of the either/or polarity is changed through the development of distinctions within one or both of the polar opposites. When this occurs, we move conceptually from a simple dual polarity (A or B) to a split within one or both of the polar opposites. Thus the possibilities move from A or B, to A and A_1 or B, or to A or B and B_1, or to A and A_1 or B and B_1. A_1 and B_1 symbolize a split within the simple polar opposites.

In the above manner distinct races, as conceptual ideals, become the classification of human beings into rigidly held segregated categories, such that they appear to be independent groups of people. The conceptual ideal of ethnicity assumes a no less rigid split across the original dualistic boundary, but a less rigid split within one of the independent groups. Thus in the context of racial and ethnic thinking, there can never be one race or ethnic group; they are, by definition, relational concepts based upon the more or less rigid segregation of two or more entities. Rigid segregation (moral and structural) can be viewed as a system of controlled interactions between groups that are assumed to be independent.

In addition to the necessary dualism of race, however, it is also logically clear that ethnicity cannot exist without race. Without race, the structure of ethnicity becomes the same as the race structure (A or B).[3] Race can therefore be seen as logically and socially prior to ethnicity, and ethnicity as logically and socially dependent upon race. Thus the two concepts are fused in logic as well as in the social world. This provides the sense of process that is lacking from the general context of vertical classification (Schwartz, 1981).

By concentrating upon one way in which social values are attached to individuals in the process of group formation, we are concentrating upon one way in which race and ethnicity – both requiring classification along structural and moral lines – are created in society. In relying upon the notion of vertical classifications, we can see that their creation embodies the internalization of moral values by all members of society based on a specific feature of the human body (e.g., skin pigmentation) that is linked to natural distinctions (e.g., dark and light).

In addition to the general acceptance of moral values, there is also a link between natural features and the structural position of the distinct groups in the social system. Thus, in the United States the natural features are seen as linked both to moral value and to structural position.

The relational basis of race and ethnic identity gets lost

The creation of ethnicity and race affects all members of a given social system, because this creation results from the formation of a vertical polarity to represent a relationship based upon economic, moral, and social inequality within a specific social system. This is an extension of the notion that there can never be just one race or ethnic group. When social groups are conceived as having developed independently, however, the assumption is that there can be only one race or only one ethnic group (i.e., vertical polarity as a relationship based upon structured inequality is ignored). This is the complete manner by which individual populations are assumed to exist as natural categories and are experienced as polar opposite categories of human beings.

The assumption that a specific social classification of human beings forms a natural category can easily occur when the natural features used as the basis for grouping individuals becomes transformed into the label for the moral and structural value of all individuals with that natural attribute (Needham, 1979). For instance, in the United States when reference is made to the race question or the race problem, it is generally acknowledged that race is a code word for Black. This formulation does not acknowledge the fact that the question or the problem is related to the entire range of those classified by race (i.e., all members of the society). In this specific example, the issue becomes what to do with the morally low and socially down group that is assumed to exist, independently, in the midst of the "normal" population. The morally low and socially down are referred to as a race in a non-relational manner, whereas the majority is composed of people in some generic sense. This type of thinking clearly illustrates the generally accepted assumption of the primordial existence of race (i.e., its independent existence).[4]

But the sense of the natural/primordial (i.e., structural and moral values resulting from nature rather than being socially constructed) can persist in general thinking even when at least two races are acknowledged. Such is the case when racial names become substitutes for the existence of structural inequality as a fundamental feature of society. In this instance one sees structural inequality as a consequence of the existence of distinct races, rather than recognizing that race is a reflection of existing structural inequality.[5] The Kerner Commission Report (U.S. National Advisory Commission on Civil Disorders, 1969), for example, talks about the danger to the United States of becoming two societies, one White and well off, the other Black and poor. Confusion is generated here by the use of racial names because it implies that if the society were all White there would be no poor. This could only be the case, however, if the structure of the social system itself were nonhierarchial. Even within the context of a segregated society, however, stratification still exists for those who are White. The use of race names does not invite an investigation of these structural issues. This has been the case, although the literature on stratification clearly indicates that both the larger society and the White subcategory is hierarchically arranged (Blau and Duncan, 1967; Kanter, 1977; Baron, 1984).[6]

It is therefore at least partially understandable how the social nature of ethnicity and race, like other socially defined designations of vertical classification, can get lost in our daily lives. This loss is manifested in the notion that racial and ethnic groups are composed of homogenous individuals classified by a natural mark.[7] Homogeneity here means that all individuals in any one group are morally and structurally more similar to each other than to any individual in the polar opposite group. This latter representation can also be seen in the Kerner Commission Report. The report conveys an image of Whites who are all well off and Blacks who are all poor. There is no room in this formulation for poor Whites or well-off Blacks. In addition, there is no room in it for Native Americans or Asians and quite a few other populations.

The representation of ethnic and racial groups as homogeneous is important in generating the sense of polar opposites between social groups. What is vital for our purposes is the way in which the establishment of those opposites serves to distort social facts by attempting to represent the human group as a series of separate categories that are internally homogenous. The use of attributes from nature as the mark of those groups provides the logic for this transformation. Behind the marks from nature, however, differential power relations assign individuals to specific structural positions within the stratified social system.[8]

Social systems in the making: the context of vertical classification

The ideal context for the analysis of the creation of ethnicity and race and of their impact upon all members of a social system is a social system in the making. Durkheim (Schwartz 1981:16) states that:

society builds a framework of knowledge only at its inception, for only in the most primitive stages of social life are group boundaries clear and compelling enough to serve as a model for mental categories.

Although Durkheim is here making reference to a very early time in human history, Douglas (1982), and Schwartz (1981) have argued persuasively that the logic Durkheim derived from those early societies is applicable to human existence generally. This is not to imply that all of Durkheim's proposals are valid, but to the extent that his propositions are valid, they are general, rather than time-and-space-specific, notions.

The concern here is with two social systems in the making, the modern world system and that of the United States. I contend that the creation and re-creation of the modern world system through the absorption of distinct geographical regions of the world and the creation of the United States provide excellent contexts for the analysis of the building of those frameworks of knowledge characterized as ethnicity and race. The analysis of the creation of the United States as a social system includes its absorption into the modern world system through the utilizing of land from one region of the world and of people from many regions of the world.

Although the concern is generally with the world system and the United States in the making, the focus of the creation of ethnicity and race within those contexts forces us to concentrate upon specific entities within them. Therefore, this work looks at the creation of the Black and the White races, which are manifested in low versus high moral values and low versus high structural positions. It also looks at the creation of the Irish and the American ethnic groups, which are also manifested in low versus high moral values as well as structural positions.

With the world system as the frame of reference, West Africa (sixteenth to nineteenth centuries), England (sixteenth to nineteenth centuries), and the United States (seventeenth century to the present) are the areas with which we will be concerned when looking at race creation. Ethnicity creation will be looked at in the areas of Ireland (from the seventeenth to the nineteenth centuries), England (from the seventeenth to the nineteenth centuries), and the United States (from the nineteenth century to the present). With the United States as the frame of reference race creation will be looked at with Blacks and Whites as categories from the seventeenth century to the present. Ethnicity creation will be looked at with Irish and American as categories from the nineteenth century to the present. Though conceptually distinct here, it is assumed, as indicated above, that there is a great deal of overlap between ethnicity and race creation within the frames of reference.

Vertical classification: power, trauma, and the creation of group identity

Vertical classification implies that moral value and structural position correlate so that a specific spatial position implies a specific moral position and vice versa. The dualistic relationship must therefore be looked at in relationship to power if a full understanding of race and ethnicity is to be achieved. Power is here viewed as a physical as well as a moral (or social) force. It is thus important to note that the dualism that operates as vertical polarity exists as an integral component of power. Although power exists as a physical force that one group uses to dominate another group, it also exists as the ability to get others to adhere to one's will through moral suasion. In the latter case, there is no overt show of force (Lukes, 1974; Weber 1978).

Thus, the use of power generates the conditions for structural inequality (the assignment of individuals to unequal structural positions within a social system). The use of power as a form of ideological manipulation is not, however, seen as the fundamental mechanism by which the process of legitimating structural inequality is accomplished. Rather, the existence of groups of individuals with similar natural marks (having been assigned specific social values) and in similar structural positions (those positions having been assigned specific social values) serves as a daily reminder of the link among marks, specific social values, and structural positions. Power thus remains in the background, although it is a critical feature in the maintenance of vertically classified social systems that are spatially and morally coherent (Berger and Luckmann, 1967; Lukes, 1974; Schwartz, 1981).

We can see significant instances of the use of power in the specific instance of the creation of race and ethnicity as forms of vertical polarities in the world system and in the United States. For instance, when English adventurers connected to the Crown took the land of the aboriginal population of North America as well as the land of the Catholic population of Ireland, power was utilized to bring new lands into the European world system. In addition, power was utilized when sectors of the West African population were captured and shipped to North America to labor upon the land. It was also utilized when sectors of the

Irish population were pushed from that country in the midst of starvation and disease. Those uses of power set the conditions for the creation of race and ethnicity in the United States, but they also were essential for the expansion of the European world system and the creation of the United States. Thus, the creation of race and ethnicity and the creation of the stratified world and U.S. social systems occurred at the same time. Unequal access and use of power were critical to the creation of the stratified social systems. Similarly, they were critical to the assignment of sectors of older stratified social systems (societies of West Africa and Ireland prior to their incorporation into the world system) into the lower structural position of the newly created nation-state and world systems.

The sociology of ethnicity and race: the view of vertical classification

The concern here is with how race and ethnicity are conceptualized (i.e., how their existence as an important feature of the social world is understood). Placing the literature into categories such as the assimilationist model, or the class model, or the internal colonial model is therefore here less important than considering to what degree do those utilizing the categories of race and ethnicity conceive of them as social facts. Within this context, there are two sociological perspectives that distinguish the understanding of ethnicity and race as entities in the contemporary United States.

One perspective, implicitly or explicitly, assumes that the social values attributed to marks by which individuals are classified into groups existed out there in the world prior to the constitution of social systems by populations with different degrees of power (see Jordan, 1968). Beyond Jordan, however, there exists an implicit belief among some scholars that antagonism toward those who are different is a natural feature of human existence (see Warner and Lunt, 1941; Myrdal, 1962; Carmichael and Hamilton, 1967; Glazer and Moynihan, 1970; Farley, 1984; Schuman, Steeh, and Bobo, 1985; Farley and Allen, 1987). Farley (1984), Schuman, Steeh, and Bobo (1985), and Farley and Allen (1987) are interesting contemporary reflections of the notion of inherent conflict. They merely report the outcome of the opinions of individuals who have accepted their racial identity without any discussion of the social basis of that identity, thus implying that they take those opinions to be inherent to individuals rather than socially constructed.

The other perspective, implicitly or explicitly, assumes that although racial and ethnic differences exist in the world, they only become manifest through the use of power in a stratified social system.[9] Park's (1950) conception of intergroup contacts as moving through a "race relations cycle" of "contact, competition, accommodation and assimilation" sets the tone for this perspective. According to him, each of the four stages of the cycle results in the social definition of race relations. Cox (1948), Patterson (1967, 1982), Van den Berghe (1967), Gordon (1971), Geschwender (1978), Wilson (1978, 1987), and Bonacich (1980) also reflect Park's social change perspective. Students of race, but less so of ethnicity, have moved away from the assimilation perspective, while maintaining the notion that change in relations is inherent to the interactions of the groups that have been assumed to exist prior to contact. Thus, the Jordan perspective can be characterized as the natural approach to race and ethnicity, whereas the Park perspective can generally be characterized as the social construction (structural) approach.

In essence, however, in both the structural approach and the natural approach research is carried out in a similar way (Geschwender, 1978; Wilson, 1978, 1987). This occurs when the structural approach takes a one-dimensional (noncomparative) perspective and thus becomes satisfied with asserting that race and ethnicity are social constructs, but does not then carry that assertion to its logical conclusion by questioning the extent to which ethnic and racial marks are themselves arbitrary.

However, the gap between the accepted truth of race and ethnicity as social categories and their use in practice does not appear to result from a lack of sincerity or from a lack of effort. Rather, it appears to result from the insufficient reexamination of the historical facts out of which those categories arose. What is at issue then is not merely placing groups in their historical contexts, but analyzing how group names, while providing the appearances of continuity and homogeneity within the thereby fractured entity of human beings, are in fact neither continuous nor homogenous (Weber, 1978). This can only be established by moving back in time and seriously grappling with the manner by which the categories of race and ethnicity became reflections of the inequality of social systems in general. Notice that this is distinct from saying that these categories are merely instances of unfairness or oppression based upon physical and cultural distinctions within otherwise fair social systems.[10]

My position is distinct from both the natural and structural perspectives. This third position, like the structural approach, stresses the power basis of race and ethnicity, but also calls attention to the fact that physical and cultural differences are two marks among many possible marks that exist among human beings. Such being the case, physical and cultural variations can be seen as similar to many other variations among human beings that carry no social significance.

This third position, therefore, not only points out the social basis of race and ethnicity, but it also stresses the need to comprehend fully the

extent to which race and ethnicity are reflections of the unequal structure of societies, as opposed to responses to particular marks that are
natural to all human beings. In this sense it is possible to suggest that
social systems not only teach their citizens how to respond to existing
identities (or groups), but rather that those identities are being created
at the same time that citizens are being taught how to respond to them.

What is at issue in this third position is the context in which race and
ethnicity, once accepted as natural entities, become substitutes for inequalities within the social structure. Also at issue is the extent to which
socially determined distinctions (premised upon high and low social
value) among the entire human group are inevitable within hierarchically stratified social systems. Those distinctions also become accepted
as real when those categories used as group labels are utilized without an
elaboration of the extent to which those labels already reflect the fractur-
ing of the human group (Durkheim and Mauss, 1963).

Under this formulation of the social construction of race and ethnicity, all sectors of a social system are affected by the existence of race and
ethnicity. However, most studies of those entities do not consistently
take this into account. Rather, the tendency, whether from a natural or a
structural perspective, is to slip into the usage of those categories as if
they naturally existed on a different plane from other logical, but less
recognized, categories by which human beings are classified.[11]

In this third approach, race and ethnicity are seen as specific instances
of a general social invention that utilizes certain marks to place sectors
of people at the bottom of a social system. Powerless and without rights,
their labor can then be utilized either entirely without remuneration or
at below market remuneration. By extension, other sectors of the human group are in the position to benefit greatly from the disadvantages
of the powerless. Weber (1978:386) characterizes this situation as "mo-
nopolistic closure." This use of power in regard to race and ethnic marks
is not the only instance in which physical differences among human
beings have become social marks within contemporary society. Rather,
all socially defined marks (e.g., gender, hair color, eye color, height)
can, and clearly have, served a similar role in human society. The critical
issue, therefore, is the existence of hierarchial stratification as the basis
of social systems, not the specific mark that is ultimately utilized to
legitimate social inequality.

I contend that the natural and structural approaches to race and
ethnicity have been relegated to the theoretical ghetto of the social
sciences precisely because they ignore the extent to which race and
ethnicity are specific instances of marks that reflect hierarchically stratified social systems. Their use of ethnic and racial categories imposes
severe limitations upon generalizing about the human condition. Their

use, in essence, has maintained the notion that race and ethnicity are natural categories and that there is no need to look at entire social systems when race or ethnicity are discussed.

This approach explains why the sociological study of ethnicity and race lacks a general theory. This deficiency results partially because the literature accepts ethnicity and race either as natural categories or as the only logical instances of vertical classification. In the first case vertical classification (the form of the stratified social system within which race and ethnic groups interact) is ignored because the assumption is that groups of people in the world are classified by nature. The second case acknowledges vertical classification, but ignores the multitude of instances of possible marks other than skin color by which moral and structural value can be placed upon and internalized by individuals. In both cases, the full extent to which race and ethnic categories reflect the larger social context is diminished.[12]

However, this third position has to be carefully stated. Throughout contemporary society there are clear signs that skin pigmentation and place of ethnic origin have social consequences for individuals in the United States.[13] This present reality appears to provide strong evidence for the assertion that the social values attached to skin pigmentation and culture in the society are natural. To ask for a discussion of this assertion is like asking for a discussion of why most people are right-handed or why up is the symbol of positive social value and down is the symbol of negative social value (Hertz, 1973; Schwartz, 1981). These attributes – including race and ethnicity – might be considered a waste of time because they appear to be natural attributes rather than attitudes which human beings, at a specific historical moment, developed and continue to reenforce within specific social contexts.

But by looking at human existence with a larger gaze, it becomes clear that skin pigmentation has not always had the significance it presently does as the social and moral mark of inequality.[14] Prior to skin pigmentation taking its place front and center as the measuring rod of human value, there have been and continue to be other measures such as age (adult/child), gender (male/female), culture (civilized/barbarians), religion (saved/damned), and language (ours/foreign) that function in social systems as marks of status (Cox, 1948; Engels, 1968).[15] What these categories have in common is their historical role as labels for the polarities of good/bad, sacred/profane, rich/poor, and value/valueless.

Indeed, skin pigmentation was not a significant measure prior to a specific historical moment (Cox, 1948; Snowden, 1983). Even if Jordan's (1968) position – that prior attitudes influenced later action – holds, it is still the case that skin pigmentation is not an inherent measure of human value. As Snowden (1983:99) states in reference to ancient Greece:

blacks suffered no detrimental distinctions that excluded them from opportunities – occupational, economic, or cultural – available to other new-comers in alien lands.

Furthermore Snowden provides ample justification of this statement, thus allowing us to conclude that skin pigmentation must have been created as a form of vertical classification rather than having existed in that form from time immemorial.

If it was created, why was it created and how was it created? Shils (1967) states:

one of the simplest and most obvious reasons for the great importance color has assumed in the self-imagery of many peoples is that it is an easy means of distinguishing between those from the periphery and those from the center of particular societies and of the world society.

He correctly points out that color has assumed importance, as opposed to permanently having importance. However, he also links skin pigmentation to prior distinctions (i.e., the center versus the periphery both in the world and in specific societies).

That link leads to some logical conclusions, such as that the periphery and center represent specific forms of vertical classification and that people in the center and people in the periphery can be distinguished from each other by the natural pigmentation of their skin. It thus leads to the conclusion that people of one skin pigment type cluster in the center, whereas people of another cluster in the periphery. Given this clustering of body features along a socially created system of vertical classification, the tendency is to replace the initial vertical classification (the structural position) with its neatly and naturally divided body marks. In this manner, skin pigmentation is seen as providing the basis for domination (Shils, 1967).

Although this approach is logical, its insistence upon the relationship between structural position and skin color is premature. It implies that color is the only, or at least the dominant, mark that distinguishes those in peripheral from those in center regions. In addition, and of extreme importance, is the fact that there is no clear sense of how centers and peripheries get created. Nor is there any discussion of the relationship between centers and peripheries. If skin pigmentation is one of various socially convenient designations for distinguishing between people, then one must logically ask, Is skin pigmentation the object of interaction (an independent variable) or is it merely the mark (an intervening variable) by which a more general type of interaction is being defined?

Shils (1967), like others, ignores a wide range of possible alternative approaches to understanding the interactions of human beings by so readily settling upon the importance of skin pigmentation. Two points need to be addressed here. One is why marks of vertical classification have persisted. Hegel (1945), Weber (1978), and Schwartz (1978) have explored this issue. The answer that is currently accepted appears to be that as long as social systems are stratified there will be marks that are utilized to classify those sectors of the social system who have access to societal rights from those who do not have access to the full range of those rights. More important for my purposes is the question of why and how, given the persistence of inequality in social systems, skin pigmentation and place of origin have become the modern measures in the United States and in much of the world by which to determine who has rights and who does not. This question clearly assumes that skin pigmentation and geographical differences are not the only potential measures of vertical classification.

The use of skin pigmentation and cultural distinctions as measures of vertical classification can indeed be seen as one among a wide range of natural distinctions between the world's peoples. They then reflect choices made from a context that has other possible marks that could perform the same function of classifying human beings. Again, just some of these alternative measures are hair (length, color, texture), height, foot size, hand size, handedness, gender, breast size, age, condition of teeth, eyes (shape, color, vision), head (shape, size), body (shape, weight, condition), and nose (shape, size, condition).

It is clear that some of the above measures are more malleable than others. It is also the case, however, that science and technology are making most, if not all, of them even more malleable over time. Therefore, characteristics that in the past have been considered natural and unchangeable (e.g., gender and eye color) have become sources of wealth for scientists (primarily medical doctors) who can transform parts of the body from a nondesired to a desired state.[16]

However, procedures designed to transform natural features of the body from the profane to the sacred will never, by definition, in and of themselves meet with full social approval. A sector of the profane population might embrace such a transformation, but the response on the part of those having the sacred body mark might be to develop more refined measures of what is sacred and what is profane. How long has one had the particular characteristic (a grandfather clause) could then become a critical social factor. The prefix "nouveau" is a reflection of the manner in which attempts at equality between sacred and profane marks are dealt with psychologically. This is a further indication of the reality of power that underlies the determination of the social value of physical features (Weber, 1978).

What is significant about all potential measures of vertical classification, however, is that they are everywhere carried around as an integral part of all human beings. Therefore, within the context of a social system, there can be a continuous evaluation of individuals based upon the permanence of the mark that has been designated, through the use of power, as the measure of moral and structural values. Schwartz (1981:75) makes this point generally when he states:

To consider each of its manifestations as a separate "shout" adds clarity to the sense in which vertical classification represents a multi-channel medium of communications. Since each channel is "saying the same thing," there must be "channel congruence," i.e, consistency between meanings broadcast at different metaphoric "frequencies."[17]

It is possible to think about vertical classification as consisting of separate manifestations precisely because of the social value placed upon permanent marks. The separate manifestations are essentially the attribution of similar social value in distinct contexts to a mark that has been socially designated as either positive or negative. Hence, a sacred (positive) response in one context presupposes a sacred (positive) response in all contexts. The degree of channel congruence is then a measure of how effectively a particular indicator (mark) of vertical polarity functions in that capacity. As a result, channel congruence also serves as an indicator of the degree of social change over time.[18]

Only by being acutely aware of potential marks other than skin pigmentation can there be a serious investigation of why skin pigmentation and cultural distinctions have become central features of social systems. By taking skin pigmentation for granted as the most logical or the only possible mark of societal inequality, the two traditional sociological approaches to race and ethnicity have tended to ignore the historical basis of those classifications as categories by which to divide the human group.

Natural body marks and marks placed on the body

Because vertical classification requires and creates a permanent visual symbol, there is the tendency to distinguish between an obvious physical difference and a subtle physical difference. It is important to note, however, that what is obvious and what is subtle are matters of social convention rather than natural fact. Hence, although the degree of skin pigmentation is seen as an obvious difference, foot size is seen as subtle difference merely because there are few, if any, social consequences of foot size.[19] It is also important to keep in mind that nonnatural distinctions can also take on the force of distinctions that are as strong as those that natural parts of the human body have. In the last analysis, human beings have the capacity to make distinctions socially significant.

Distinctions of dress, such as those made by placing symbols on clothes (scarlet letters, yellow stars, pink stars), tattooing (numbers, objects), scarring the body, wearing jewelry, and wearing makeup, are a few methods utilized in social systems to set apart certain individuals by means of a clear mark of distinction. It is also true that structural positions within a social system leave their marks on individuals. In that manner a group mark is also formed. Class marks, for example, are manifested in such diverse forms as dress patterns, body posture, speech patterns and general behavior. Such marks easily become accepted as the natural features of individuals within a particular structural position in a society.

Of course, all natural body marks and marks placed on the body affect all members of any society. It is thus true that a mark of any derivation provides a social value for all individuals in a specific social system. In this manner, everyone can theoretically be placed on a scale as measured by their skin pigmentation, type of body scar, symbols on their clothes, or posture.[20]

Whether marks are found upon clothing or are a natural feature of the human body, they can function as clear and fixed indicators of the mark of social value and the valueless mark. In this manner individuals become a living measuring rod by carrying the symbol of social and moral worth around with them. The essence of vertical classification is the existence of a mark by which to legitimate the placement of persons in high and low positions within a social structure. The focus of the approach to race and ethnicity taken in this book is that they represent specific historical and structural instances of marks of vertical classification. We now turn to a discussion of the specific social contexts and historical moments in which skin pigmentation and culture related to Blacks and the Irish became socially significant in the United States.

2 Historical structures and social marks as systems of hierarchical classification

To get a clearer understanding of how skin pigmentation and culture became marks of vertical classification in the United States, we must initially discuss some of the similarities among groups defined by skin pigmentation (race, ethnicity) and the national context of those groups (nation-states – specifically the United States) as well as the international context in which the United States developed (i.e., the modern world system). I contend that the modern world system, nation-states, and race and ethnic categories are linked to each other through the existence of hierarchically stratified social systems. Beyond their high and low polarities, these entities are characterized by variations in moral/status value.

Similarities in how these three entities classify is therefore not accidental. The existence of vertical stratification and classification at the level of the world system is linked to vertical stratification and classification at the group level precisely by the existence of vertical stratification and classification at the level of the nation-state.

Classification at the level of the world system

Wallerstein (1974:15) starts his discussion of the creation of modern world systems by contrasting them with empires.[1] He points out that although both are hierarchically organized social systems, the units out of which empires are composed are held together by political (military) links, whereas the units of a world system are held together by economic links. In the latter case, political links do not disappear. Instead they become subordinate to economic links. The similarities as well as the differences between these two types of units are important in aiding our understanding of how skin pigmentation became used as the mark of the modern form of vertical classification.

At the general level, world systems and empires function to reproduce inequality (i.e., some goods and services that are traded have more value that others). This occurs despite the fact that many goods and services are important for all regions of world systems and empires. As is

15

the case with all forms of social classification, the value of items traded is not determined by nature. Rather, the value of products are socially determined through the use of power (Marx, 1974). It is therefore no accident that the value of traded items correlates with the vertical strata in which a region is located. Highly valued items are in the upper strata regions (more powerful state structures), whereas low valued items are in the lower strata regions (weaker or nonexistent state structures) of the world system.[2]

The shift in the basis of surplus flow from military power to economic power indicates that the flow of surplus from weak to strong regions of world systems is functional for the existence of such systems (Stinchcombe, 1978).[3] If this is indeed the case, we would expect to see similar social strata of the world system performing similar functions (producing surplus or absorbing surplus) as well as having a similar value attached to their position within the system. That is, the absorbers of surplus value will be similarly valued (stronger, higher), and the producers of surplus value will be similarly valued (weaker, lower) throughout the system.[4]

The immediate concern here is with England, the United States, West Africa, and Ireland during the "long-sixteenth" (fifteenth to seventeenth) century (Wallerstein, 1974; Braudel, 1976). During this period, England was becoming a core (upper-strata) state within the forming European world system. During the period of concern, what was to become the United States was an external region of that system. Also during this period, West Africa was an external region and Ireland was making the move from an external region to a peripheral region in the European world system.

Although forms of hierarchical stratification, as reflected in vertical classification, existed in the core and periphery as well as the external regions of the emerging European world system, the marks used to indicate where individuals were to be placed in the hierarchical system did not always include skin pigmentation. I am concerned with precisely how skin pigmentation became that dominant mark. That process occurred simultaneously with the integration of land and people from non-European parts of the world into the European world system. I propose that the use of skin pigmentation and culture as the dominant marks of the modern world resulted from the absorption of a larger and larger proportion of the world's people, consisting of a wider range of physical and cultural types, than existed in Europe alone. This absorption was not peaceful, however, and could not have occurred without the use of power. Because the emerging European world system was hierarchically stratified, in reality absorption meant the assignment of populations into the unequal slots of that system. This fact, in conjunction with the physical and cultural diversity of the human group, provided the conditions that allowed skin pigmentation to become the modern mark of vertical classification.[5]

As a core region of the developing world economy, England was the locus of surplus accumulation – a place where capital and naval power eventually became centralized. We observe this by examining how lands throughout the world came under the influence of the English elite as well as how the English utilized labor from throughout the world for surplus production. This expansion by England initially looked very much like that of an empire, but eventually it took the form of a world system.

Land in Ireland and in what became the United States became integrated into the world system through the efforts of English traders, soldiers, and the Crown. In both Ireland and the United States the domination of land resulted in significant benefits to specific social groups in England, particularly traders and innovative members of the nobility. At the same time, however, land domination had significant negative results for social groups in Ireland and North America who had occupied the land prior to the imposition of outside domination. The position a region eventually occupies within the world system therefore has a fundamental impact upon the social groups within those regions.[6] Unlike Adam Smith's (1976) proposed model for the explanation of the wealth of nations – one that assumed the independence of states and therefore concentrated primarily upon internal factors – the concern here is with both internal and external factors that resulted specifically from the interdependence of states and regions within the world system.[7]

As has been suggested, intergration into the world system as a core state or as a noncore state results from state power differentials and therefore results in different outcomes (structural position and moral value) for groups within distinct state structures and regions. Whereas in England, for example, the upper classes benefited from integration under core status, in Ireland and North America integration resulted in a peripheral status. In the latter cases the existing elites incurred losses as the focus of surplus value extraction was transferred away from local markets and toward the world market.

Ireland's peripheral status was the result of direct military conquest. With it, land ownership and land use were transformed. Initially, we can follow the conventional use of religious labels to demonstrate this significant shift in land ownership. Indeed Catholics did lose land while Protestants gained it during the seventeenth century (Bottigheimer, 1971). This use of religious labels is adequate in demonstrating that a fundamental transformation took place during that period in Ireland. However, to obtain a clear understanding of the impact of Ireland's integration into the world system as a peripheral region we must utilize other categories.

During the mid-seventeenth century, Catholic landowners were primarily self-sufficient producers linked to local markets (Bottigheimer, 1971). On the other hand, the new Protestant landowners were primarily capitalist farmers who were linked to the European world market through England. This distinction, more than religious affiliation, served to generate a population that migrated to the United States, as *Irish* and eventually *White,* during the mid-nineteenth century.

After the shift toward capitalist farming in Ireland, the land was utilized primarily to produce commodities that would bring the highest price in the world market. It is therefore not surprising that as the profit margin for locally consumed goods dropped, the emphasis upon growing crops that could be eaten took a secondary position for the new owners of the land. Thus, concern in Ireland, as early as the middle of the seventeenth century, moved away from the use of land to feed the existing population and toward turning the highest profit in a wider market.

These changing conditions in Ireland show what has historically happened when cultivated land is integrated into the world system as a peripheral region. The use of the land became transformed primarily from local production to production for the national and international markets. In turn, the nonelite population occupying the land was transformed from subsistence producers to marginal workers on the land. These workers were producing goods that were sold beyond the local market.[8]

The indigenous elite population was replaced as a distinct entity – because a new elite from the core controlled the land and the workers. That new elite found itself in an ambivalent situation, however. To the extent that it became increasingly dependent upon the world market either to maintain or expand its social and economic positions, its peripheral status hampered its ability to compete with the elite of the core.[9]

It is also important to note that in the Irish case, integration as a peripheral region of the European world system created a division between the indigenous social classes that was far wider than had previously existed. This division provides one of the basic contradictions to the attempt to utilize racial, ethnic, and religious names to designate groups as primordial categories.

I argue that despite the fact that race and culture are commonly used as explanations for the domination of Ireland by the English, they were not the dominant forms of vertical classification in Ireland during the seventeenth century. The form of vertical classification can best be seen by looking at the way in which the rural peasantry was placed in a structural position relative to the new elite (Protestants as well as Catholics). The form of vertical classification can also be seen by the way in which the surviving indigenous Catholic elite became increasingly dependent upon the same system of capitalist competition that hampered the new Protestant elite in their competition with the elite Protestant members of the core state. Both forms replicate the structural relationship of Ireland to England.

The point here is that Ireland's position in the world system was assigned through force and that there were specific social, economic, and political consequences of that process. It is therefore important to see that populated regions of the world were not placed untransformed into their structural positions in the world system and that interests among populations in a region can diverge, with some groups becoming more dependent upon the world market for their relatively elite social position, and others becoming increasingly subordinate to that dependent elite precisely through their role in the world market. In turn, despite moments of contradiction, power was unequally distributed between those who stood to benefit from world market links and those who stood to lose from it.

In addition, the identification of a peripheral (dependent) elite with the nation-state is problematic because the nonelite population is ignored in such a formulation.[10] On the other hand, the structural position of the nonelite within the peripheral state parallels the structural position of the peripheral region within the world economy. Not only are there structural parallels, there are also moral/status parallels. Thus the creation of a national identity based solely upon the nonelite population is also problematic because it ignores the existence of the peripheral elite as well as the peripheral status of the society.

It is therefore important to stress that inequality exists at the world system as well as at the nation-state level. The types of relations that develop from that inequality are a function of the structural position of those regions in the world system. Furthermore, these relations ultimately affect those who migrate, where they migrate, and how they are integrated into the host country.[11]

In North America, integration into the European world economy was also achieved through military conquest. However, it achieved its external, then peripheral, status in a different manner than in the Irish case. Crucial to the distinction between North America and Ireland here were differences in their people-to-land ratios (even when concentrating only on the east coast of North America).[12] The impact of this distinction was that the integration of North America into the world system was more significant as an integration of land than of people.[13] Thus the land in North America eventually became crucial to its integration into the European world system, even though that process was far from straightforward.[14]

But although there were people to till the soil in Ireland, it was precisely a lack of people – once the lands were taken from the native population – that proved to be the formidable problem in establishing the United States. It was, in fact, the ongoing process of solving the people (labor) problem that provides the immediate focus for our analysis of the creation of skin pigmentation as the mark of contemporary vertical classification in the United States.

To people the land (i.e., provide laborers who would be producing for the world capitalist market), it was also deemed necessary to reach into Africa. Initially, however, the native population of North America and the lower classes from England were used as the cheap unskilled labor force that cleared and planted the lands that were newly integrated into the European world system. Only later were sectors of populations from West Africa brought in to perform that labor.

As the United States began to change from an agriculturally based and merchant-based economy to an agriculturally based and industrially based economy during the 1840s, however, there arose another problem connected to the need of cheap unskilled laborers. This time, sectors of people from northern European societies (Ireland in particular) were utilized as important sources of labor. Late in the nineteenth century, as the U.S. economy shifted away from agriculture and toward industry, sectors of people from southern and eastern European societies became the primary sources of cheap unskilled labor.

These labor supplies were not generated merely because of demand from the United States, however. Indeed, just as the United States was being transformed, so were other nation-states and regions of the European world economy. Thus, by logical extension, the world system was itself being transformed. Hence, this approach to the rise of the skin pigmentation mark of structural inequality concentrates upon the expansion (through the absorption of an ever-increasing proportion of the peoples and regions of the world) of the world system and the impact that this process had upon the different sectors of those regions.

West Africa's relationship to the developing European world system and to the development of the United States primarily consisted of supplying labor. On average, that labor force had more skin pigment than either the Europeans or the aboriginal population. Some thus find it easy to conclude that skin pigment determined the role of West Africans in the world economy generally and specifically in the United States to be that of unfree laborers. Such an assumption leads one to the notion that if there were no people with dark skin in the world, there would not have been slavery in the United States. Even further, it implies that there would not be inequality in the United States today if there were not people with a great deal of pigmentation in their skin.

These notions follow logically from the manner in which race and ethnicity are conceptualized.[15]

However, to explain the enslavement of *a sector* of the West African population by its skin pigmentation is to assume that the attitudes and needs of European merchants and landowners alone could determine who would and who would not be enslaved (i.e., that one need not look into the social systems in West Africa for a complete understanding of the vital aspects of the enslaving process) and that European merchants and landowners were morally restrained from enslaving individuals with little pigmentation in their skin, but had no such restraints about enslaving people with a dark pigment.[16]

In both cases there is little if any acknowledgment of the existence of hierarchical structures in the world system or nation-state level. In addition, there is a lack of discussion about the specific historical details surrounding the enslaving process as well as the use of unfree labor in the United States generally. For instance, skin pigmentation as the central position ignores the fact that until the 1680s sectors of populations from Europe were used as indentured servants at the same time as sectors of the African population were so used in the United States. Thus there is some need to explain why Africans were not immediately treated as legally different from the light-pigmented indentured servants during this early period.

To discuss the integration of West Africans into the European world system is therefore to discuss a situation that was almost the opposite of the integration of the developing United States into that system. This can be seen most directly by the fact that in the African case it was labor, not land, that was crucial to the continued development of the European world economy and the United States.

The fact that West Africa supplied labor rather than land presents an ironic, though controversial, twist to public opinion in the United States about the process by which skin pigmentation became the mark of vertical classification in the modern world. Because although land in both Ireland and North America was integrated into the European world economy by force, the process by which a sector of the West African population was integrated was somewhat more complicated. It was warfare (force) and trade between elites from West Africa and Europe that accounts for the actual transfer of sectors of the West Africa population to the New World.

Such a statement obviously demands elaboration. First, I am *not* saying that those who were enslaved were not taken by force, and therefore willingly consented to slavery. I *am* saying, however, that the transfer of a group of people from West Africa to the New World was primarily the result of trade between two groups, both of whom utilized force in order to obtain people. The African elite were of a skin pigment similar to those who were enslaved. The other group, European traders and merchants, were of a lighter skin pigment. The use of race as a central argument concentrates upon the power of those with the lighter skin pigment. Indeed it even expands them into all Europeans regardless of structural distinctions, while ignoring the power of those with darker skin. In this process all the dark-skinned people can be viewed as being available for enslavement.

This is an important issue because it has the potential of taking us out of the simplistic notion that skin pigmentation was the primary, if not the sole, basis by which some people from West Africa were enslaved. It is also important because it will allow us to see that some of the elite in West Africa acted out of economic self-interest. Thus, they acted in a fashion identical – with almost identical motivations – to elites in England and Ireland when gains were felt to be available from "shoveling out" a sector of their societies.[17]

In West Africa, the nonelite sectors of the societies could not prevent themselves from being shipped across the Atlantic. They could not call upon the similarity of the pigmentation of their skin to prevent the African elite from enslaving them. Where is the unifying function of skin pigment here? In a similar fashion, where was the unifying function of skin pigment when the English Parliament refused to save the lives of millions of dying Irish peasants during the nineteenth century? The point therefore is to focus upon stratified social systems as the central feature in the understanding of how skin pigmentation gained its existing role in the vertical classification of human beings.

As long as we close our thoughts to the fact that Europeans and Africans had interacted before the sixteenth century on terms that were not determined by skin pigmentation, we remain forever stuck with the notion that the present skin pigmentation mark is a natural phenomenon.[18] If it was possible for Europeans and Africans to interact based upon a form of classification that was not determined by skin pigmentation, then it is even possible that some individuals from those skin-pigment-classified groups interacted – even if only out of self-interest – on terms other than skin pigmentation.[19]

Rather than seeing the present as a moment in which attitudes toward skin pigmentation differences are better than they have ever been, (i.e., human beings are becoming more tolerant of each others' pigmentation differences), this perspective points toward the notion that human interactions in regard to the skin pigment mark are cyclical rather than linear. If such is the case, it adds support to the assumption that race and ethnicity are two among a multitude of potential marks that can function as alternative labels for levels of social stratification.

To assert that trade between elites was the basis of the process by which a sector of the West African population became integrated into the European world economy is therefore to assert that there were interests of specific groups in certain West African societies that led some of them to engage in the trade of people with a specific sector of Europeans, but not with all Europeans. It is also to assert that skin pigmentation was not, and could not have been, the dominant cause of the enslavement of a specific sector of the West African population.

Turning to the history of United States is then critical for our study because through it we can clearly see the process by which people from throughout the world were pulled and stratified in a specific region of the world. It is by concentrating on that process that we can visualize the process that moves from the assignment of nation-states into specific structural positions at the world system level to the assignment of individuals into specific structural positions at the nation-state level.[20]

3 The hierarchical context of the creation of the United States

The United States became multiracial when the Africans entering U.S. society were made slaves by law, with that condition being hereditary (Higginbotham, 1978; Alpert, 1987). Contrary to general notions, however, this did not take place when Africans first entered the society. As we look closely at the creation of the Virginia colony during the early seventeenth century, we see that the African population in the United States was initially on the same legal footing as European indentured servants (Hurd, 1968).[1]

The differentiation of status between European and African indentured servants in the United States was accomplished through making the African's skin color the mark of the slave labor category. This process could only have been accomplished by the simultaneous creation of the image of the free, White European in contrast to the unfree, Black African. By thus equating skin pigmentation with the contrasted conditions of free and unfree, all individuals in the society were, in theory, placed into one and only one of these categories. The roots of that process remain the basis for racial identity in the United States today. This continuing fact has had a tremendously distorting impact upon the study of the early U.S. society.[2]

Attitudes toward the first Africans brought into the Virginia colony are unclear; even their legal status has been seen in different ways. The general assumption, however, despite evidence to the contrary, has been that the first Africans in the colony came as slaves in 1619 (Frazier, 1949; Hollander, 1963; Smith, 1965; Craven, 1971; Galenson, 1981).[3] The document reporting that arrival bears closer inspection, however.

That document is a letter from John Rolfe, one of the representatives of the Virginia Company in Virginia. It is addressed to Sir Edwin Sandys in England and is a general account of the movement of ships in and out of the colony in 1619. In the midst of this account Rolfe states:

About the latter end of August, a Dutch Man of Warr of the burden of a 160 tunes arrived at Point-Comfort, the Comandors name Capt. Jope, his Pilott for the West Indyes one Mr. Marmaduke an Englishman. They mett with the Trere in the West Indyes, and determyned to hold consort shipp hetherward, but in their passage lost one the other. He brought not anything but 20 and odd

Negroes, which the Governor and Cape Merchant bought for victualles . . . at the best and easiest rate they could [sic]. (Kingsbury, Volume III, 1933:243)

Those asserting that the 1619 ship carried slaves must rely upon existing notions about the skin pigmentation mark, combined with the statement that they were "bought." The fact that they were bought does not, however, prove that they were slaves. Indentured servants in the seventeenth century were routinely treated as private property (Smith, 1965; Galenson, 1981; Main, 1982).[4] This thus makes any easy movement from being "bought" to being a slave problematic.

Whatever the status of the specific Africans brought into Virginia in 1619, there is ample evidence that Africans even later than 1619 lived in that colony as indentured servants. Smith (1965: 243–4), for instance, reports that as late as 1691 one Benjamin Lewis sued his master, contending that he was under contract as an indentured servant, but his master was attempting to treat him as a slave. In this instance, the court found the claims of the African valid and granted his freedom.[5] This example attests to the fact that at least some Africans were not slaves during this early period. Thus we may logically question the assumption that skin pigment, as presently viewed, determined the movement of the African population to the United States.

We can thus more confidently state that the United States became a multiracial society when skin pigment legally became the mechanism used to separate the population into free and unfree structural slots toward the end of the seventeenth century (Handlin,1950:203; Hurd,1968:226–47; Alpert,1987:191). During the seventeenth century, the unfree labor category was transformed from indentured servitude to slavery. That transformation was paralleled by a shift from some Europeans as the predominant group occupying the unfree labor slot to some Africans being that group. Here, *race* is given its essence by the classification of people based upon distinctions in their skin pigment. That classification was manifested through placing people in distinct structural positions, either free or unfree, within the society. Prior to that point, differences in skin pigment did not constitute the absolute mark they later took on.

Some crucial questions concerning the rise of the United States as a society stratified by race are brought up in this context. Because an unfree labor slot existed prior to the creation of the slave labor slot and because it was not populated by groups with different skin pigments, it is important to know more about the relationship of unfree labor slots, in general, to the developing society at large. It is also important to find out why the earlier unfree labor slot was replaced by the later one, as well as why the populations assigned to that slot changed. Additionally, it is important to find out what was the attribute analogous to race that was utilized to assign individuals to the earlier unfree labor slot. These questions can easily appear trivial if race is accepted as the undisputed explanation of the social transformation cited above. If that explanation is not accepted, however, such questions become vital for the full understanding of the history of the United States and the concept of race.

Wallerstein (1974) gives us a clue to the general understanding of the multiracial results of the peopling process of the United States when he asserts that the enslavement of the African was rooted in the need for labor from outside the existing European world capitalist economy. He states that there were areas of the world during the early seventeenth century that were not yet integrated into the European capitalist economy, and as such they were vulnerable to European desires. That is to say, there were areas, hence labor, in the world that were not explicitly generating goods for sale through a European-dominated capitalist market that could readily be forced into that relationship.[6] This is a partial view, however, because it ignores the fact that indentured servitude existed prior to slavery. Just as important, it ignores the relationship of integrating land into the world capitalist system to the need for unfree labor in general. The stress should thus be placed upon the need for unfree labor, and not upon Africans who were brought to the United States.

The historical evidence indicates that New World lands were integrated into the expanding English empire before African laborers were integrated into that system. Although the first charter of the Virginia Company was drawn up in 1606, sectors of the African population had not yet been introduced into the colony. It was, in fact, well over half a century later before Africans outnumbered their European counterparts as unfree laborers (Galenson, 1981).

Because the land of the New World was introduced into the English empire and because unfree laborers were forced to work on it, the discussion correctly begins with how and why land became integrated into the system before taking up the use of unfree labor in the colonies. Virginia, the first successful settlement of the colonies that became the United States, is a prototype of the land and labor structure that gave rise to the use of unfree labor. We begin therefore with the world context within which the Virginia colony arose.

Trade and plunder: the basis of the Spanish and Portuguese empires

The English Crown provided the legal basis by which New World lands were annexed into the developing English empire. England's interest in establishing colonies in North America during the sixteenth century was rooted in the desire for wealth. Struggle for control over New World lands was deemed legitimate because they were viewed as being outside of the "civilized" European world and, as such, were available to the strongest members of that world. During that period Europeans referred to the New World as the "Heathen Lands."

The Papal Bull of 1493 brought that struggle for land to a momentary close by dividing those lands between Spain and Portugal. The western half (with the exception of Brazil) was granted to Spain, and the eastern half was granted to Portugal. This meant that Spain was granted the lands of what are presently North and South America, with the aforementioned exception, while Portugal was granted the lands of Africa, India, and parts of Asia.

The Portuguese nobility, primarily through its merchants, developed trade along the African and Indian coasts, the Persian Gulf, and the Malay Archipelago and the China Sea. This resulted in the concentration of great wealth in Portugal. The lands in the west were not as settled as those granted to the Portuguese in the east. Spanish trade with native populations in that region was therefore not as profitable as the Portuguese trade. Spain did not fundamentally suffer from this lack of trade, however, because Spanish merchants, with the blessing of the Spanish Crown, turned to conquest, plunder, and piracy as the means of gaining wealth.

The acts of conquest yielded tremendous gains in wealth. Cortez conquered the Aztec empire of Mexico during 1519. Pizarro conquered the Incan empire in Peru during 1534. Gold and silver were found in large quantities in both regions. During these conquests the native populations were enslaved and forced to work the gold and silver mines. From this exploitation of unfree labor, gold and silver flowed into the treasury of Spain (Braudel, 1966). This influx of mineral wealth greatly increased Spain's power within the European world. It even increased Spain's trade with the lands granted to Portugal in the east. Spanish expansion was indeed so great that by 1581 it dominated the trade routes that had been developed by the Portuguese.

Trade was the basis of the Portuguese empire. Conquest and plunder were the bases of the Spanish empire. Under the provisions of the Papal Bull, however, neither trade nor conquest nor plunder were legally open to the English (Brown, 1890).[7] This put severe pressure upon the English Crown to devise a mechanism by which to benefit from the lands beyond its borders (i.e., lands dominated by Spain and Portugal).

England's expansion during the sixteenth and seventeenth centuries

Given the above conditions, it is not surprising that during the early sixteenth century, the economic development of England was not as dynamic as that of Portugal or Spain. It is even the case that a series of economic downturns and depressions during that period were attributed by the English to their exclusion from the trade and mineral riches of the "Heathen Lands." The few moments of upturn, on the other hand, appear to have been by-products of the need of the Spanish for English goods and the illegal plunder of Spanish and Portuguese ships (Brown, 1890; Osgood, 1958).

But all did not remain bleak in England's economy during the sixteenth century. Changes in the wool industry illustrate some of the positive results of aggressive action on the part of the Crown to defend the national economy. Until the middle of the sixteenth century, England was the chief supplier of unfinished wool in Europe. On the other hand, Flanders and France were the centers of wool cloth production. Two actions by the English Crown changed that structure. First, unfinished wool was prevented from legally leaving England, thus allowing the domestic woolen industry to develop. Second, the Crown directly supported the Company of Merchant Adventurers that traded finished woolen goods throughout Europe. The combination of the two actions aided England in becoming the center of wool cloth production and trade by the end of the sixteenth century.[8]

In addition to developing a strong wool trade, the English Crown acted in other ways to expand its economic position in the world. Significant in that regard was the turning of a blind eye toward the actions of English sailors and merchants on the high seas. Those Englishmen pirated gold and silver on the way from the Spanish colonies, sacked Spanish settlements in the New World, and raided Dutch ships bringing textiles and spices from the east. Thus, in spite of England's legal exclusion from the new sources of wealth, benefits were still to be had, although indirectly. Such benefits were limited, however, by the greater than usual risks of such enterprises. This meant that the benefits were not only obtained at a great loss in human life, but that they were also very sporadic.

The possibility of gaining direct access to the gold and silver mines of the New World was therefore not ignored by the English. According to the Papal Bull of 1493, they were specifically excluded from colonizing any western lands below latitude 44 degrees north.[9] But, there were no gold or silver mines to be found on or above that latitude. Hopes for settlements that may have contained mines could then only mean deceiving the Spanish or confronting them directly in war. Either action required the support of the English Crown, however, because both could eventually result in war.

Getting the support of the Crown for potential open conflict with Spain was not easy, however, (Brown, 1890, Volume II: 15).[10] One enterprising soul proposed getting that support by explicitly offering a return tithe to the Crown. An unsigned letter dated November 6, 1577, reads:

A discourse on how Her Majesty may annoy the Kings of Spaine by fitting out a fleet of Shippes of war under pretence of Letters Patent, to discover and inhabit strange places, with special proviso, for their safeties whom policy requires to have most annoyed – by which means the doing the contrary shall be imparted to the executors fault; your Highness's letters Patent being a manifest show that it was not Your Majesty's pleasure so to have it.

If you will let us first do this [destroy the Spanish fleet while it fished off the Newfoundland coast] we will next take the West Indies from Spain. . . . You will have the gold and silver mines and the profit of the soile. You will be Monarch of the seas [sic]. (Brown, 1890, Volume I: 8–9)

For the English Crown to have acted upon this idea of hiding the actions of the English from Spain would only have delayed an eventual war with Spain. But despite the fact that this letter does not appear to have been acted upon, it clearly indicates that there were individuals giving thought to the reformulation of the results of the Papal Bull of 1493.

Toward the close of the sixteenth century, the English Crown became bolder about dismantling the Papal Bull of 1493, with the complete understanding that it made war with Spain inevitable. On April 9, 1585, Sir Walter Raleigh sailed from Plymouth, England "under the letters-patent of Elizabeth, Queen of England to take possession of a land claimed by Spain under the Bulls of the Popes of Rome (Brown, 1890, Volume II: 14)." In July 1585, Captain Thomas Cavendish set sail on an around-the-world voyage to raid Spanish ships in the Pacific (Brown, 1890, Volume II: 18).

As a result of such actions, England was at war with Spain within a year. That war raged in the Atlantic Ocean for two years. Its outcome was ultimately determined by battles between the English navy and the Spanish Armada from July 29 to August 7, 1598. The Spanish Armada was defeated and the English swiftly claimed land in the New World below the north forty-fourth latitude.

The settlement of Virginia: the search for profits without a large labor force

Once the English had access to the New World below latitude 44 north, some practical problems involved in taking advantage of it had to be faced, not the least being how to finance the colonizing expeditions. The initial method of financing relied upon a small number of large investors. Because the project did not generate an immediate profit, an alternative method of financing had to be sought. By 1609, the joint stock company became the means of involving small investors and thus decreased the pressure on the company to provide a quick return to the investors.

Determining how investments would be utilized to generate profit from the exploitation of the new lands was as important as the financing of the projects. Initially the desire for establishing a settlement in Virginia was tied to extracting wealth in the form of precious metals. The Spanish success in dominating native cultures that were based upon extracting gold and silver was the ideal, because there was no need to engage in the time-consuming process of importing labor to grow or produce commodities. The exploitation of the new lands in North America by the English became inextricably tied, however, to the production of commodities for sale on the world market.[11] We will see that the mechanisms utilized to return a profit to English investors indeed had a significant impact upon the use of labor and the creation of group identity in the United States.[12]

The ultimate factor that had to be addressed by the Virginia Company was the type of organizational structure that would represent the investors, most of whom remained in England.[13] As was the case with the aims of the settlement, the stratified organizational structure, which was the centerpiece of the creation of the United States, was critical in the creation of group identity in the society.

By looking at how the Virginia settlement was financed and organized, we will gain a detailed understanding of the relationship between social stratification, land, labor, profits, and group identity based upon specific marks during the beginning of what became the United States.[14] Three types of evidence will help us in this process. First, the three charters granted by King James I of England in 1606, 1609, and 1611 illustrate the extent to which the Crown was willing to make concessions in the conditions of the settlement to benefit itself and the grantees. Second, the records of the Virginia Company and the orders given to the settlers by the investors in England show the methods by which the investors hoped to obtain profits from the settlement. Third, the history of the settlers themselves – their responses to conditions in Virginia – show that when practical decisions contradicted the desires of the investors, changes were made to maintain the loyalty of the investors and ensure the existence of the settlement.

The first charter was granted by King James I in 1606 to Sir Thomas Gates and Sir George Somers (Osgood, 1958, Volume III: 24). This charter called for the settlement of two colonies/plantations between latitudes 34 degrees and 41 degrees north in the New World. Once the settlement was established, the first colony, eventually called Virginia, was granted all lands, woods, soils, grounds, havens, ports, rivers, mines, minerals, marshes, waters, fishing, commodities, and property within fifty English statute miles along the coast to the west and the southwest and fifty miles along the coast to the north and northwest. In addition, they were granted all of the islands within one hundred English miles off the coast of the first settlement (Brown, 1890, Volume II: 54). There was no mention in the charter of the aboriginal population or its claim on the land (Brown 1890, Volume II: 54; Osgood 1958, Volume III: 36).

This first charter gave the grantees the right to mine for gold, silver, and copper. Most of the benefits from the mines were to go to the investors. In addition, the grantees were given a monopoly over all trade between the colony and the rest of the world for twenty-one years. At the end of that period, all benefits from trade were to pass to the Crown and its heirs. The Crown and its heirs also reserved to themselves one-fifth of the gold and silver and one-fifteenth of the copper found during these explorations (Kingsbury, 1933; Neill, 1968). Those were indeed generous terms for both parties, assuming that precious metals or an easily produced commodity were to be found. The overall tone of the document clearly demonstrates that the use of the land, as far as the Crown was concerned, was premised upon generating wealth through mining precious metals and through trade (Scott, 1951).

Such was the position of the Crown, but what were the ideas of the grantees as they sent forth the original settlers (Lacey, 1979:70)? On December 10, 1606, before the settlers sailed for Virginia, "Certain Orders and Directions" were issued by the Royal Council for Virginia (Neill, 1968). The first part of that document set the rules of leadership while the settlers were aboard ship. It gave total power to Captain Newport, commander of the voyage.

Part two of the document, entitled "Advice for the Colony on Landing," suggested the best place to settle, laid out the rules of leadership upon landing, listed methods by which to treat the natives, advised that labor should be used for the company before being used for private functions, and in the paragraph before the last stated:

You shall do well to send a perfect relation by Captain Newport of all that is done, what height you are seated, how far into the land, what commodities you find, what soil, woods and their several kinds, and so of all other things else to advertise [sic]. (Neill, 1968:13)

We see that the grantees were concerned (in addition to being able to find the site again) that the settlers immediately get to work determining what commodities were readily available in the area of settlement. This would help demonstrate the value of the enterprise for present and future investors (Scisco, 1903:260; Osgood, 1958, Volume I: 33–4).

Early reports of products and their value were contradictory, however. Captain Newport remained at the Virginia colony for one month during this first trip (May 13 to June 22, 1607) and then set sail for England with minerals and specimens from the forest. In his letter to Lord Salisbury, one of the investors and a member of the Royal Council of Virginia, he stated that the country was rich with gold and copper. He also stated that he had such minerals for the king's inspection (Brown, 1890, Volume II: 105).

The statement from the Council of Virginia (the governing body in Virginia) to the Royal Council in England, however, indicated that the easiest product to gather and the most abundant product found was sassafras. It added that there was an abundance of trees in the area, but only referred to gold in regard to the Spanish. This statement was clearly a cry for help:

We entreat your succors for our seconds [the second shipment of supplies for the colony] with all expedition least that all devouring Spaniard lay his ravenous hands upon these gold showing mountains, which if we be so enabled he shall never dare to think on [sic]. (Brown, 1890, Volume I: 108)

It would appear that because the settlers did not initially have gold, they thus found it necessary to pose the issue of a second shipment (requiring further investments from England) within the context of benefits to the grantees.[15]

Between Newport's return to England in 1607 and the signing of the second charter in 1609, two additional supply voyages went out to the colony. The first, consisting of two ships, arrived in early 1608. The second arrived in October 1608 and was composed of only one ship. During this period, the settlers constantly complained about the conditions in the colony and the use of the supplies. In fact, the situation became so desperate at one point that the settlers felt compelled to act against orders and rely upon trade with the natives between the arrival of shipments from England.[16]

On his return from his second and third voyages, Captain Newport took back commodities that were merely variations upon those brought back from the first trip. The existence of pitch, tar, glass, potash, clapboard, and wainscot on board indicates, however, that labor was being utilized on a small scale to produce commodities to send to England. These products did not indicate the existence of great riches, however (Brown, 1890, Volume I: 205).

The problem clearly stated

In addition to the products brought back on his second and third voyages, Newport took back reports of the difficulties faced by the settlers in developing a stable society in Virginia (Brown, 1890, Volume I: 341–2). One report was John Smith's letter to the treasurer of Virginia, written in 1608. The letter summarized the position faced by the settlers and gave a clear sense of the distinction between the settlement of the colony as a purely commercial venture concerned with trade and the appropriation of valuable resources as opposed to the establishment of a stable colony that would utilize labor to produce commodities for the English market (Osgood, 1958, Volume I: 52, 55).

Smith stated that the letter would speak to the assumption of the treasurer that the settlers were merely involved in divisive acts and were sending "ifs, ands, hopes, and some few proofs" of commodities that could be derived from the colony. He intended to explain to those in England why there were difficulties in turning a profit in Virginia. He also stated that factionalism within the colony resulted from the desire on the part of some of the settlers to leave and divide up the land, which like trading with the natives, was strictly forbidden by orders of the council (Brown, 1890, Volume I: 201). Smith further pointed out that there was no way to give a quick return on the thousands of pounds that had been invested in the colony. He saw all of the above issues as resulting from the fact that with the small group (approximately 150) of settlers, there was no way to search for gold mines above the falls in the river, produce commodities, and set up a stable society (Brown, 1890, Volume I: 201).

In his letter Smith indicated that the production of goods such as pitch, tar, and glass had begun, but that the difficulties the settlers faced as laborers were great. He reminded them that:

if you rightly consider what an infinite toyle it is in Russia and Swethland where the woods are proper for naught els, and though there be the helpe both of man and beast in those ancient Commonwealths, which many an hundred years have used it; yet thousands of those poore people can scarce get necessaries to live, but from hand to mouth [sic]. (Brown, 1890, Volume I: 202)

Once again Smith explicitly stated that the colony lacked the type of labor force necessary to perform those duties that were viewed by the council in England as important to the investors. In addition, he argued that even with the correct form of labor the living conditions of those involved in such forms of industry would continue to be marginal. His point therefore was that more important than there not being the correct type of labor, there was not enough labor.

At the most basic level Smith took the position that if the choice was between food for the settlers and commodities for England, the settlers would have to decide upon food. There was just not enough labor to provide both. He then made this proposal:

When you send again I entreat you rather send but thirty carpenters, husbandmen, gardeners, fishermen, blacksmiths, masons, and diggers up of trees, roots, well provided; then a thousand of such as we have; for except wee be able both to lodge them, and feed them, the most will consume with want of necessaries before they can be made good for anything [sic].

He continued:

Thus if you pleas to consider this account, and of the unnecessary wages to Captain Newport, or his ships so long lingering and staying here . . . or yet to send to Germany or Poland for glasse-men and the rest, till we be able to sustaine ourselves and relieve them when they come. It were better to give five hundred pound a ton for those grosse commodities in Denmarke, then send for them hither, till more necessary things be provided. For in overtoyling in our weake and unskillful bodies, to satisfie this desire or present profit, we can scarce ever recover ourselves from one supply to the another [sic]. (Brown, 1890, Volume I: 203–4)

From the above picture, it is clear that the difficulty in obtaining labor was creating a crisis that threatened to destroy the entire colonial undertaking.

It also appears that the crisis was partially the result of the fact that the structure of the organization of people sent to the Virginia colony was geared toward the model of conquest practiced by the Spaniards in Mexico and Peru. A closer look at that structure and how it was transformed through crisis is now important to isolate the basis of skin pigmentation as the mark of vertical classification in the United States today.

4 Structural slots and identity creation in seventeenth-century Virginia

Continuing with our notion that identities are created within specific social structures, it is important to stress the type of social structure that was the basis of the first successful English colony in North America – the Virginia colony. The prevailing notion is that the English colonies in North America – the origins of the United States – were composed of oppressed European groups seeking a haven for themselves. On the contrary, however, we have seen that at least in the Virginia colony, profits rather than political protection was the basis of settlement. Even further, the organization of that settlement was hierarchical. It did not conform to the image that a haven for the oppressed would immediately suggest.

The hierarchical organization of the group sent to Virginia can be seen by the distinct separation between those in positions of authority and those sent to perform physical labor (Kingsbury, 1933; Diamond, 1958:465–568; Morgan, 1975). There was a small upper group exercising authority in the name of the Virginia Company in England in command of a larger group of laborers. It was through that separation that the investors in England initially desired to transform their funds into profits if precious resources were found and exported from the new lands.

But despite the creation of such an organization, early communications between those in the colony and those in England clearly demonstrate that the process of setting up the colony required some specific adjustments. One fundamental adjustment centered around the insufficient supply of laborers to meet the needs of the settlers as well as the investors. What is important here is that the labor needs of the colony resulted from the same force that led to the existence of a hierarchical organizational structure (i.e., the desire for profits).

We know that sectors of the African population were eventually used to meet the labor needs of the Virginia colony. In addition, we know that this group was eventually enslaved. We also know that skin pigment differences were eventually utilized to justify placing some people in the unfree (slave) labor slot, while others were placed in the free labor slot.[1] These facts provide us with the basis by which to investigate three important questions.

1. Was slavery the only form of unfree labor utilized to meet the labor needs in the colony?

35

2. If not, were Africans also utilized in those unfree forms?
3. What mechanism was utilized to justify the assignment of individuals into the low unfree labor slot when skin pigment differences between free and unfree laborers did not exist?

The point is that relying upon skin pigmentation as a *natural opposition* to explain why sectors of the African population were utilized as the exclusive slave labor force in the United States is severely limiting. It is historically limiting because it prevents us from clearly examining the period between the settling of Virginia in 1606 and the legal establishment of slavery in the 1660s (Higginbotham 1978). In addition, it is theoretically limiting because we are prevented from determining whether and to what extent the use of skin pigment functions as a specific instance of a more general category of marks used to assign individuals to structural slots in hierarchical organizations. Thus, approximately a half century gets relegated to the periphery of our national consciousness. In addition, it is theoretically limiting because we are prevented from determining whether and to what extent the use of skin pigment – among various other mechanisms – was used to assign individuals to structural slots in a hierarchical organization.

The specific focus of this position is that if the group assigned to the lower structural slot of an organization has the same range of skin pigmentation as those in the upper structural slot, skin pigment will not become the *natural* mark used to justify the assignment of individuals to different groups. Rather, some other contrast between those individuals in the two slots would become the commonly utilized mark of distinction. Strong evidence for this position is provided by Davis (1966:49), who states:

Although slaves in most ancient societies were not distinguishable by skin color or other racial characteristics, their masters often marked them with *visible symbols of their lowly status*. No doubt the original purposes of such labeling were identification and prevention of escape. Some slaves merely had their heads shorn or wore an identification tablet of clay or metal, which could be broken when they were freed. But more permanent branding or tattooing was also common in Egypt, the Neo-Babylonian Empire, Roman Sicily, and even fifteenth century Tuscany. From the earliest times such *skin markings* became indelible signs of a servile status, and *suggested a deformity of character which deserved contempt* [emphasis added].[2]

It is significant that Davis here links skin markings with "lowly status" and "contempt." This not only supports the basic point that specific marks are relied upon to demarcate the occupants of the upper and the lower structural slots, but it also supports the notion that marks can replace preexisting structural slots as indications of social value. I assert that we can thus explain why specific groups of people routinely evoke an emotional response along a continuum of contempt and envy. As such, marks, regardless of what they are, function as broadcasters of social value, social position, and economic, social, and political power for all members of a society (Douglas, 1982:67; Schwartz, 1981:19).

With this frame of reference we can trace the transformation of the low structural slot in the Virginia colony and the people placed in it to pinpoint the marks used to justify the assignment of the powerless to the low structural slot as laborers.[3]

The Second Charter: proposed solution to the labor problem

The response of the investors, if not specifically to Smith's letter expressing concern about labor then at least to the ideas put forth in it, can be seen in two documents. One is the Second Charter issued to the Virginia Company by King James I in May 1609. The other is "A True and Sincere Declaration," written by the governors and councillors of the colony in December 1609.

The Second Charter establishes new conditions under which the colony of Virginia was to be held. While the First Charter had been issued to private individuals, the second was issued to a corporation. Its heading is "King James the I's Second Charter to the Treasurer and Company for Virginia, erecting them into a Corporation and Body Politick, and for the further Enlargement and Explanation of the Privileges of the said Company and first colony of Virginia." This charter directly confronts the project's lack of resources, labor, and focus (Brown, 1890, Volume I: 238–40).

It asserts that to bring in additional resources, more investors would be sought. Toward that end, the project was no longer confined to those close to the Crown; indeed, 56 city companies of London and 659 new individuals were incorporated into the charter. Included among the signers were 21 peers, 96 knights, 11 doctors and ministers, 53 captains, 28 esquires, 58 gentlemen, 110 merchants, and 282 citizens and individuals not classified (Brown, 1890, Volume 1: 228).

The extension of the charter into a corporation had some important implications for the method by which profits were expected to be generated in the colony. Most important, the inclusion of large numbers of people under a joint-stock company eased the overall burden on the individual investor. There was, therefore, less urgent pressure for immediate returns on the investment. Such a decrease in pressure, in fact, enabled the Virginia Company to begin to view the colony as a long-term investment rather than as a source of quick wealth. Changes made by the Second Charter supported this shift.

The movement toward a longer time frame can be seen by the expansion of the land area granted by the Second Charter from ten thousand square miles to one million square miles. In addition, a commission was authorized to survey and distribute the land to the adventurers and planters when such distribution became the object of the company. The importance of these changes is their implication that the company was beginning to think about utilizing land, rather than mining gold and silver, to entice and eventually pay off investors.[4]

The issue of laborers was confronted directly in the charter:

It shall be lawful and free for them [the treasurer, company and their successors] and their assigns, at all and every time and times hereafter, out of our Realm of England, and out of all other our Dominions, to take and lead into the said voyages, and for and towards the said plantation, and to travel thitherward, and to abide and inhabit there in the said colony and plantation, all such and so many of our loving subjects, or any other strangers, that will become our loving subjects and live under our obedience. (Neill, 1968: Appendix)

There is a clear distinction between the loose attention paid to the need for labor that Captain Smith criticized in his letter, and this document, which sets the stage for transferring English subjects as well as others to the colony.

The organization of the colony from afar

The "Instructions" to Governor Gates in 1609 were more detailed than those written by Richard Hakluyt as "Advice for the Colony on Landing" in 1606. The second set of orders attempted to regulate the social, economic, and physical structure of the colony. A demonstration of the company's vision of the colony as hierarchical can be seen in Section Sixteen of the charter, which states that towns that were sufficient to house the new settlers were to be established under the authority of commanders, whose job was to make sure that the workers were engaged in their designated tasks (Kingsbury, 1933, Volume III: 17). Similarly, force would be utilized to keep the workers in their position (Diamond, 1958:467).[5] Thus it was determined that those sent to establish the Virginia colony were to operate like a military hierarchical structure.

While such plans were being made for the Europeans, thought was also given to the manner in which relations with the natives were to be conducted. The "Instructions" state:

For Powhaton [the main native leader in the region of settlement] and his warriors it is clear even to reason beside our experience that he loved not our neighborhood and therefore you may no way trust him, but if you find it not best to make him your prisoner yet you must make him your tributary, and all other of his warriors about him first to acknowledge no other lord but King James, and so we shall free them all from the terror of Powhaton – Upon them every Lord of a Province shall pay you and send you into your fort where you make your chief residence so many measures of corne at every harvest, so many baskets of dye so many dozens of skins so many of his people to work weekly, and of every thing somewhat, according to his position in greatness of territory and men, by which means you shall quietly draw to your selves an annual revenue of every commodity growing in that country and this tribute payed to you for which you shall deliver them from the *exactions* of Powhaton, which are now burdensome and protect and defend them from all their enemies shall also be a means of clearing much ground of wood and of reducing them to labor and trade [sic]. (Kingsbury, 1933, Volume III: 18–19)

Thus, in addition to obtaining laborers from England, the members of the corporation also hoped to use the natives in the attempt to solve the labor shortage.[6]

It appears that the council planned to have the natives produce food for the settlement and clear the land, thus leaving the settlers free to perform other functions. This extra labor force would certainly have been valuable to the settlers. Ideally, by integrating the labor of the natives into the economic structure of the Jamestown settlement as the producers of foodstuffs, the European laborers would have been allowed more time to produce commodities for export without having to compromise their survival. They would also have been able to continue to look for gold and silver. Therefore, the efficient control of the European laborers as well as the use of native laborers were seen by the investors as vital to the success of the colony.

The reality

There were difficulties in assigning the nonelite settlers as well as natives into the low labor slot during the first years of the settlement of Virginia. This can be seen by the deteriorated conditions in the colony during the summer of 1609. By that time some of the nonelite settlers had already traded their tools, swords, guns, and, in some instances, their houses to the natives in return for food (Stith, 1969:98). It is even reported that nearly eighty persons left the fort at Jamestown and formed a new settlement twenty miles away (Neill, 1968:31). These actions were taken in the face of prohibitions that threatened the galleys or death for engaging in such activities. Another example of the difficulties in successfully assigning the nonelite settlers to the labor slot is indicated by the actions of the passengers abroad the *Swallow,* one of the advance ships from the first supply of the 1609 charter. After their arrival in Virginia, they took the ship when it was on a mission to trade with the natives for corn and joined a band of pirates.

The native population was not easily assigned to the low labor slot during the early period because there was no general sense that protection was needed from native chiefs (like Powhaton). In addition, the desperate state of the settlers brought them to the natives rather than the other way around. Tied to both points is the fact that the native population controlled access to land near the coast as well as further inland.

As a result of this breakdown in the development of the lower rung of the social structure, the nonelite settlers worked less and depended more on trade and personal interactions with the natives for their survival. Such difficulties in assigning people to the labor slot remained a threat to the survival of the entire settlement as an investment venture.

The condition of the colony by May 1609, as reflected in the behavior of those who were potential members of the lower rung of the social structure, clearly indicated that the colony's labor problems were far from solved by making it legal to bring in more people from England or by schemes designed to trick the natives into becoming serfs. Significant changes had to be implemented if the assignment process (the creation of a stable labor force) was to occur. The "Instructions" of 1609 attempted to impose such conditions from afar, but the actual conditions in the colony made their implementation virtually impossible.

To make matters even more difficult, by the time Governor Gates arrived some of the advance ships had already returned to England without commodities and reported that it was possible that the governor's ship had been lost. The new start set forth in the 1609 charter, supported so strongly by the merchant community of London, was quickly coming to an end before the plans could be implemented (Neill, 1968:39; Brown, 1890, Volume 1: 330–1).

Investors' confidence was shaken because the organizers of the colony were unable to create a stable labor force. Those investors who persisted despite the failure of the 1609 charter therefore attempted to rescue the colony by calling upon the people of England in "A True and Sincere Declaration" during December 1609. That document argued that investment in the colony still made sense and described how workers could be assigned to the labor slot in Virginia and thereby generate profits from the colony.

According to the declaration, the colony had three aims:

1. "To preach and baptize into christian religion, and by propagation of the gospell, to recover out of the armes of the divell, a number of poore and miserable soules [sic]."

2. To build a settlement in Virginia for the king by transporting the unemployed and poor surplus laborers to the colony. In this manner, the poor of England would serve as a defense against England's enemies, while their transportation to Virginia would decrease the possibility of mass death from a lack of subsistence in England (Brown, 1890, Volume I: 348–9).

3. "[To provide] the appearance and assurance of private commodity to the particular undertakers, by recovering and possessing to themselves a fruitful land, whence they may furnish and provide this kingdom, with all such necessities and defects under which we labour, and are now enforced to buy [sic]."

Despite the selfless, moral tone of the language, it is clear that the success of the colony would accrue to its investors and English society in general. Success could not be had without assigning people to the predesignated low structural labor position within the colony.

As we have seen from earlier documents issued during the seventeenth century, the struggle to set the colony on a stable footing was far from determined by the above proclamation. On the one hand, prior to 1616, no profitable commodities were produced in the colony[7] and the assignment of people to labor slots remained a difficult task.[8] This was due to two factors:

1. Merely because there were people in England who were potentially available as laborers did not mean that these individuals could be economically transported to the colony on a large scale.[9]

2. Before confronting the problem of economically transporting large numbers of individuals from England to Virginia, some mechanism had to be established to make sure that those transported remained tied to their assigned labor slot.[10]

The development of tobacco as an export crop by 1616, the shift toward granting land based on the Headright system in 1617, and the establishment of indentured servitude were the critical and interconnected mechanisms by which the social system in Virginia eventually gained stability. During this period the clamor for quick profits died down entirely.

Tobacco and labor

By 1616, tobacco was being commercially cultivated for export in Virginia and there is no doubt that it was crucial to the survival of the colony (Perkins, 1980:20; McCusker and Menard, 1985:118–20).[11] In fact, during this period the tobacco plant paid for most imports into the colony. As a result tobacco took on the role of the coin of the colony. Settlers were therefore compelled to produce it if they were to survive (Main, 1982:16).

As was the case throughout this early period, taking advantage of the favorable position of tobacco could not have occurred without the availability of labor. For although tobacco production did not require large tracts of land or a large labor force, it did require a large labor force relative to the amount of land needed for the crop. Therefore, discussions stressing the large number of small holdings should not deter us from seeing that approximately 75 percent of the settlers in early Virginia were indentured servants before they became small holders (Craven, 1971:5). In addition, "the majority of servants in the early period lived and worked as common field hands in an all-white environment."[12] Main (1982:106–8) adds that skilled individuals made up fewer than 4 percent of all male servants and that most servants were field hands.

Tobacco produced for export not only enriched the colony, but it also provided most of the work for indentured servants during much of the seventeenth century in British North America. This insight also permits us to move away from the tendency of ignoring the existence of a hierarchically stratified social system in the colonies. It specifically leads to the observation that despite the greater chances for mobility in the colonies, as opposed to England, there clearly existed different degrees of wealth, status, and labor that were not primarily determined by what we have come to characterize as distinctions between Blacks and Whites.

At the root of the distinction within the colonial social system between the third and eighth decades of the seventeenth century were differences in the ability to supply the necessary goods to feed, clothe, and shelter people beyond oneself and one's immediate family. This meant having access to land, labor, and a product that would turn a profit in the marketplace. Once tobacco and other staples became valued in England, the basic components of social distinction were in place. Within the context of developing a product that generated wealth, having a large, cheap labor source became even more important to the colony.

The Headright system, which was established in 1616, was specifically designed to confront the cost of transporting individuals to the Virginia colony (Craven, 1932:32). Under that system those who were able to pay the passage for a laborer to the colony received approximately fifty acres of land for each laborer transported. Those with large amounts of money to expend on transporting laborers got large grants of land. Those with few resources, on the other hand, received a small holding and those without resources were relegated to being indentured servants with the possibility of obtaining land only as payment for seven years of labor for a master. The Headright system was thus an important mechanism in creating and peopling the social structure of colonial Virginia. But while providing the conditions for generating a stable population for the labor slot of the developing society it was providing people for the structural slot at the bottom (landless, unfree, indentured servants) of the social system (Craven, 1971:13–17).

Unfree labor

Now we can begin to understand the rise of unfree labor as a structural position outside of the context of skin pigmentation marks and social value. The early form of unfree labor was clearly indentured servitude and clearly not based on skin pigment. The tendency toward ignoring the existence of the beginning of the United States as hierarchically structured prior to the use of skin pigment has moved us too quickly through this crucial period of U.S. history.

It is generally assumed that the period of indentured servitude as the dominant type of unfree labor from 1609 to 1680 was so brief that it is overshadowed by the period of slavery. If we look more carefully at the history of this young country, however, it becomes obvious that indentured servitude legally existed for approximately one century, from the early seventeenth century to the early eighteenth century, and slavery legally existed for approximately two centuries, that from the late seventeenth century to the late nineteenth century. The twentieth century has been legally devoid of unfree labor forms. Thus indentured servitude comprises nearly one-fourth of the history of this country and therefore cannot legitimately be characterized as insignificant.[13]

General remarks on colonization and unfree labor

In 1776 Adam Smith stated that the prosperity of new settlements was assured by "plenty of good land." He assumed that this land would lead to the production of commodities that would in turn enable the planter to obtain more laborers to whom he would be able to give higher wages. Through this ideal cycle of change in which the planter accumulated more capital, obtained more land, and employed more laborers, Smith saw the development of wealth within colonies (Smith, 1976).

Missing from Smith's analysis, however, is a specific discussion of the relationship between land and labor in newly settled export-oriented areas.[14] In the early Virginia colony, there was an abundance of land, but that land was covered with timber and bush. In fact, the more fertile the land, the greater was the growth of trees and bush. This, in addition to the labor needs discussed above, put a premium on labor (Wertenbaker, 1959:31). It was the scarcity of labor that prevented the planter from cultivating large amounts of land. In addition, the scarcity of currency in the colony meant that planters were limited in their ability to pay wages to free laborers. Land as payment was a possibility, but that would have had the immediate drawback of pulling labor away from the lands of the planters (Bruce, 1935:585).

The prosperity of a settlement like that of Virginia, which depended upon the production of commodities for export, was therefore far from assured merely by the existence of "plenty of good land." Good land provided the potential for prosperity, but it was labor power, manifested as cleared land and a product for market, that ultimately stood between the planter and profits. Thus, access to the labor of others marked the distinction between those at the top and those at the bottom of the social structure. Within this context, control over labor would be a significant feature of life in colonies such as seventeenth-century Virginia.

Hence, while Adam Smith (1976) assumed that free labor (wage labor) would be the normal form utilized in new undertakings, free labor did not fit the reality of the Virginia colony. Merivale (1967:261) gives us a clearer image of what went on in colonial Virginia in his discussion of land-labor relationships in settlements producing staples. He stated that during the early phase of such settlements, production takes place on a small scale with the use of some unfree laborers. Over time, however, there is a transition from small land holdings worked on by a few unfree laborers to large land holdings worked on by many unfree laborers. Key to the discussion is his assertion that unfree labor rather than wage labor is utilized during both periods of production.

In fact, bonded labor was absolutely critical to the stabilization of the Virginia colony, because there was a dearth of laborers combined with a surplus of land. Because the planters had to pay for the transportation and subsistence of individuals coming over as laborers, there had to be some way to protect their investment.[15] This translates into the fact that new immigrants were restrained from striking out on their own once their passage had been paid for (Main, 1982:100).

The existence of a surplus of land was connected in three ways to the use of indentured servitude as the early form of unfree labor. One connection is that land served as payment to those who could pay for the passage of another to the colony. This was an immediate gain. Another connection is that the land served as payment to the servant at the end of the labor service. This was a future gain. The third connection is that surplus land served as a means by which the servants might escape from the full period of their service. This was a constant threat of loss.

Connections one and three made some form of unfree labor a critical feature of seventeenth-century capitalism in Virginia. But connection two made indentured servitude possible (with the existence of a labor force, of course) in its specific form. Under different conditions, such as the lack of land to pay for labor, slavery or wage labor would have developed (Merivale, 1967).[16]

When looking at the links between structural position and the mechanisms by which individuals were assigned to specific social slots during early colonial America, we have to keep in mind the need for labor and the existence of surplus land in the colonies as well as the availability of labor (i.e., the existence of surplus labor) in England.[17]

Structural position and attitudes

After the native population had been subdued and moved from the Virginia coast, indentured laborers became even more prevalent. At that time the lower group was primarily composed of individuals with the same range of skin pigmentation as the upper group (i.e., landlords and indentured servants were similar in skin pigment, especially when compared to the general landlord-slave differences). This accounts for the lack of skin pigmentation as the mark of distinction between the upper and lower European group during the seventeenth century in Virginia. On the other hand, there were not many struggles over other marks either. One reason why the attributes used to assign individuals to the upper and lower structural slots were not more obviously drawn during the early period of colonial settlement is that defining the characteristics of the two groups had already been accomplished in England.[18]

Stone and Stone (1984:397) characterize English society from the sixteenth through the nineteenth centuries as hierarchically organized, based upon deference to the privilege of birth. Wrighton (1982:19) describes the stratified system of seventeenth-century England as having four levels consisting of gentlemen, citizens and burgesses of the cities, yeomen of the countryside, and, at the bottom, day laborers, poor husbandmen, artificers, and servants. Of particular interest are his descriptions of the highest and lowest strata. Gentlemen are described as "those whome their *race* and *blood* or at least their vertues doo make noble and knowne."[19] Day laborers are described as "people who had neither voice nor authorite in the common wealthe, but are to be ruled and not rule others" (Wrighton, 1982:19).

The attributes for assigning individuals to social slots in sixteenth- and seventeenth-century England were perceived as natural, (i.e., in the "blood") and were defined by life chances, styles of dress, address, and behavior. Those features were directly transplanted to the colonies.

Smith (1965:16) points out that by 1619 – slightly over a decade after the settling of the Virginia colony – servants had become a distinct part of the colonial community. Because it is clear that the stratification of early colonial society was based upon a mark other than skin pigmentation, the period between 1607 and the 1660s is critical for our understanding of the relationship between structural positions and moral values (i.e., marks of vertical classification). Williams (1966:16) states that:

servitude, originally a free personal relation based on voluntary contract for a definite period of service, in lieu of transportation and maintenance, tended to pass into a property relation which asserted a control of varying extent over the bodies and liberties of the person during service as if he were a thing.

This transition follows logically from the attitude expressed within English society toward those at the bottom of the classification system as people without voice or political power within the social system.

In calling our attention to the manner in which the structurally and morally low group was perceived in colonial America, Perkins (1980:70) states:

In the tobacco colonies, planters constantly complained about the poor quality of servant labor. Masters invariably described their white indentures as lazy, ignorant, and alcoholic idlers, who were universally ungrateful, unruly, and irresponsible.[20]

This perception of the lower group in the colonies parallels the view of the lower group in seventeenth-century England.

We can get another view of that lower group from the debates surrounding the English poor laws. Crucial to that debate was the distinction between *the deserving poor* and *those who would not work*. The deserving poor were sent to work houses, but the others were characterized as "idle, debauched, and profane" (Hill, 1961:24).

Debates about the poor laws reflect the strain in English society between the importance of the poor as a vital resource for the economy (i.e., the poor should remain poor) and the sense that the poor should be kept "adequately and properly employed" (Coleman, 1956:280). On the one hand, the poor were a source of labor for producing necessary goods. On the other hand, there was also a perception of the danger of the existence of a large number of poor in the society.[21] The general notion was that "casual labour is a good basis for a mob, and a mob a valuable part of a well-organized riot." This attitude was expressed through the notion that if the poor did not work, they would develop habits of idleness, laziness, and debauchery (Coleman, 1956:291).[22]

In this case, when it is argued that idlenesss, laziness, and debauchery will result if the poor are not kept laboring, it is not surprising that the poor are perceived as always being at the bottom of the society as laborers. And it is also not surprising that the poor were defined as that sector of the population that was to be ruled. Such was the attitude in seventeenth-century England and its colonies in North America.

We would thus be legitimate in looking at this early period of U.S. history as one in which the attribute used to justify the assignment of individuals into structural positions moved from skin pigment/culture (White/civilized and Red/uncivilized) and class (upper class and lower class) to one in which class in the form of the rise of indentured servitude became the dominant mark.

The decline of skin pigmentation/culture as the early mark of vertical classification in colonial America, not surprisingly, coincided with a decline in the native population due to death from wars, disease, and forced migration from the Atlantic coast. This decline meant that there was a diminishing pool of labor available from among the native population. In addition, of course, the role played by the native population as a source of social cohesion by supplying food for the settlers became less significant as more laborers were brought in from England and as food cultivation developed more extensively (Williams, 1966:9; Morgan, 1975:19). In effect, because the labor of the native population did not long remain important to the social structure of British colonial North America, they were pushed to the outskirts of the social system and thus were less important.[23] The decline of skin pigmentation/culture as the early mark of vertical classification resulted in more functional prominence of the upper-class and lower-class marks.[24]

But once we have established that unfree labor in the colonies was related to the perceived labor needs of the context and times, it is legitimate to move toward a discussion of the shift from servitude to slavery. In addition, because unfree labor as the lowest slot (negative pole) in the early colonies had moral values attached to it, the expectation is that if the structure of the lowest slot changed, or if those peopling that slot changed, there might be a change in the mark of vertical classification. Without this understanding we easily slip into the existing mode of thinking, which tries to explain the utilization of Africans as the exclusive unfree labor force after the late seventeenth century primarily by skin pigmentation differences.

The process of filling the lowest slot of the early colonies relates directly to the fact that the class structure in England was transposed to the colonies. The tension between the need for a large number of poor and the fear of the mob behavior of the nonlaboring poor became acute in seventeenth-century England as more and more poor flooded the cities because "the decline in English foreign trade and the stagnation of home industry had brought unemployment and suffering to every class of workers" (Wertenbaker, 1959:30). At this point, fear of the mob won out and the same forces that drove migrants to the cities generated the context within which they were transported to the colonies.

The indentured servant slot was primarily, but not exclusively, peopled by the surplus population of England's social structure. The poor were fine as long as they were working; out of work, they were viewed by the upper group as a threat to the stability of the social system.

Attempts at portraying how the lower slot of early colonial America was peopled is greatly caught up in the process of maintaining an image of the creation and development of the United States as equal and nonhierarchical until the introduction of sectors of the African population. It is clear, however, that not only was the structure hierarchical, but that the peopling process from England was not without its trauma for the poor who came and worked as indentured servants.[25]

Following the structure laid out by Merivale (1967), the shift from using unfree labor on a small scale to using it on a large scale is the basis of the shift from indentured servitude to slavery. This shift can clearly be seen through the changes in the structure of production from tobacco to rice and cotton as well as in the passage of laws that made slavery legal. But before moving to the creation of the slave labor slot, it is important to look at the social systems in West Africa.

5 The hierarchical structure of West African societies: some theoretical notions

The introduction of African people into hierarchically stratified, European-dominated North America provided the historical basis for the modern use of skin pigmentation as the mechanism that determines the identity (social value) of individuals in the United States. It is important, however, that we not rely upon our present notions of distinctions between Africans/Blacks and Europeans/Whites as explanations for that introduction. Thus the assignment of people from Africa to the slave labor slot in the North American social structure needs further investigation.

I have demonstrated that an unfree labor slot already existed in the North American colonies for reasons having nothing to do with Africa or Africans and hence their skin pigmentation. In addition, I have shown that there existed mechanisms of identification that were congruent with distinguishing between groups that occupied the top slots and groups that occupied the bottom slots of the social system in Colonial Virginia.

Within this context, we can distinguish between the movement from the indentured labor slot to the slave labor slot and the movement from a majority European population to a majority African population in those slots. The shift from indentured servitude to slavery was a transformation in the structure of the unfree labor slot. In the most simplistic terms, it was a shift from laboring without pay for seven years to laboring without pay for life.[1] The shift from Europeans to Africans as the dominant population occupying the unfree labor slot transformed the people who occupied the unfree labor slot. The fact that these transformations occurred at the same time does not in and of itself justify the assertion that the shift to slavery was fundamentally determined by the existence of the skin pigment differences between Africans and Europeans.

The assumption throughout this work is that an understanding of the introduction of people from Africa into the slave labor slot (which set up the conditions for the use of skin pigmentation as the identification of one's structural and status place in society) needs to be separated from the existence of an unfree labor slot in the Virginia colony. Within this context, the shift from indentured servitude to slavery can be analyzed largely from the perspective of conditions in the developing English empire.[2] It can be seen largely as the result of an existing structural compulsion to assign people (without an essential regard to their skin pigmentation) to a particular labor slot in North America.[3]

The shift from Europeans to Africans cannot be solely analyzed within this English empire context, however, because the availability of Africans to fill the unfree labor slot cannot be primarily accounted for by conditions within the English empire. Africans were external to that social structure, (i.e., were external to the power relations that characterized the interactions of the weak and the powerful in that specific social structure). This externality therefore makes necessary a specific analysis of those African societies that provided the people who were used as slaves in North America.

Although the above position is logical, it is clearly not the only conceivable approach to explaining the issue at hand. It is certainly possible, especially from present societal perspectives, to argue that the need to assign people to the unfree labor slot in North America was indeed the dominant factor in the use of Africans in that slot.[4] This position, which I characterize as the European power and attitude position, results in an important implicit conclusion that warrants further discussion. It implies that there is no need to look at the impact of social structural factors in Africa in regard to the rise of skin pigmentation as the basis of present identity (or social value).[5] The implicit assumption of that position is that the context out of which sectors of the African population were brought to North America needs no investigation.

The European power and attitude position presents us with conceptual as well as historical contradictions, however. Conceptually, it poses the existence of a homogenous European population as well as a homogenous African population. I have already addressed the fact that seventeenth-century England as well as the Virginia colony were far from homogenous in terms of the very significant variable of class. They indeed were hierarchically stratified social systems. But homogeneity here, as we know, refers to skin pigmentation. Clearly the use of skin pigmentation in this context camouflages the existence of at least one other basis of evaluating the extent of the homogeneity of life chances within a specific society.[6]

Historically, a significant contradiction in the European power and attitude position can be found in the existence of the trade in people from Africa. As was the case with other regions external to the European world system, Europeans did not penetrate far into the West African coast until the nineteenth century. European power, even during the seventeenth century, was primarily naval and as a result was incapable of extracting the large numbers of individuals from the inland societies of West Africa without the aid of mechanisms that directly interacted with those societies.[7] Hence, European power and attitude alone could not have sufficed as the bases upon which people from West Africa were transported from their communities to the Atlantic coast (Wallerstein, 1974:330).

Given these conceptual and historical contradictions of the European power and attitude position it is legitimate to assume that we can gain from looking more carefully at the social structures in North America and in West Africa to avoid having to rely solely upon the European power and attitude perspective when analyzing the process by which some Africans were assigned to the slave slot in the North American society during the late seventeenth century.

The following points are important in this chapter. First, I do not view the use of a sector of the African population to exclusively fill the unfree labor force as having been inevitable, regardless of the differences in skin pigmentation between Europeans and Africans. Second, the fact that Africans entered the Virginia social structure did not in itself create the mechanisms by which to characterize those at the bottom of that structure with a negative collective identity and those at the top with a positive collective identity.

The world system

The above assertions by no means negate all of our contemporary general notions about slavery and skin pigmentation, however. It is certainly true that a need for unfree labor on the plantations of the English colonies was an important factor in the use of a segment of the African population as unfree labors in North America. But it is also true that limitations on the available technology necessary for the transportation of large numbers of people by way of the ocean was another factor (Bowen, 1961; Braudel, 1976). The fact that the colonization of North America was simultaneous with the colonization of Ireland was also a factor in the exclusive use of a sector of Africans as unfree laborers by the beginning of the eighteenth century.[8] In addition, a decline in the population of England during the late seventeenth century also contributed to the enslavement of a segment of the African population (Helleiner, 1967).

Beyond expanding upon the idea of the need for labor, however, the crucial point here is that the above factors individually or in combination (all factors external to African societies) could not have resulted in the movement out of Africa of segments of the population on the scale that it took place (Williams, 1966; Curtin, 1975). What needs to be addressed is how the existence of hierarchically structured social systems in Africa contributed to the process that assigned a segment of the African population to the lowest slot of the developing North American social structure. To the extent that this is true, it implies that the transfer of one segment of the African population to the New World required the organized and systematic interaction of at least one segment of the African population with at least one segment of the European population as trading partners.

This perspective is by no means an attempt at forcing Africans to take the blame for the trade in humans, which is generally mislabeled the slave trade. Quite the contrary, at the broadest level the point is to dispel the notion that Africans, as an undifferentiated group, were assigned to the slave labor slot in North America at the whim (power and attitudes) of Europeans as a homogeneous group. In this manner we can move beyond the screen that race puts between historical facts and our perceptions. Such an exploration forces us to look more carefully at what happens when hierarchically structured social systems interact with each other without the basic structure of either being destroyed by that interaction. This type of interaction is therefore in marked contrast to the type of interaction that occurred when English settlers went into North America and eventually carved out a stable settlement, such as in Virginia. In this case, we have people from a sector of a world economy (traders from England) interacting with people from a sector of a region external to that world economy (traders from West African societies).[9]

The fact that the interaction between English traders and West African traders was the interaction of people from a developing core structure with people from an external region distinguishes between the type of domination that occurred to Native Americans during the seventeenth and eighteenth centuries and that which occurred to that sector of West Africans who were enslaved. The temptation is to characterize the two forms of domination as the same, thus reinforcing the notion of a homogenous European group dominating and capturing all Africans as a homogenous group. Wallerstein (1974:339) here greatly helps our thinking when he states: "Handling oneself in the periphery and in the external arena are different skills. It is only in the periphery that the economically more powerful group is able to reinforce its position by cultural domination as well." We can take this to mean that because West Africa was an external region of the European world economy during the seventeenth century while the Virginia colony was a peripheral region, there would have been different degrees and forms of domination in the two regions. The interactions with which we are concerned cannot therefore be simply lumped together as instances of European domination.

Indeed, something distinctive and lasting occurred as the representatives of the upper sectors of stratified West African social structures traded with representatives of the upper sectors of the stratified European and North American social structures. But again, we should not confuse the results of that phenomenon with their cause. It is, therefore, important to keep in mind that this interaction occurred within the larger context of the creation of a European world system. With this clearly fixed in our consciousness, it is easier to see how hierarchically stratified social systems in various parts of the world interacted during the creation of the European world system and in turn created skin pigmentation as the significant modern mark of identity.

In this approach, skin pigmentation is less important than the existence of hierarchical stratification as a form of organizing social structures in attempting to explain the phenomena of social inequality in the modern world. We therefore return to the importance of viewing the structure of social systems (the organization of differentially valued slots) as existing prior to the process by which groups of people with specific physical features are assigned to those slots.

Hierarchical stratification in precolonial West Africa

The historical evidence concerning the social structure of West African societies prior to and during the Atlantic slave trade appears, on its surface, to be contradictory. There are, for instance, statements concerning the communal ownership of land, whereas at the same time there are statements about kings and chiefs. There are statements about the existence of empires, whereas nonstate societies are also discussed. Long-distance trade is highly significant in some writings, whereas others stress the fact that local barter systems were key to those societies. Some writings stress the importance of slavery to the internal development of societies, whereas it is ignored in other writings (Lovejoy, 1979).

Out of these contradictory views have come many different positions on the relationships between the internal structure of African societies and the trade in people that began in earnest during the seventeenth century. After all, it makes a difference if the West African social systems that were the source of people who were assigned to the slave labor slot were stratified or nonstratified. If they were nonstratified social systems, it would be expected that the population was fairly homogenous in power relations and as a result all individuals were available for enslavement. On the other hand, if they were stratified social systems, it would be expected that there would be some inequality in how individuals were made available for assignment. The need to resolve this issue is therefore critical to a larger understanding of how people were uprooted from one social system and transported to another.

What appears to be a set of contradictory facts on the surface, however, can be given unity by using a logical framework that does not negate their essence. That framework consists of focusing upon the combination of methods by which labor was organized for production and surplus appropriation within the diversified group of West African societies.[10]

Despite the fact that various forms of labor organization and surplus appropriation can coexist, one form is always dominant (Marx, 1965; Terray, 1972; Amin, 1976:16–22). This understanding allows us to look systematically at the methods of production and the appropriation of value within the geopolitical units of the West African empires prior to and during the Atlantic slave trade (Cipolla, 1970; Wallerstein, 1974:15).[11]

Three factors are important in helping us to understand how African societies provided the population that became assigned to the slave labor slot in North America and thus created the basis for skin pigmentation as the mark of identity (social value) in the United States:

1. The predominance of a communal method of labor organization with a slave labor organization subordinate to it.
2. The centrality of long-distance trade.
3. The existence of an empire (with tribute payment as an important basis of surplus extraction) as the geopolitical unit within which the methods of labor organization and long-distance trade operated.

These factors indicate the existence of a hierarchically structured social system (an empire) within which communally organized forms of labor occurred alongside the use of slave labor. The important point here is that the seeming contradiction between communal and hierarchical systems is resolved, because the communal system of labor organization in fact existed within the context of a hierarchically organized political system. This system has been characterized as a type of world system held together by military force (i.e., a world empire), as is indicated by Wallerstein (1974:348) when he asserts that world empires have a single political system over most of their areas, although there exists a division of labor as well as multiple cultures within them.

The existence of a single political system (an empire) accounts for the fact that different forms of labor were used to pay tribute to the central administration. The upper group within such a social system was distinguished by the fact that they were the recipients of tribute and, therefore, the recipients of the results of the labor of others. As is the case in all empires, military force was used to extract tribute. Empires in fact are built upon the military conquest of people who are rooted to the land. In the resulting social organization, the dominant group extracts tribute from the weaker regions. But during that process there is no transformation of the basic methods by which production takes place in the conquered region.

Because they are premised upon military conquest without the disruption of traditional forms of production, empires have some inherent weaknesses. One significant weakness is that the upper group within empires is fundamentally dependent upon the ability of the dominated group to produce goods efficiently. This gives leverage to direct producers. Indeed, this leverage can provide vital insights into the interaction of communal and stratified organizations of production in West Africa that contributed to the trade in humans.[12]

The communal form of labor organization

As an ideal type, the communal form of labor organization exists before the beginning of class distinctions within society. In fact, even in their earliest form, there were distinctions within that form that indicate the seeds of stratification (Marx, 1965:19–20). Thus, in actual communal societies, labor has been organized partly on an individual basis and partly on a collective basis. The individual organization is generally centered around individual families (as opposed to individuals), with the division of labor being along age and sex lines (Bucher, 1912:54; Krader, 1972:75). The collective organization is generally centered around the extended family, the clan, or the village. Projects affecting units larger than the family are carried out with this collective method of organizing labor (Bucher, 1912:55).

Land is the dominant unit to which labor is applied in the communal form of production. Within that form, land is collectively owned by the clan and granted to all families as it is needed. The major restriction upon land use in the communal form is that it cannot be sold and therefore can never become the private property of an individual or group.

Despite this image of the ideal communal society, however, hierarchical distinctions do exist within this form of labor organization. These distinctions are rooted in the unequal distribution of quality land, the unequal distribution of goods, the unequal use of the labor of women and children, and the use of slave labor. Hence, in spite of the fact that land within this form of organization is not privately held, inequality can and generally does exist within it (Krader, 1972:22).

Hierarchical distinctions are specifically manifested in the form of families and clans gaining access to more fertile land holdings, better situated holdings, and monopoly over the use of the labor of others. These privileges are generally gained from the existence of religious and political (military) power within a community (Neibor, 1910:7). Some of the problems involved in the different perceptions of scholars studying early African societies can be resolved by understanding the differences between the ideal version of the communal organization of labor and the historically developed form (Anderson, 1979:400).

Tribute-paying surplus extraction

Tribute paying distinguishes between those who have less power within the communal social structure and those with slightly more power within it. This is achieved when the surplus (that which is above and beyond what is necessary for the reproduction of those at the lower level of the social structure) of the direct producers of the communal social structure is transferred to those at the top. This allows us to see that even while direct producers (laborers) remain organized in communities based upon production for need, goods can still be extracted from them through the use of force without interrupting the basic organization of their production.[13] Thus, the communal form can exist on the surface of an exploitative system of surplus extraction.

Tribute paying can develop in two basic ways. On the one hand, those to whom tribute is paid (the upper sector) can arise as a family or faction within the community and then separate themselves from the rest of the community. On the other hand, a distinct group from outside can impose itself upon an existing community. In both cases, tribute paying is distinguished by the superimposition of a social and political apparatus upon an existing community to exploit that community (Amin, 1976:16).[14]

Regardless of its origin, tribute is extracted by force, be it ideological or material. However, the possession of land by the direct producers allows resistance, which can result in limitations upon the amount of goods that can be extracted from the community by the upper sector. This fact is very significant for our understanding of the relationship of this type of hierarchical structure to the availability of sectors of the African population that would be assigned to the slave labor slot of the North American colonies.

The slave-owning organization of labor

The slave-owning organization of labor is distinct from the mere use of individuals as personal servants. Slave owners own individuals who produce goods that are valuable for exchange. Slaves used in agriculture, mines, industry, and crafts are examples of such a form of organization.[15] In this context a person is turned into a permanent producer, a commodity.

Amin (1976:16) argues that slavery in West African societies prior to European contact was always subordinate to tribute paying as the mechanism by which surplus was transferred from the lower sector to the upper sector. Thus, forms of labor organization other than slavery (i.e., other than unfree labor) were generally the bases of labor organization during this period in West Africa.

An additional point needs to be made, however. Because both tribute paying and slavery are based upon geographical conquest, one would expect to find them together in specific contexts (Anderson,1979:28). Thus, although slave labor was a feature of some West African social structures between the sixteenth and seventeenth centuries, it was not central to the process by which a sector of the West African population was shipped to North America.[16]

Long-distance trade

Long-distance trade was a critical feature of West African societies prior to contact with Europeans along the Atlantic coast. That early long-distance trade was through the Sahara Desert and was critical to the social structure of societies in West Africa. This long-distance trade does not include the trade between the forest region and the savannah region, nor the trade between the coastal region and the forest region during the precolonial period.

Discussions of the makeup of the social structure of African societies prior to European contact through the Atlantic have drawn a direct link between long-distance trade, tribute, and the power of the ruling group. The fundamental emphasis has been upon the fact that the extent and type of tribute were the bases of the long-distance trade that in turn influenced the power of the ruling group within those societies (Amin, 1976:16; Coquery-Vidnovitch, 1976b:106–7). This formulation, however, ignores the varying organizations of labor indicated above that existed in Africa during that period. Just as important, it also ignores the necessity of the long-distance trade for salt, even for groups that were not integrated into a tribute-paying system. Bucher (1912:67) speaks generally to this point when he discusses the bases of trade between local societies. He states:

The object of the interchange is to obtain products that cannot be produced in one's own tribe at all, or at least cannot be produced as well and so artistically as in neighboring tribes. This must again lead each tribe to produce in greater quantities than it requires those products which are valued among the tribes not producing them, because in exchange for these it is easiest to obtain that which one does not possess one's self, but which others manufacture in surplus quantities.

Within this context we can see that although trade may be significant to an understanding of the structure of early African social structures, trade did not consist merely of tribute extracted by the ruling elite from direct producers. For instance, the necessity of salt required trade for some societies, regardless of whether tribute was one of its essential features.

More to the point, long-distance trade was ultimately under the control of the state bureaucracy of the early as well as the late empires in West Africa.[17] This was so even though traders who were independent of specific states were the dominant merchants of the long-distance trade, because the political and military force in the state bureaucracy ensured the safety of the traders and kept the trade routes in good order. This was not done out of generosity, however. In the bargain, the ruling elites benefited from the organized taxation of goods traded and from the stable system used to trade goods obtained through tribute.

Long-distance trade grew in importance as the societies in general and the ruling groups in particular came to depend upon the exchange of the surplus of their direct producers for goods from outside of the social system. This trade therefore became less important when the desired goods could be produced locally.[18] Long-distance trade within this context is therefore best characterized as the method by which goods produced under the various methods of labor production in West Africa were linked with other world systems. Thus, long-distance trade was critical to the process by which the West African societies and the European world system interacted. The relationship of that interaction to the process by which sectors of the West African societies were made available for enslavement in North America is the next topic of discussion.

6   The logic of a trade in humans

There are some significant points that will guide our discussion of the specific impact of African social systems upon the availability of a sector of its population to fill the unfree labor slot in North America. But unlike most discussions of the African slave trade, we will focus here upon the interaction between empires (or world systems) and state structures (the components of empires). This specifically means that we will look at the existence of hierarchical stratification at the level of the empire as well as at the level of local production communities, or state structures. This approach allows us to look more broadly at some of the transformations that made the export of people logical at an economic level for some sectors of the societies under discussion. At the same time, it will provide the historical grounding for the theoretical notions that were introduced in Chapter 5.

Here we will concentrate upon transformations in the social structure of the Mali empire (thirteenth to late fifteenth centuries) and the Songhai empire (late fifteenth to late sixteenth centuries) in West Africa. By looking at both empires we will be able to illustrate generally the structure of West African empires and at the same time show how specific historical moments and structural forms resulted in significantly different responses by ruling groups to shifts in their ability to extract surplus.

Divisions within the Mali empire

The Mali empire was based upon a center-periphery political administration. The center was inhabited by the Mandingo people and was, in turn, divided into three geographical sectors. The largest sectors, called provinces, were always governed by relatives or trusted friends of the king of the empire. Provinces were also divided into regions referred to as districts. Each district, in turn, had a leader. Districts were further divided into village communities. At each level, starting with the village communities, the leaders were required to collect the annual tax on agricultural produce and livestock, as well as to make sure that tribute was sent to the central government and that each sector sent its requisite number of men to the central army (Levitzion, 1980).

The peripheral areas were composed of the conquered people of the tributary states. The conquered people were ruled indirectly. Toward

59

this end, the traditional ruler of the peripheral state would be granted the right of office by the king in an elaborate ceremony. In turn, the local leader would then pledge allegiance to the central government. Thus, the central government could continue to utilize the socioreligious influences of the traditional leader. Through this local influence, the bureaucracy of the empire could function without having to occupy every conquered province, district, and village community with an army that was directly loyal to the central government (Levitzion, 1980:15). In turn, the central government maintained order along trade routes so that traders and travelers could move about in safety. Its positive role toward the tribute payers took the form of protector. The tribute payers were protected from raids by other groups who might be inside or outside of the empire. This system resulted from the need to maintain the local organization of production.

Revenue was gained by the central government from tribute for protection in the form of food, clothing, and craft items, the imposition of tolls on trade routes, and a monopoly on all gold nuggets and war booty. One significant war booty was the ability to obtain workers, sometimes as slaves (Levitzion, 1980:51,156; Stride and Ifeka, 1971).

Additional sources of revenue included plantations that used slave labor. These plantations were specifically organized to supply the needs of the king and his court (Levitzion, 1980:59). Revenue was thus obtained in traditional ways (through tribute) as well as in nontraditional ways (by producing commodities through the use of slave labor on plantations). The existence of plantations in the Mali empire indicates a clear separation between the central government and the local communities as sources of surplus. Their existence can also be seen as a sign that the upper (or ruling) group was aware of some of the limitations involved in collecting tribute from communal societies and was taking steps to address those limitations.

The production that took place on plantations did not interrupt the traditional production methods of the conquered peoples, however. Rather, some individuals from the conquered populations were utilized specifically for generating the exchange and consumption needs of the crown (Levitzion, 1980:175). The rise of a slave-owning method of production was, therefore, secondary to local production at the same time that it pointed toward providing some economic independence for the central government. Nonetheless, tribute remained the essential feature of the revenue base of the Mali empire throughout its existence.

As has been pointed out in the previous chapter, trade was a very important feature of the process by which tribute was transformed into revenue. In addition to the centrality of trade as a mechanism for transforming tribute from the local level, it also was a direct source of revenue for the ruling group. Trade provided revenue to the Empire as a result of the tolls placed upon the goods. Thus, local as well as the more lucrative long-distance trade generated revenue. Local leaders taxed agriculture, fish, cattle, and other goods as they passed between peripheral groups. Stride and Ifeka (1971:239; see also Levitzion, 1980:117) state: "Farmers, fishermen, and cattle breeders lived close to each other and exchanged their products. The diversity of primary products stimulated local trade and also broadened the economic pace of the Empire."

At another level, taxes were collected on rice that went from Gambia to the hinterland in exchange for iron. Millet and sorghum, which were grown in the savannah region, were taxed as they went to Timbuktu, Waluta, and the salt mines of Taghaza (see Figure 1). These examples indicate that local as well as middle-distance trade were taxed as goods moved along the routes of the empire. They also indicate, however, that the ruling groups of peripheral areas were structurally separated from local producers. This was the case precisely because those ruling groups had to use the direct producers in order to generate tribute for the central government. These local ruling groups tended to utilize the military support of the central government to tax items that were necessities rather than luxuries. When we move to the Trans-Sahara trade – and into long-distance trade proper – we see a different situation.

Long-distance trade through the Sahara was generally a reflection of the needs of the central government. Salt, horses, and military weapons were brought from the north to the south. Salt was a necessity for the general population, and horses and military weapons were necessary for the continual expansion of the empire. High-quality textiles, preserved foodstuffs, copper, glassware, beads, and the occasional foreign slave were other nonnecessities that were imported south of the Sahara. Gold, expensive cloth, pepper, iron, kola nuts, and leather goods were sent in exchange for the goods from the north.

This geographical division of labor made trade at the local-, middle-, and long-distance level necessary. Through trade the military-based empire could ultimately generate revenue from its rule over communal groups. Because trade was the root of its power, the ruling group of the Mali empire needed to ensure that communities remained specialized producers. Therefore, communal and slave-owning methods of production limited technological advances in the empire. In addition, the methods that generated revenue in the empire also made advances in production (outside of slave villages) a liability for the ruling group.

The decline of the Mali empire by the sixteenth century has the ring of the ideal type of decline of empires. One after another, the vassal states revolted against the central state and the local ruling group was no longer forced to send tribute to the center. The central government thereby lost its military and economic power and became unable to enforce its rule. It was largely excess taxation and raids into the vassal states by the rulers of Mali that gave rise to the revolts.

The loss of power by the Mali rulers did not result in the continued independence of all of the rebellious states, however, because also as in the ideal case of empire decline, a central administration was re-created as one region was able to utilize its superior military power to subordinate other regions. Thus, the decline of the Mali empire resulted in the rise of the Songhai empire.

Divisions within the Songhai empire (1490 to 1595)

The Songhai empire (from 1490 to 1595) encompassed fertile regions suited for agriculture and cattle raising. In addition, fish was available from the Niger River region. Trading, fishing, agriculture, cattle rearing, and hunting were the basic arenas in which the population produced goods for survival. Its southeast border extended through what is presently Guinea, touching slightly the northwest corner of what is now the Ivory Coast, through Upper Volta, the northwest tip of modern Benin, and into the northern part of modern Nigeria and most of modern Niger. The empire also extended north, taking in most of modern Mali and the salt-mining region of present-day Algeria. It even had access to the Atlantic Ocean in what is presently Senegal (Figure 1).

The upper (or ruling) sector of this empire controlled the three major trade routes through the Sahara during the fifteenth and sixteenth centuries and also controlled the salt, iron, and gold mines over the wide expanse of the empire. Thus, the size of the empire was matched by the complexity of the methods that enabled the central bureaucracy to benefit from the labor of others through the extraction of surplus. According to Boahen (1966:29) revenue was basically generated by:

1. *Royal estates worked by slaves.* Each estate had to produce a fixed quantity of a particular commodity per year. Slave labor was the norm here.
2. *Tribute from vassal states.* A fixed amount of tribute was determined after the period of conquest. Although tribute was paid by the states, the specific goods were initially obtained by the local upper-class group in the form of tribute from local (or direct) producers.
3. *Regular contributions from generals.* These contributions by military commanders were obtained through taxing peasants and farmers. This revenue was in addition to that obtained by the local elite.

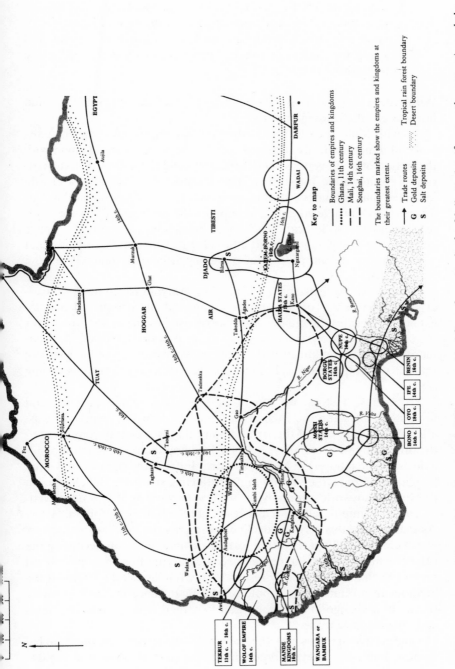

Figure 1. *A map of West Africa, showing the Ghana empire (eleventh century), the Mali empire (fourteenth century), and the Songhai empire (sixteenth century) and trade routes to the north. Source: Michael Kwamena-Poh, J. Posh, R. Waller, M. Tidy. African History in Maps. London: Longmans, 1982. Used with permission of the publisher.*

4. *Custom duties.* To ensure maximum income from tolls and custom duties, trade and commerce were promoted. Routes were
made safe by controlling groups known to be troublesome, and
a uniform system of weights and measures was put into place
throughout the empire.

Within the empire gold and ivory were the chief exports, while salt and
horses were the leading imports.

As with Mali, such factors in the Songhai empire illustrate the existence of a hierarchically stratified social system that is inconsistent with
the notion of homogenous social structures and the notion that all Africans were available for slavery. The existence of royal estates clearly
indicates that the upper strata intervened in the arena of production.
There, slaves produced goods to support the army and for trade. This
resulted in the solidification of class distinctions, because the upper
group was thereby able to build a base for its economic well-being that
was distinct from the process of obtaining tribute payments from the
vassal states.

In addition, the existence of a standing army, in which military leaders from the center of the empire dominated the conquered people,
explicitly indicates the greater control exercised by the upper group over
the conquered regions. Once a standing army was established, the center of the empire no longer had to depend exclusively upon the sporadic
services of conquered people to assure the extraction of surplus for the
center.

From these factors, we can observe a few fundamental structural
distinctions between the Mali empire and the Songhai empire. It was,
after all, the breakup of the latter empire that was closely connected to
the process by which sectors of the African population were made available as unfree laborers in North America. Indeed, the significance of the
Songhai empire is to be found in its distinctive structure and changes in
the European world economy, as well as in the way it was destroyed.

The Mali empire fell apart as a result of rebellion by peripheral states.
As mentioned, this form of decline represents the classical method by
which empires fall apart, with a former peripheral region becoming the
center, while the former center becomes a tribute-paying peripheral
region. Such a decline rarely results in any fundamental changes in the
methods of production or tribute or in long-distance trade. It basically
results in a change in the group that benefited from tribute payments
and long-distance trade.

Routine change was not the case with the decline of the Songhai
empire, however. Indeed, rebellion on the part of peripheral regions
was not the problem for the ruling group. Rather, the empire was con-

quered by Morocco, from the outside.[1] This difference in the decline of the Songhai empire is significant for our understanding of the relationship of factors within West Africa to the process that made people available for assignment to the slave slot in North America. The manner in which the Songhai empire was destroyed made it necessary for ruling groups in the local communities to respond to the production of revenue and trade in ways that were new to the region. The hierarchical structure of the empire and contact with the European world economy made a successful response possible.

The shift of trade toward the Atlantic: the rise of small states

Unlike what had previously occurred in the classical decline of empires, the Moroccans did not step in to replace the destroyed central state structure of the Songhai empire. In fact, they utilized their power to prevent the reunification of any large empire immediately south of the Sahara. The resulting lack of a central government generated a chaotic situation in which the ruling groups of peripheral regions were relegated to continually fighting among themselves for control over tribute and trade.

These struggles had a significant impact upon the region. One indication of this was the decline of traditional trade routes to the north. This lead to merchants struggling for alternative routes through which to exchange tribute for other goods. The development of alternative routes at the end of the sixteenth century resulted in the creation of possibilities for communities near the Atlantic coast to benefit from trade with European merchants. By that time, the Dutch and English were on the Atlantic coast looking for opportunities to trade in gold and ivory as well as people (Rodney, 1964; Polanyi, 1966; Curtin, 1975).

The existence of European merchants on the Atlantic coast provided an alternative outlet for trade, which was already an established method of generating wealth for the ruling group of West Africa. The Dutch and English merchants were therefore the initial European benefactors of the African traders' search for ways to salvage their essential long-distance trade that had been destroyed by the breakup of the Songhai empire. With the destruction of that empire, the major trade routes within West Africa eventually shifted from the Sahara Desert to the Atlantic Ocean.

This shift is an indication of changes within Europe as well as within West Africa, and again illustrates how the two were interconnected on bases other than skin pigment differences. Within the European world economy, the shift of the focal point of trade from the Mediterranean/ Sahara to the Atlantic Ocean resulted from the decline of Portugal (part of that decline resulting from its defeat at the hands of the Moroccans) and Spain and the advance of the Dutch and English as world powers (Braudel, 1976:486).

Shifts in the occupation of hierarchical slots in the European world economy influenced the rise to power of inland societies near the Atlantic coast of West Africa. These small societies (acting independently of a central government as intermediary) were in the position to trade directly with the outside world because of the shift of the European focus from the Mediterranean Sea to the Atlantic Ocean (Davidson, 1961).[2] The important point here, however, is that the destabilization of social systems within West Africa coincided with the shift of European traders away from the Mediterranean and toward the Atlantic. The combination of those factors set the stage for the transfer of people out of West Africa and to North America (Braudel, 1976, Volume I: 486; Rodney, 1964; Curtin, 1975; Polanyi, 1966).

After the destruction of the Songhai empire, the major trade routes within West Africa moved toward the Atlantic (Figures 2 and 3). This situation significantly changed the conditions of societies near and on the Atlantic coast (Boahen, 1966; Davidson, 1961; Levitzion, 1980).[3] Because these societies could trade directly with the outside world, state systems that grew up along and near the Atlantic coast were able to participate in the trade of humans.

The following descriptions of some participating state systems indicate some of the relationships between factors within those West African societies and the process of making people available for enslavement in North America. We can see some similarities, and differences, between the small states developing toward the Atlantic during the seventeenth century and the larger empires organized around the Sahara trade routes. The major similarity was the systems' reliance upon trade premised upon a military-based bureaucratic tribute system. The major difference was in the size of the structures.

The Akan states grew up at the end of the sixteenth century between the Volta River and the basin of the Pra River and their tributaries. One of the larger states, Bono-Tekyima (sixteenth to eighteenth centuries), developed at the end of the trade route from the Jenne and the Niger region. The central area was around the Banda gold fields, which were a major source of the gold that for centuries had been traded to the Arabs and Europeans though the Sahara. The ruling group of Bono-Tekyima dominated the weaker societies in the area, as well as the trade routes. Domination took the specific form of extracting tribute from the direct producers. In this society, the direct producers were able to control production because they occupied the land, but they did not control the trade routes. By 1723, Bono-Tekyima was conquered by the Asante group and reduced to a vassal state.

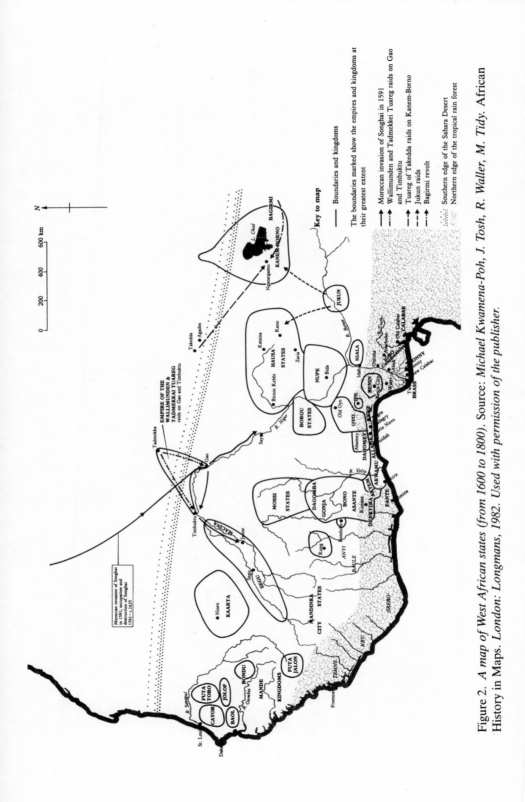

Figure 2. *A map of West African states (from 1600 to 1800).* Source: *Michael Kwamena-Poh, J. Tosh, R. Waller, M. Tidy. African History in Maps. London: Longmans, 1982. Used with permission of the publisher.*

The following labels appear on the map:

Key to map

Boundaries and kingdoms

The boundaries marked show the empires and kingdoms at their greatest extent

Moroccan invasion of Songhai in 1591
Wallimunden and Tadmekkei Tuareg raids on Gao and Timbuktu
Tuareg of Takedda raids on Kanem-Borno
Jukun raids
Bagirmi revolt

Southern edge of the Sahara Desert
Northern edge of the tropical rain forest

BAGIRMI
L. Chad
KANEM-BORNO
Nguarugamu
JUKUN
Takedda
Agades
Kano
Katsina
HAUSA STATES
Zaria
Birnin Kebbi
NUPE
Bida
IGALA
Itah
BENIN
IFE
OYO
Old Oyo
BORGU STATES
Saye
R. Niger
Tadmekka
Gao
EMPIRE OF THE WALLIMUNDEN & TADMEKKAI TUAREG raids on Gao and Timbuktu
Timbuktu
MOSSI STATES
DAGOMBA
GONJA
BONO
ASANTE
Kumasi
Bondu
Kong
ANYI
BAULE
GREBO
KRU
R. Volt
AKWAMU ALLADA
DENKYIRA
FANTE
DAHOMEY
Abomey
Porto Novo
Whidah
Accra
Anomabu
Axim
KAKONA
Jenne
MANDINKA CITY STATES
Segu
SEGU
KAARTA
Nioro
MANDE KINGDOMS
BONDU
PUTA TORO
CAYOR
BAOL
JOLOF
FUTA JALON
R. Senegal
Gambia
St. Louis
Dakar
Freetown
TEMNE
R. Benue
CALABAR
Old Calabar
New Calabar
BONNY
BRASS
IGBO

Moroccan invasion of Songhai in 1591; occupation and destruction of Songhai 1591 – c.1625

N

0   200   400   600 km

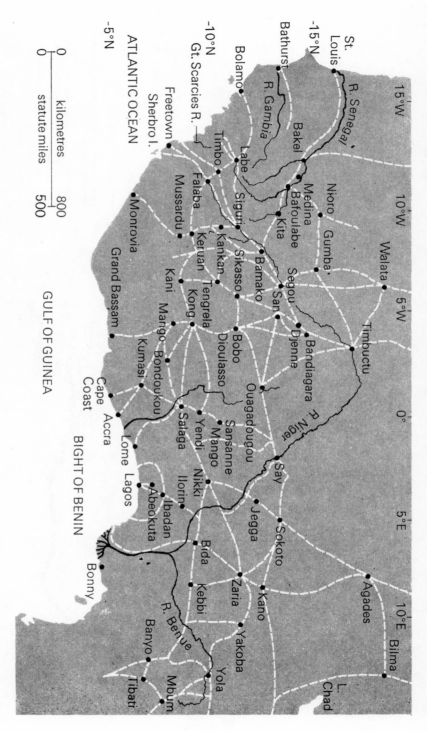

Figure 3. A map of trade routes to the Atlantic Ocean (nineteenth century). Source: A. G. Hopkins. An Economic History of West Africa. New York: Columbia University Press, 1973. Used with permission of the publisher.

Twifo, unlike Bono-Tekyima, was one of the smallest states of the inland region. It also developed in the rich gold-producing region along the Pra River and thus relied upon the trade routes extending north to the Sahara and west to the Atlantic. The ruling group of the Twifo state was able to extract tribute as well as tax trade until it was conquered by the state of Denkyira near the end of the seventeenth century. At that point, Twifo also became a vassal state that was forced to pay tribute.

Assin and Denkyira were similar to the states discussed above. They financed themselves by controlling trade and extracting tribute from conquered groups who could continue to occupy their land. These states were in turn defeated by a stronger state and reduced from tribute takers to tribute payers. Boahen (1966) makes this statement about Denkyira, which became powerful during the second half of the seventeenth century: "By the end of that century Denkyira had conquered Aswin and Sefwi and Wassa to the south-west, Assin, Twifo, Abrambo and Fetu to the south, Adamsi and all the pre-Asante states to the north, and had gained possession of the note for the rent for the Elmina castle" (p. 62). Elmina castle was one of the major forts for holding people prior to their sale to Europeans as slaves. Shortly after 1700, however, Denkyira was defeated and reduced to a vassal state.

The coastal states were also numerous and relatively unstable during the seventeenth and eighteenth centuries. Fante, for instance, flourished from the late seventeenth to the eighteenth century. It expanded between 1660 and 1690 in an attempt to gain control over trade between the interior societies and the European traders. Its expansion consisted of conquering smaller inland societies to extract tribute and dominating trade routes to extract taxes and control the flow of arms. The Akwamu state, prominent during the same period as the Fante state, is described in this manner:

The Akwamu were able to gain a firm control of the trade routes from the region of Accura into the interior by the middle of the seventeenth century, and were able, therefore, to impose duties on traders passing to and fro. The wealth which they derived from this source enabled them to purchase arms and ammunition which greatly facilitated their imperial expansion (Boahen, 1966:67–8).

As was the case with the others, the Akwamu state did not last long. It was defeated in 1730 when the vassal states joined forces to free themselves from the heavy taxes and tribute demanded by the ruling group.

The Asante empire and the empire of Dahomey, both important in the trade of humans from West Africa, did not differ greatly from the above state structures in how they extracted surplus from the population. Tribute and taxes, extracted with the force of arms, were the order of the day. The shift in the long-distance trade routes from the Sahara/

Mediterranean to the Atlantic coincided with and in turn resulted in a situation of constant changes in control over trade routes and tribute in West Africa. What did not change, however, was the extraction of surplus from dominated peoples through tribute and the control over trade. There were also no changes in the methods of production in the area, because the direct producers maintained their hold over the land.

The human trade

To further our discussion, we need to show the links between the structure of the empires that developed below the Sahara desert and those smaller state structures that gained power as trade routes shifted toward the Atlantic. As we have already seen, the larger Saharan empires as well as states involved with Atlantic trade were able to gain revenue through forms of surplus extraction (taxation). Taxation took various forms, including tribute to the central government from conquered states, taxes on all goods passing through the societies, and taxes on long-distance trade.

What stands out is that the central administration in both types of systems depended largely upon trade and tribute from conquered communities to meet its costs. Neither the ruling groups of the empire nor those of the smaller state structures controlled the process of production. Thus, their ability to gain and maintain domination over conquered people rested heavily upon trade within the empire and between the empire and other world systems.

Trade was thus an important mechanism that led to a fundamental distinction between the ruling groups and the direct producers. This is not to imply that long-distance trade created the tribute-paying vassal states. Instead, the ruling groups utilized the revenue gained by trade to increase their independence from the limitations imposed by the fact that land (the means of production) was controlled by the direct producers. By plugging into the world market, the ruling groups were able to grow in strength and develop different interests in regard to relationships between the society and outside world systems.

The empires as well as the later smaller state structures used political/ military methods to extract surplus from the direct producers of goods. As has already been pointed out, the ability of the ruling groups within such systems to expand their power base was inherently limited. Because both the empires and the small state structures were premised upon the maintenance of strong military-based bureaucracies, they operated within a context of production that they did not fully control. The tribute-paying societies of West Africa, like the empires, were thus unstable organizational forms (Polanyi, 1966; Cipolla, 1970).[4]

Because the administrative units of the ruling groups could not control production, but instead gained their surplus from tribute and taxation on trade, it was potentially in their interest to trade the producers and thereby overcome this limitation. If we focus upon factors internal to West Africa, it becomes clear that the trade of humans became full-blown when the tremendous degree of instability that resulted from warfare made it increasingly difficult for any ruling group to institute an efficient administrative staff to determine legitimate amounts of tribute (the essential feature of a tribute-paying system).

To use the conquered peoples as laborers within societies that were primarily based on the communal use of land (or in which the direct producers had control over the land) would have been problematic because of the ability of the population to move away and utilize free land. From the West African perspective, the logic of trading humans was that it allowed for the expansion of trade with the outside world and thereby gave the ruling groups greater independence from the tribute-paying system. The direct link to the outside world system therefore provided the ruling group with a greater degree of control over the local population.

The trade in humans did not create the ruling groups in West Africa. Rather, the trade in humans enabled an already developing state structure to continue to separate itself from the limitations of extracting surplus from the direct producers. Rodney (1970:117) supports this general idea when he states:

It could scarcely have been simple coincidence that the Djolas and the Balantas who produced the least slaves either by raiding or by preying upon each other, were the very tribes with an amorphous state structure from which a well-defined ruling class was absent.

The trade in humans thus appears as an extension of the hierarchical relations existing within West Africa. Those relations were partially based upon control over trade. Thus, the trade in humans clearly benefited certain groups in West Africa, while harming others.

The limitation of basing surplus extraction on trade is inherent to empires. Faced by this limitation, the upper-class groups of West African societies found the trade in humans more profitable to continue their domination. The exchange of humans thus became a method of expanding surplus extraction, given its roots in long-distance trade.

The class basis of a trade in humans

The classical notion of the transfer of people from Africa to the New World is derived from the accounts of the three voyages of John Hawkins. His first voyage took place between 1562 and 1563, the second occurred between 1564 and 1566, and the third and last voyage took place between 1567 and 1568. As a result of his three voyages of piracy, approximately 1,200 people were forcibly taken from the Upper Guinea Coast and transferred to the Spanish colonies in the West Indies as slaves (Donnan, 1965:46,51,68).

The account of the second voyage gives us a clear picture of Hawkins's methods. He stated that he sailed to an island off the West African coast and captured some of its inhabitants by burning and destroying their homes (Donnan, 1965:47).[5] In that instance a small group of Europeans captured a small number of Africans through an act of piracy. Judging from reports of the sixteenth century, this method was not uncommon (Donnan,1965:18–72).

But along with the indications of how many Africans were taken, we find other statements in Hawkins's reports that point toward the difficulties involved in using piracy as the primary method of obtaining laborers. The report states that while attacking a town during the second voyage, Hawkins and his men were counterattacked and in the process seven were killed and twenty-seven were hurt (Donnan, 1965:50).

Such counterattacks help explain why there eventually was a shift away from piracy to legitimate trade as the primary method of obtaining people for enslavement in the North American colonies (Manning, 1979). Despite that shift, however, there has been a persistent belief that the Hawkins type of voyage was the dominant form used to obtain people from Africa.[6]

Only by maintaining that the Hawkins type of voyage was the dominant form used to assign Africans to the slave slot in North America can we assume that all Africans were available for enslavement. But once we observe the existence of an organized, systematic trade, we are forced to look more carefully at the role social organizations within Africa played in the process of assignment.[7]

Between the rise of the ancient Ghana empire in the eleventh century and the fall of the Songhai empire in 1591, there are constant references to the existence of a trade in slaves, gold, food, and cloth from the savannah region of West Africa to the north through the Sahara Desert. Slaves were used in the salt mines of the Sahara, and they were also exported into the Mediterranean region to work on sugar plantations (Curtin, 1976:308). Descriptions of the means used to obtain slaves fixate around one particular point: "The majority of slaves were recruited through force (kidnapping, raids, and warfare). Broadly speaking, the larger states of the Savanna preyed upon the decentralized people living south in or near the forest" (July, 1975:228). That description of the method used for obtaining people for the trans-Saharan trade also applies to how people were obtained for the Atlantic trade. War was the dominant method.[8] Within that context, however, what was the role of social stratification in determining who ended up assigned to the slave slot in North America?

Daaku (1970), discussing the methods by which people were captured inland from the Gold Coast, lists debt, captivity in war, and criminal offenses as the dominant forms of assigning people to slavery. But as we look more closely at how people were captured for eventual shipment to North America, we see that all Africans were clearly not available for assignment and that some indeed benefited to the detriment of others.

In discussions of the Atlantic trade, there is no argument that war captives were the largest source of people who were eventually assigned into slavery: "All the evidence suggests that it was the victims of wars and raids that provided the main bulk of the slaves. In such a situation even the most powerful member of society could not be said to be immune from becoming a slave" (Daaku, 1970:30). Although Daaku here appears to take the traditional view that all members of society were available for assignment, two additional points have to be stressed concerning war captives, enslavement, and the market through which one was transformed into the other.

The organization of war was determined by the upper-class group. This was true of the wars in which obtaining slaves was secondary as well as those in which it was primary. The ruling element of the victorious group monopolized those who were captured, but did capture automatically result in assignment to the slave slot? A further quote from Daaku (1970) is in order here: "The uncertainties of the trade affected all concerned, for after these wars *all who could not redeem themselves were liable to become slaves*" (Daaku, 1970:30). Like Daaku (1970), Curtin (1976), initially draws a link between being captured in war and enslavement, but then distinguishes between what actually occurred to those so captured. He states that they were either ransomed at the end of the war, became domestic slaves, or were sold into slavery. Therefore, the ability to ransom oneself was crucial to escape enslavement, though not to escape capture. This is a significant distinction.[9]

Rodney (1970:115–16) discusses the ability of the ruling class in the Upper Guinea coast to ransom themselves after they were captured in war. He states that the ransom could be paid in the form of gold, weapons, other valuable merchandise, or by replacing the ransomed individual by others who would be enslaved in their place:

The noble suffered a minimum of disadvantages through the degeneration of the customary law and the rise of slave trading, and if he was sold he stood a very good chance of regaining his freedom; the commoner was the target of all the abuses of the law, he was the victim of slave raids, and when he was sold his position was desperate. (p. 115)

Clearly everyone was not ransomed. To be ransomed, an individual either had to have wealth or access to wealth. Members of the upper-class group that won a war benefited from war captives, while members of the upper-class group that lost the war were generally given the opportunity to ransom themselves. The differentiation between those who became enslaved within Africa before the march to the coast was therefore quite real.

Not all who were made available for assignment to the slave slot were obtained through warfare, however. It was possible that people were randomly gathered up through illegal (nonelite sanctioned) captures. Unlike war, kidnapping was not generally organized in a systematic manner. Such acts occurred when the opportunity arose. Some were taken while working in fields, while in defenseless villages, or while on a trade route away from a protected region (Curtin,1975:181).

But members of the upper-class group did not work in fields and were rarely alone outside of protected areas. It is possible, however, that wealthy merchants or a member of the ruling group could have been ambushed along a trade route. The significant point, however, is that although there are examples of merchants and members of the elite being taken and assigned to the slave slot in the New World, they appear to stand out because they are the exception to the rule (Alford, 1977).[10]

Like the system of ransom that existed after wars, there existed a ransom system that could obtain the release of most members of the upper-class group before they got to the coast. Therefore, even if these individuals reached the coast, there were still mechanisms to secure their release (Mahdi, 1979).

Conclusion

To study the process by which Africans came to the United States without knowledge of African history distorts one's ability to understand fully that process. Within the societies of Africa, those who were eventually assigned to the slave slot in North America first had to be made available for enslavement. The need for labor on the colonial plantations and other factors mentioned at the beginning of this chapter represent significant aspects of that process, but certainly not its totality.[11]

In West Africa, the process of making people available for assignment to the slave slot in North America was intricate. It could not have existed in such a systematic manner without the participation of groups within African societies. At best, the merchants from Europe, as indicated by

Hawkins, could have engaged in sporadic raids upon the coast and enslaved some people. That type of operation could not have continued indefinitely, however, because the inland regions of West Africa were not accessible to Europeans until the nineteenth century. The environment of the west coast of Africa thus offered ample means for the indigenous populations to protect themselves from slave traders from the sea (Davidson, 1961:157; Hopkins, 1973:108–9).

However, I do not intend to portray those Africans who engaged in the trade in humans as worse than others who have engaged in such activities throughout human history. After all, during the seventeenth century, when English traders were trading in people from Africa, they were already shipping people to the colonies through such processes as kidnapping as well as shipping out dissenters from Ireland, Scotland, and Wales. In addition, paupers in England were routinely imprisoned and even hanged (Kingsbury, 1933).[12]

My position has been that the wealth of the African societies that engaged in the trade of humans was generated through the exchange of people, tribute, and the exchange of commodities. Therefore, the question that has to be confronted is, Why was it deemed more profitable to ship out potential laborers than to engage them in productive activity? The trade in indentured servants, the shipping out of convicts and political dissenters, as well as the shipping out of children from England during the same period of history poses a similar question.[13]

Within the European context, there are assumptions that provide answers to that question. The following explanation is generally offered. Because there was no employment for the surplus population, it was best for them as individuals (so that they would not starve or be sent to debtors prison) to leave the country. Another position holds that it was good for the colony as well as for England for this sector of the society to leave the country. Thus, the excess population was viewed as providing the needed labor force for the economic expansion of the colonies. Shipping people out was also seen as a way of keeping down political unrest. The benefits to European societies of shoveling out the poor have therefore been well argued. The political and economic logic for the society are taken for granted, along with the implicit assumption that any dominant class will want to maintain its rule.

Within the African context, the assumption of the existence of a social system with political and economic logic dominated by an upper-class group is greatly downplayed. There is, of course, this difference; the population shipped out of West Africa was not transported on ships controlled by Africans and was not sent to regions of the world dominated by Africans to produce wealth for Africans. Within this frame of reference it would appear to be illogical to argue that the use of Africans as laborers in North America resulted partly from the self-interests of a segment of West African Societies.

West African societies in which the upper-class groups engaged in the trade in humans were following the economic and political logic of their social structure, however. This logic was indeed distinct from that of upper-class groups in England and Europe generally during the seventeenth century, but not so distinct as to negate some fundamental similarities. The trade in people, from the perspective of the upper-class group in West Africa, represented an adaptation to the conditions under which the means of subsistence were being produced and distributed. It was thus a reflection of the manner in which people within those societies were vertically classified. As the upper-class group saw alternative means of obtaining wealth, the people assigned to the lower-class slot became utilized in a different manner. Rather than waiting for them to engage in the process of production, the upper-class group sold them directly to obtain goods desired by that dominant group.

What was occurring there, as was the case in early seventeenth-century England, were changes in the assignment of people to the lower-class slot within social systems. In some instances, people were being assigned to slots within the vertical classification structure, whereas at other times they were being moved out of those slots. In this manner we can see that the process by which people are assigned to the lower-class slot of a new social structure is mirrored by the movement of people out of lower-class slots in other social structures.

The significant point here, therefore, is the similarities in the behavior of the most powerful groups in Europe and the most powerful groups in West Africa. Concentrating upon skin pigment differences among all Europeans and all Africans merely leads us away from seeing those similarities. We can now conceptually address the creation of a slave labor slot in North America as distinct from the assumption that Africans and their skin pigmentation were its determinants.

7 The creation of the slave labor slot in Virginia

From small holdings to plantations

An emphasis upon differences in skin pigment as the basis for the rise of the slave labor slot in North America takes us away from more fundamental and far-reaching changes that occurred during the seventeenth century. Here the argument continues with the assumption that structures can be analyzed separately from the people who have historically occupied them. More specifically, the use of skin pigmentation as the modern mark of identity (social value) resulted from forces larger than preexisting European attitudes toward Africans.

There was indeed a fundamental shift in the social structure of Colonial Virginia as a result of the English Revolution and its aftershocks (1642 to 1689). That shift resulted in the transformation of the land as well as the labor needs of the ruling group in the colony. As has already been pointed out, the Virginia Company was a joint stock venture, initially designed to gain quick profits. During the early period of the colony (1606 to 1616), ownership of land was controlled by the company rather than by individuals. Approximately fourteen years after the Jamestown Settlement was established, however, land was passing from the company and into individual hands. In this transition, land was used as payment to the investors in the Virginia Company as well as a method of providing laborers for the land. The latter point has been discussed in regard to the Headright system (see Chapter 4).

Once land entered private hands it was vital that the individual holders establish their investment as an income-producing enterprise. Thus, because the Virginia Company was being dissolved, as indicated by the fact that land was being given to individual investors, any return of investment had to come from the use of the distributed land. The rising value of the tobacco plant as an export commodity was critical in that regard. Reliance upon tobacco production meant that land was valuable only to the extent that it was arable. Land was therefore valuable primarily when it was cleared by labor and made ready for planting. This established a particular type of agricultural organization as manifested in land and labor use in early seventeenth-century Virginia.

The social composition of the Virginia Company is also important to our understanding of how labor and land were utilized in the colony. The members of the company's council were primarily Puritans, but there were also a few Presbyterians in that group. Indeed, between 1607 and

1660, the Virginia colony was ruled, with few exceptions, by Puritans. After 1660, however, the Puritan rule in Virginia was permanently replaced by the rule of Cavaliers and their world view (Talpalar, 1960:78–81).[1] The importance of this transition for our understanding of the shift from indentured servitude to the slave labor slot becomes clearer once we look closely at the Puritan and Cavalier groups during the seventeenth century. The type of social system established by seventeenth-century Puritans in Virginia favored the use of indentured servants (temporary unfree laborers). The Cavalier's orientation toward a feudal social system, on the other hand, was geared toward the use of a permanent unfree labor force. Thus, I contend that this structural shift from small to large holdings was the significant factor in our understanding of the rise of a slave labor slot in the Virginia colony. Furthermore, this understanding supports the notion that labor slots arise within the context of social systems rather than as a result of those who are eventually assigned to the slot.[2]

The social and economic position of the early seventeenth-century English Puritans was generally determined by their involvement in trade. Their successful pursuit of trade generated a group of Puritans who were wealthy merchants with commoner and gentry backgrounds. As merchants they benefited from the national policies of the monarchy, which was geared toward the monopolization of the internal as well as the external trade of England by Englishmen. On the other hand, they were socially limited because of the feudal restrictions on obtaining land and the status that came with it. To the extent that they reflected the immediate economic interests of their class, the Puritans favored the monarchy because of its position on trade, but opposed the monarchy because of its feudal position on land. The rigid class system of England, as reflected in the laws of primogeniture, therefore generated an extreme ambivalence among the Puritans. Cavaliers of the period, on the other hand, had no such ambivalence. Their economic interests coincided with that of the monarchy because they were members of the feudal aristocracy. The Cavalier insistence upon "no land without a lord" aptly points to their sense of place in English society. It was inconceivable to them that land ownership could be posed as separate from feudal relations.[3]

Tensions between the Puritans (wealthy merchants) and the landed English aristocracy made the Virginia colony look appealing to the Puritans. Restrictions upon the mobility of the wealthy merchants has partly served as the basis of the myth that the United States was settled by people seeking religious freedom. However, the wealthy merchants were far from the most oppressed sector of seventeenth-century English society. Indeed, the bases of their oppression were economic and social rather than religious. As such, the Puritans sought access to land, but within the context of the fact that their wealth had been obtained through trade.

Puritan domination of the Virginia colony (1607 to 1660), not surprisingly, resulted in the development of a system in which land was important to the extent that it could produce goods for the market. In addition, because all citizens had the right to land, this system permitted commoner freemen to become socially mobile. This meant that farms were only composed of land that could be planted, because land that could not be planted had no immediate value within this context. The low value placed upon uncleared land meant that it was very cheap for farmers to exchange land in seven years (the end of the term of indentured servitude) for the immediate use of an individual's labor. As a result of this world view, the lack of capital and the abundance of land in combination with the need for labor produced the conditions for an indentured servant unfree labor slot in the colony.[4]

Cavalier domination of the Virginia colony (after 1660, the year of the restoration of the monarchy in England) resulted in fundamental changes in the conception of the value and use of land.[5] This, in turn, had a significant impact upon labor needs in the colony. Both coincided with changes in the labor supply inside the European world economy. These factors, along with the availability of people from West Africa, combined to create and people the slave labor slot in the North American colonies.

With Cavalier domination came major changes in the legal system of Virginia in regard to land. Talpalar (1960:80) states: "The commoner farmers lost their status as leaseholders, and they had the choice of remaining on their lands as tenants of the proprietary overlords or of leaving the jurisdiction" (c.f. Main, 1982:123). In addition, there was a tremendous shift in the amount of land legally owned by the citizens of Virginia. Under the Puritans, stress upon arable land of necessity held down the number of acres that were of value. In 1660, approximately 20,000 acres of arable land became available in Virginia. After the restoration of the monarchy in England, however, the Cavalier political leaders obtained grants of millions of acres of land from the Crown (Talpalar, 1960:83).

Thus, large feudal estates became the dominant economic unit of the colony during the late seventeenth century. These estates were premised upon the English manor, which stressed self-sufficiency.[6] Here, the value of land was not limited by its capacity to produce goods for market. Instead, land was looked upon as having a long-term as well as immediate economic value. With this change, uncleared land was more valuable than under the system that was oriented toward indentured servitude. This did not decrease the need for labor in the colony, however. Rather it required an increase in laborers and a fundamental shift in the mechanism by which laborers were to be obtained and held in their structural slot. Thus, the shift from independent farmers to large estates provides the conditions for the shift from a temporary unfree labor slot to a permanent unfree labor slot.[7]

It is here that the importance of distinguishing between the shift from temporary unfree (indentured servant) to permanent unfree (slave) labor and the shift from a predominately European to a predominately African population assigned to the unfree labor slot comes into play. The Cavaliers created a social structure that led to the creation of a permanent unfree labor slot. Permanent unfree laborers were needed because there continued to be a dearth of currency in the colony to pay laborers and land was no longer available as payment. This certainly did not require the use of Africans (especially premised upon their skin pigmentation) in that slot.

The tendency to see the rise of the slave slot and its occupation by Africans as one and the same is evident in the investigation of explanations for the shift from the indentured servitude slot to the slave labor slot during the late seventeenth century. Perkins (1980:71–2) offers these explanations for that shift. First, improved economic conditions in England resulted in the decrease in the availability of servants. Second, the planters in the North American colonies were imitating slaveholders in the Caribbean. And last, slavery resulted in a sense of solidarity among Whites. Galenson (1981:152–4) offers more limited, although similar, types of explanations to those of Perkins. He sees the shift as rooted in (1) increased opportunities in England, (2) an increase in the price of servants, and (3) a decrease in the price for slaves. Alpert (1987:221) adds different elements when he states:

The law of servants was readily amenable to extension to slaves. Such an extension and gradual rigidization may not have been inevitable. A number of non-legal factors, however, encouraged this development. These factors included 1) the manpower shortage; 2) the value of the servant as a capital asset; 3) the feeling that blacks were different and consequent fear of them;[8] 4) the general desire of the colonists to retain their servants as long as possible.

From Perkins, Galenson, and Alpert, we can see that the explanations fall into two basic categories. One category emphasizes the shortage of Europeans to fill the servant labor slot and the resulting increased cost of servants. The other category explains the shift in terms of racial attitudes.

What is significant about both categories is that ultimately they rely upon the assumption that the slave labor slot was premised upon the existence of the African. The racial attitudes category clearly takes this position. The shortage of Europeans as servants explanation is premised upon the notion that only Europeans were servants and ignores any possibility that Europeans could be used as slaves. It is assumed that Africans could not be substituted for Europeans as indentured servants; rather, if Africans were coming into the system, they had to come in as slaves. This position uses servant as synonymous with European and slave as synonymous with African. But indeed, not all Africans who were brought into early seventeenth-century Virginia were slaves. Therefore, the decrease in the availability of Europeans as indentured servants does not suffice as an explanation for the shift from indentured servitude to slavery, unless it can be demonstrated that Africans could only be slaves. Given the fact that some were already indentured servants, to assert that they could only be slaves is clearly historically inaccurate.

Connected to the above discussion is the fact that there is insufficient attention paid to the actual destruction of the indentured servant labor slot and its replacement with the slave labor slot. The shift from the former to the latter is assumed to have occurred because of the shift from Europeans to Africans as the dominant group in the unfree labor slot. As a result, structural issues such as those connected to the struggles between Puritans (independent farmers) and Cavaliers (feudal estates) is ignored in favor of the racial explanation for the shift.[9]

At another level, the two explanations entirely ignore discussions of the impact of social transformations in West Africa upon the availability of people for the slave slot. In this regard, it is important to notice that the issue of availability in England is not ignored, but is instead given a central place in the shift. This means that people in seventeenth-century England have not been conceptually frozen into the indentured servant category, but people from Africa have been frozen into the slave category.[10]

It might be argued that the flexibility of the indentured servant/ European category and the rigidity of the slave/African category reflects the real conditions under which they existed. Such an argument would be problematic on two counts, however. On the one hand, Africans were also servants until the destruction of that labor slot. On the other hand, our ability to conceptualize the existence of slavery requires that we see that the rigid slave/African form occurred at a historical moment rather than having existed throughout human history. In addition, not all Africans were available for assignment to the slave labor slot. This means that there is no natural equality between slave and African, because slavery is a labor category into which any human being could be placed.

Perkins's mention of solidarity among Whites as an explanation for the shift from indentured servitude to slavery is very suggestive. In fact, it calls attention to Bacon's Rebellion of 1676, which was an indication of the schism within the ruling group of Europeans in Virginia. Perkins's point is that slavery was a device that unified different strata of the European population around their Whiteness. Once again, however, slavery is viewed as inherently fused with African/dark skin pigmenta-.tion. The existence of a structural necessity for a permanent unfree labor force (regardless of its skin pigmentation) is not conceptually explored. This is no doubt one reason why the participation of Africans in Bacon's Rebellion is ignored (Andrews, 1952).[11] What is usually emphasized as the explanation for the shift to slavery thus ignores as much as it explains and, most important, assumes what most needs to be explained.

Legislation and the creation of social identity

As a final look at the creation of the slave labor slot and its identification with skin pigmentation, we will briefly view the legislation upon which it was based. The existence of such legislation poses a fundamental prob-lem for those assuming that slavery was premised upon the Africans' skin pigmentation. The ultimate question becomes, If slavery was funda-mentally based upon the skin pigmentation of the African, why would there have been the need to pass laws identifying skin pigment with slavery? Linked to that question is the issue of those Africans who served as indentured servants and were not enslaved as the transition to slavery occurred. The point is that skin pigmentation does not fully deal with the historical realities of the United States (Alpert, 1987:189; Hurd, 1968:226–47; Smith, 1965).[12]

All Africans in seventeenth-century Colonial America were not slaves, and all slaves during that period were not Africans (Alpert, 1987; Galenson, 1981; Smith, 1965).[13] Alpert indicates how the fusion be-tween African and slave in our consciousness could have led us to ignore the above facts. He states:

The legislation clearly distinguishes slaves from servants. it also seems to indi-cate that even Christians may be slaves. Probably in 1639 "slave" as a matter of law simply meant a person who was obligated to serve his master for life. Although slavery may have been hereditary by 1640, perhaps it was not, because in 1664 legislation was enacted apparently to establish that characteristic.

He then adds: "The recognition of slavery by 1640 was more important for the Indians than for the few Negroes then in the province" (p. 191). These are not trivial points, although their lack of general dissemination has resulted in the slavery/African/skin pigment fusion that is so preva-lent today.

The important point is that even after the 1660s, when legislation in various colonies was being passed to link rigidly skin pigmentation with slavery and to make that condition hereditary, all Africans in the colonies were still not slaves. In fact, as late as 1744, an amendment was passed in Virginia stating: "Any free Negro, Mulatto, or Indian, being a Christian, shall be admitted in any court of this colony, or before any justice of the peace, to be sworn as a witness, and give evidence for or against any other Negro, Mulatto, or Indian, whether slave or free" (Hurd, 1968:243). Although it is clear that there were restrictions upon the testimony of these three categories of persons, it is equally clear that slavery and skin pigment were not absolutely fused, even in Virginia at that late date.

The history of seventeenth-century Virginia indicates a social system within which unfree labor was an essential feature. It does not indicate, however, that unfree labor was tied exclusively to the skin pigment of the African. Indeed, by keeping the unfree labor slots separate from the people who occupied them, we have been able to justify our position that skin pigment appears as a mechanism to rationalize the placement of individuals into a low (socially devalued) structural slot (Alpert, 1987:194–8) rather than as the cause of the creation of that slot.

As has already been demonstrated in the discussion of the relationship between the European settlers and the native population, skin pigmentation can serve as a convenient mechanism of identity (social value) because of its ability to establish distinctions between those assigned to distinct structural slots of social systems. This contrast between hierarchically structured slots – rather than physical or cultural distinctions in and of themselves – has been stressed as we continue to unravel the process by which skin pigment became a mechanism of identity in the United States.

By the end of the seventeenth century in the Virginia colony, there had evolved a White identity and a Black identity. The White identity was largely based upon the criteria used to assign people to the free structured slot of the society. The Black identity was the mechanism that legally assigned individuals to the unfree structured slot of the society. With that contrast White had a positive social value while Black had a negative social value. They served as indicators, from birth, of the social value (identity, life chances) of individuals. These distinct social values persist today. They exist with a force that implies that there is something natural about the Black/White distinctions. What we have seen as a result of our discussion of England, Virginia, and West Africa during the seventeenth century, however, is that the creation of racial identities (social values) as natural has been achieved by historical distortions.[14]

The White group was created out of the unequally stratified European, primarily English, population that came to North America in search of profits. This White identity could only be created in contrast to another idealized color identity. The lower class of England occupied the unfree labor slot during the seventeenth century. Within that context, free and unfree were not based on skin pigment, but instead were based upon many factors that were overtly centered around access to power. With the pervasive use of White as a primordial category in the contemporary world, those distinctions are lost and the stratified European settlers become lumped together as a homogenous group. In addition, the global category free gains its homogeneity only in contrast to an unfree category. But being free in the colonies did not mean that there was equality among the free/White population. As a result, fundamental distinctions get obscured by the use of the global categories free and White as homogenous equivalents. Main (1982:123) in a general reference to the tobacco colonies after the mid-seventeenth century demonstrates this fact when he states: "Men with both capital and connections gradually built a more familiar society in the meanwhile, one more stable and more stratified, and one into which freed servants could fit only as landless, voteless, voiceless tenants or else leave in search of yet another frontier."

Du Bois (1965) in his work on the opposition to the trade in humans from Africa between the seventeenth and nineteenth centuries demonstrates that all Whites who were free laborers were by no means convinced of the economic validity of slavery, because slavery had an adverse impact upon their ability to gain wage work. Even by the nineteenth century, at the height of the power of the slave owners and hence the justification for slavery, there continued to be contrasts within the White/free group. For example, most slaves were owned by a very small proportion of the White population. The stress upon the equivalence of White and free entirely hides these real facts from our daily lives (Du Bois, 1977).

The Black group came to North America in large numbers partly because ruling groups in the hierarchically stratified societies in West Africa were able to exchange their surplus populations for more economic, military, and political power. The sector of the population that benefited from that trade in people and the sector that was eventually assigned to the unfree labor slot nonetheless get lumped together as unfree and Black. Thus, the creation of *Whites* as well as *Blacks* fundamentally obscures structural distinctions.

Skin pigment, social stratification, and the evolution of ethnicity

The lumped White and the lumped Black groups have thus become ideal contrasts that transcend time and place. Despite this fact, however, those categories do little for our understanding of this society and the people who live in it. The image of seventeenth-century America is one of a haven from oppression for the idealized White group. There is little discussion of the distinctions between feudal lands and independent farmers or between both groups and indentured servants. According to the image, there were equal individuals with unlimited possibilities before them. Distinctions, when acknowledged, appear to rest upon work habits rather than social structures and unequal power relations.

The image of the ideal Black group is of an uncivilized population that had to be enslaved so that they might gain the civilization they so sadly lacked. Lost in this image is any sense of social systems within West Africa. Indeed, lost is the fact that social systems were so developed that their hierarchical structures greatly influenced the extent to which people without power could be made available for assignment to the slave labor slot being developed in North America.

These images were developed from the existence of the two significant labor slots in the vertically classified society of seventeenth-century America: the free slot and the slave slot. The free slot was identified with the skin pigment of the upper/ruling group, those who had structured the society in their interests. The slave slot was identified with the skin pigment of those who were assigned to that slot. Thus, the modern concept of race – the human group divided fundamentally between White and Black – was historically grounded in the consciousness of the members of the society.

Two points need to be kept in mind regarding the incorporation of this dualism into the modern conscious, however. One is that there were distinctions within the free/White group. That group was initially stratified along economic, political, and social lines. It would eventually also become stratified along cultural lines. The persistence of the notion of "poor White trash" is a graphic and cruel indication of the strength of those distinctions.

Because the free/unfree structural positions were the legal context of American society from the late seventeenth century to the late nineteenth century, it is understandable how a belief system about the unity of the free/White category could supersede the historical reality of the existence of stratification within the group. Thus, despite the clear sense of the distinction exhibited by the term, "poor White trash," the free/White category was made conceptually (never historically) homogenous in the context of being opposed to an unfree/Black category.

The second point is that the mark of skin pigmentation is not a precondition for the creation of race. There is a wide range of potential marks of vertical classification. The historical fact is that skin pigment was a convenient mechanism to distinguish between those who were allowed to benefit from the existence of the social organization and those who were assigned to the lower slot. Thus, the unfree labor slot could have existed without the assignment of Africans to it. If Europeans had been assigned to that slot, the mark of vertical classification (the basis of identity, social value, and race) would have been something other than skin pigmentation.

Once skin pigmentation became the mark of vertical classification, however, it became a social fact. In turn, it helped in the continuing stratification of the society. This can be seen in the creation of the free/White/ethnic group. This group eventually filled the free low structural slots of the society during the latter part of the nineteenth century. Their existence is an additional indication of the existence of stratification within the free/White sector in U.S. society.

The creation of race was thus the creation of two distinct but interdependent vertically stratified social systems. The unfree system was composed of slaveholders, overseers, and slaves. The free system was composed of merchant capitalists, farmers, laborers, and industrialists. They were distinct in that the labor force of one was excluded, by skin pigmentation, from becoming the labor force of the other.[15] Their interdependence rested with the ability of both upper groups to invest in controlling labor in the other's realm. This ability was intimately linked to the domination of the colonies by England and later by the creation of the United States.

Thus, the two vertically stratified social systems developed different complexities of stratification, different high and low slots, different populations occupying the lower slots, and thus different marks of vertical classification. Because the entire society was already premised upon skin pigment as the most fundamental mark of classification, there were not two distinct conceptions of race, but rather class and then ethnicity (religion, language, culture) became the mark of vertical classification within that social system, which was built upon the free labor slot. That form of vertical classification provides some sense of how marks of social value operate when the skin pigmentation between those assigned to the upper and lower structural slots of a social system is similar. It only provides a partial sense, however, because of the initially dominant unfree labor system that was marked by skin pigmentation.

Ethnicity became the mark of vertical classification in the free labor system when the upper group of that free system began to struggle with the unfree labor system for control over the national economy. One sign of the growth of the economic strength of the elites in the free labor system was precisely its need for more labor. Like the split between temporary unfree and permanent unfree labor, we can also see a split between skilled and unskilled labor. A new population was brought into the society to fill the unskilled labor slot of the free labor system. Because the unskilled labor slot was then the lowest structural position within the society, the ethnicity of those who were assigned to it – when contrasted with those in the upper slot – provided the mark of vertical classification within the free labor system.

In the United States, the Irish were moved from being the lower race (Irish and Catholic as opposed to English and Protestant) into the lower slot of the upper race (Irish and White as opposed to African and Black). The creation of skin pigmentation as the dominant mark of vertical classification in the late seventeenth century made their nine-teenth century identification possible.[16]

We now move to a look at the general labor needs of the United States during the nineteenth century. The society was being economi-cally transformed during that period and one result of the transforma-tion was the need for cheap unskilled labor. In the same manner that I have argued that the creation of the slave labor slot can be seen as distinct from those Africans who eventually filled it, such is also clearly the case in the development of this later labor slot in regard to the Europeans who eventually filled it.

8　The United States on the eve of mass migration from Ireland

Seventeenth-century Virginia was the social structural focus for our discussion of the rise of race (skin pigmentation) as a modern mark of group identity in the United States. For our analysis of the rise of Irish ethnicity (skin pigmentation combined with culture) as a mark of group identity, we will focus upon the social structure of the mid-to-late-nineteenth century United States. During that time period a large number of immigrants from Ireland entered U.S. society. Initially, we will look at some of the social forces within the receiving society that encouraged that mass movement from Ireland.

As was true in the case of the movement of people into Colonial American society from West Africa, there was a tremendous labor need in the United States that had to be filled to ensure the continued development of a specific sector of the society. The desire for a specific type of labor (the need to create and people a specific labor slot) was also the case here. As we shall see later, however, conditions within Ireland (which had been influenced by its place in the European world economy) were significant in determining that a sector of the Irish population would become available as the cheap unskilled labor force in the United States during the nineteenth century. Thus, we will see that the creation of an Irish ethnic identity (a group of individuals with a specific social value, as reflected in stereotypes) in the United States was similar to the process by which a sector of the African population became Black.[1] Here we again have a situation in which a sector of a population is transformed into the totality of a people because of the narrow range (specific slot) of the social positions that population was allowed to occupy in the receiving society. In this chapter, I lay out the social context within which that transformation occurred.

The first mass migration of the Irish into the United States occurred between 1840 and 1860 (Carrier and Jeffery, 1953). Within the United States, that movement has been viewed as resulting from a humanitarian gesture on the part of U.S. citizens toward the Irish, who were experiencing a the potato famine (Clark, 1973:30). Notwithstanding the surface validity of that view, I will show that the movement of the Irish to the United States during the famine period was fundamentally a reorientation of capital and labor within the expanding European world economy.

For purposes of analysis, we have to look at shifts within the U.S. economy as well as shifts within the Irish economy and their connections to the English economy. We thus can illustrate the reorientation that was occurring within the world economy at large.

The United States in the world economy: 1800 to 1860

During the period from the end of the Revolutionary War and the establishment of a constitutional government to the beginning of the Civil War, significant economic change occurred within the United States. One indication of that change was the large increase in the country's population from five million to thirty-one million people. It is important for our purposes that the greatest external increase to that population occurred between 1840 and 1860, the period of the Irish migration (Table 1). In addition to the increase in population, there was a population shift toward the West along with the beginning of the concentration of the eastern population into urban areas.

There were also significant structural changes in the society. An indication of the structural changes was the extensive work done in the areas of transportation and communication. There were government investments in the building of highways, as well as in the Erie, Philadelphia, Pittsburgh, Chesapeake, and Ohio canals that were all built between the 1820s and 1850s. In addition, steamboats became regular sights on the rivers while railroads increased from a total of 32 miles in 1830 to a total of 32,000 miles in 1860 (Graf, 1952). There were also significant increases in the agricultural and manufacturing sectors of the economy between 1800 and 1860. One result of that rise was a shift toward domestic trade and away from foreign trade between 1800 and 1860. Despite the shift toward domestic trade, however, the country remained overwhelmingly dependent upon foreign trade during most of the nineteenth century (Graf, 1952: Chapter 10).

Those internal changes, in conjunction with changes in other areas of the nineteenth-century European world economy, specifically within Ireland and England, set the stage for a shift in the position of the United States in the larger network of the European world economy. On the whole, that shift was from a peripheral to a semiperipheral state system.[2] There are three areas of internal change through which this transformation can be observed. First, the economy of the United States was transformed from depending on merchant capital to relying on industrial capital as the dominant source of wealth. This gives us the overall view of the development of capitalist production methods in the society. Second, the organization of production was transformed from the home-

Table 1. *United States census data by region (1800–1900, in thousands)*

	1800	1820	1840	1860
New England[a]	1,233	1,660	2,234	3,135
	(23.23)[b]	(17.22)	(13.09)[c]	(9.97)
Middle Atlantic	1,403	2,700	4,526	7,459
	(26.43)	(28.01)	(26.53)	(23.72)
East North Central	51	793	2,925	6,927
	(.96)	(8.23)	(17.14)	(22.03)
West North Central	–	67	427	2,170
	–	(.7)	(2.50)	(6.90)
South Atlantic	2,286	3,061	3,925	5,365
	(43.07)	(31.75)	(23.00)	(17.06)
Other	335	1,358	3,025	6,388
	(6.31)	(14.09)	(17.73)	(20.32)
Total	5,308	9,638	17,062	31,444

[a]New England: Maine, New Hampshire, Vermont, Massachusetts, Rhode Island, Connecticut. Middle Atlantic: New York, New Jersey, Pennsylvania. East North Central: Ohio, Indiana, Illinois, Michigan, Wisconsin. West North Central: Minnesota, Iowa, Missouri, North Dakota, South Dakota, Nebraska, Kansas. South Atlantic: Delaware, Maryland, Virginia, West Virginia, North Carolina, South Carolina, Georgia, Florida.
[b]Numbers in parentheses are percent of total population.
[c]Due to rounding, these percentages total 99.99 percent.
Source: Based upon U.S. Bureau of the Census, *Historical Statistics of the United States, Colonial Times to 1957* (Washington: U.S. Government Printing Office, 1957), pp. 12–13.

spun method to the factory system. This gives us a detailed insight into the early form taken by capitalist production in the society. Finally, the economy was transformed from relying on independent producers who were skilled craftsmen to relying on cheap and unskilled wage laborers. This allows us to see how the transformation to capitalist production affected the population and how the surplus labor force from Ireland became a valuable resource.

From merchant capital to industrial capital

One of the origins of merchant capital in the United States was participation in the trade in people from Africa. Merchants gained wealth by supplying people as slaves to work on the plantations that produced sugar, coffee, tobacco, and rice as well as to work in the mines and on the plantations of South America. Merchants also transported the luxury goods that were being imported from Europe to all regions of the Americas.

The transactions that resulted in the origins of merchant capital during the eighteenth century existed in different forms, but existed nevertheless in the United States at the beginning of the nineteenth century. During the latter period, merchant capitalists speculated in the West by buying up large tracts of land and selling them in smaller plots to individuals who saw Western expansion as the route to their social mobility.[3] In addition, merchant capitalists were extensively involved in financing canal and railroad construction (Hidy, 1970). Such merchants were also involved in speculative trading and household manufacturing operations for the developing internal market of the United States. Their involvement in the carrying trades, however, was their most significant contribution to the U.S. economy during the eighteenth century. Wheat (including flour), naval stores, gum, resin, raw cotton, and a few manufactured cotton items were the major items exported, whereas coffee, sugar, manufactured cotton goods, fruits and nuts, hides and skins, manufactured wool, and copper were the major items imported (Graf, 1952).

We can therefore see that in the early 1800s, the United States depended on the foreign market for finished products while it supplied raw materials for that market. The dilemma for the economy was clear. Capital was not being invested in industrial production, that is, a home market was not being developed at the same rate as capital was being invested in the carrying trade. The net result was that the costs of the imported finished products were greater than the profits from the raw materials exported. Thus, between the Revolutionary War and the Civil War the U.S. economy faced a serious balance of payment problem. The ability to make money through merchant ventures therefore had the contradictory impact of prolonging the dependence of the U.S. economy upon England.

Although profits were to be had from trading raw materials, there were also problems. In 1791, Alexander Hamilton stated:

The embarrassments which have obstructed the progress of our external trade, have led to serious reflections on the necessity of enlarging the sphere of our domestic commerce. The restrictive regulations, which, in foreign markets, abridge the vent of the increasing surplus of our agricultural produce, serve to beget an earnest desire, that a more extensive demand for that surplus may be created at home. (Cole, 1968:247)

Hamilton's solution of extending the manufacturing sector of the U.S. economy during this early period was far from immediately successful, however. The conditions necessary for manufacturing on the scale envisioned by him did not occur until the 1840s.

There was more to the problem than merely convincing a segment of the population to invest in industrial production. In the first place, around the beginning of the nineteenth century greater profits were to be made in the commercial arena than in manufacturing. Second, the technology necessary to make the transition to large-scale industrial production was not available in the United States, because it was dominated by English capitalists.[4] In addition, there was a scarcity of labor, especially skilled labor, in the United States, and as a result the wages of such laborers were higher than in England. This combination created a fundamental hindrance to industrial production in the United States during the nineteenth century.[5]

Another significant problem that stood in the way of large-scale manufacturing was the existence of domestic household production, which remained competitive with factory production until the 1840s (Lippincott, 1973:153). The transition from capital investments in commercial ventures to industrial ventures was therefore slowed by internal as well as external factors during the early nineteenth century. As a result, the economy of the United States remained in a dependent position during this period.

Because profits in the carrying trade continued during the nineteenth century, investments in commercial ventures also continued. Downturns in the carrying trade also had a negative impact on the U.S. economy. For example, although the Napoleonic Wars (1796 to 1815) were very good for the society's position in the carrying trade and as a world supplier of raw materials, the end of those wars resulted in a contraction of the position of the United States in the commercial arena and greater competition in the domestic market from British manufactured goods.[6]

Partly as a result of the world depression after the Napoleonic Wars, the transition from merchant capital to industrial capital in the United States was not fully achieved by the beginning of the nineteenth century. By 1821, however, there was another upturn in the U.S. economy. This upturn was fueled by population increases, the use of canals to open markets in the interior of the country, and the movement of foreign capital into public works programs. Cotton production also expanded in the southwest regions of the United States, fueled by demand for cotton in England. The carrying trade expanded as a result of this greater demand for cotton, and profits from that trade were invested in land companies and merchant textile ventures (Graf, 1952:206).

As long as there were expansions in the demand for the agricultural products of the United States and profits from investing in the infrastructure to transport those products, the ups and downs of the economy remained dependent on the fortunes of merchant capital in the world market. The new cycle, starting with 1821 and ending with the Depression of 1837, went in this manner, according to Hacker (1966:327): "From 1821 to 1825, revival and prosperity, followed by about a year of setback; from late 1826, again good times, to be interrupted once more by a year of recession and depression; revival late in 1829, prosperity during 1830–1833, and depression in 1834; and then a boom period which lasted until the collapse of 1837." Once again, we see that the concerns Hamilton voiced in 1791 remained important between 1821 and 1837. The basic point was that the industrial sector of the society was not being invested in as rapidly as was necessary to facilitate economic independence. Hence, the world market continued to dictate the economic fortunes of the United States.

The Depression of 1837 resulted from the drying up of capital for commercial ventures in the West and a slackening of the carrying trade. As profits in commercial ventures decreased, merchants were more and more reluctant to invest in those markets. Booms tended to be followed by downturns because profits could not continue to rise at an absolute rate. As a result, investors were concerned with finding the highest rates of profit and thus were reticent to remain in a field of investment once the rate of profit began to diminish. Booms resulted in abnormally high rates of profit, but the decrease that followed only served to drive investors out of the market more quickly (Cochran and Miller, 1961:43–7). It is therefore not surprising that by the end of the 1821 to 1837 cycle, the United States was still a debtor nation. Graf (1952:206) states: "Looking only at the trade in merchandise, on the export side, the American credit was one billion, three hundred and eighty-nine million dollars. On the debit side (cost of imports) the figure was one billion, five hundred and seventy four million dollars." This $186 million deficit was not a trivial problem for the society's economic well-being. In addition, the deficit weakened the political power of the merchant capitalists.

A clear indication of the changing status of merchants' capital was the fact that from the start of the upturn in the U.S. economy in 1843, the expansion of the internal market was just as significant a factor in the economic turnaround as was trade with the external market. An important factor preventing the full transformation of the society into a capitalist industrial economy had been the lack of political strength of the industrial group. Nonetheless, they were clear as to what they needed to succeed. Hamilton, in fact, had outlined the necessary program over a half century before it even became a possibility. Therefore, despite the fact that the issue was not resolved at the national level until the end of the Civil War, that struggle was well underway before then.

Between the beginning of the nineteenth century and the 1860s, the U.S. economy shifted from depending upon merchant capitalism to depending upon industrial production. This resulted from the development of a home market. The potential for a home market grew as the population grew, as industrial production became more efficient (cheaper products), as the labor force grew, and as protecting the manufacturing sector of the economy became a major concern of the national government. There were also external factors that aided the shift, however.

One major factor, ironically, revolved around changes within the English economy. As the industrialists in England became more powerful, they searched for cheap means of feeding their work force. They found that it was no longer profitable in the 1840s to rely solely upon the agricultural production of British and Irish farmers. Their search for the cheapest agricultural commodities led them to advocate free trade and thus to attempt to transcend national boundaries. One way of obtaining cheap agricultural goods was through the repeal of the corn laws in 1846, which gave U.S. agriculture greater access to the English market. Thus the agricultural sector became the strong foreign-exchange earner during the mid-nineteenth century and, in turn, fueled the internal industrial economy through the demand for machinery and farm implements. The coming to power of the industrialists in England thus paved the way for the later rise of industrialists in the United States.[7]

From homespun production to factory production: 1800 to 1860

At the beginning of the nineteenth century, homespun manufacturing was the most pervasive form of textile production in the U.S. economy. Primarily, it was production in the home for use in the home. The labor used in such production was restricted to the members of the immediate family and servants or slaves, if any were available. The scale of production was generally small and the number of laborers used in such operations was correspondingly small.[8]

Clark (1949) estimates that nearly two-thirds of the textiles consumed in the United States as late as 1820 were produced under the homespun system. Foodstuff production was also dominated by household production. As we move toward the 1840s, however, increased population and the introduction of the power loom resulted in a significant decline in homespun production and the rise of the factory, especially in New England.

Textile industries were the basis of the first factories in the United States. The invention of the power loom and the use of the Waltham organizational system transformed those older methods of production into full-fledged capitalist enterprises. Clark (1949:529) states:

The Boston Manufacturing Company erected the first modern factory in America. It differed from previous establishments of equal size, either here or abroad, in performing all operations of clothmaking by power at a central plant. Labor was specialized and workers were organized by departments. Wages were paid in cash, output standardized, cost accounting introduced, and buying and selling systematized.

In this instance, manufacturing clearly could no longer be conceived of merely as a household industry.

The successful rise of factories required a large market, a good system of transportation, and a labor force that was, like the system of production, entirely removed from the household. A large market for the first factories in the United States was found in the plantations in the South, with their large slave population (Aronowitz, 1973:145).[9] Despite assertions that those who were enslaved were less than human, slaves still had to be clothed. Ironically, much of the merchant capital invested in the early New England textile mills and in the transportation system necessary for the distribution of goods was produced in the carrying trade. In turn, however, some of the investments in the carrying trade came out of profits from the slave trade. Therefore slavery, one of the initial sources of wealth for the new society, was an important institution in the development of the home market for textile goods.

The need for unskilled labor

The labor force that powered the factories of the early 1840s in New England was derived from native-born young women and children. By midcentury, however, immigrants from Ireland were beginning to provide the labor for those factories. Hamilton had long before stated that the labor force that would generate an industrial economy was to come from immigrants. He did not know, however, that the immigrants would be from Ireland or the conditions that would transform them into immigrants.

With the removal of manufacturing from the household, the problem of obtaining specific types of labor arose. The independent craftsmen were no longer desired. The full-time wage earner became essential to this system of production. Within the classical framework, such laborers are homegrown. They generally are viewed as the surplus labor force from the agricultural sector of a society (Marx, 1974, Volume I).

But the transformation of the agricultural labor force in the United States during the 1840s was hampered by the low population in the Western agricultural regions, the predominance of slave labor in the agricultural South, and the tendency of farmers in New England to move west to re-create the conditions of independent production. There were also problems involved in transforming the independent craftsmen into wage laborers. They were generally committed to their position of independence within the society and resisted becoming wage earners by moving West and by developing associations that attempted to monopolize production (Turner, 1920). Thus, although the factories of the 1840s could not function without a steady labor force, it was not readily available in the United States.[10]

Industrial capital and ethnic labor stratification

While the homespun industry flourished in the rural United States at the beginning of the nineteenth century, the urban areas were dominated by handicraft and household production. Journeymen and master mechanics were significant sources of labor in that urban sector. There were some restrictions preventing the movement of journeymen up to master mechanics, such as the necessity of paying a large price for the freedom to work in the large cities, but such restrictions were loosely enforced. Journeymen could become itinerant artisans and could move to a smaller town having fewer skilled craftsmen. The craftsmen of the early nineteenth century, therefore, had a great deal of independence as small producers. Because their skills were much in demand and their numbers were small, they could command relatively high wages for their services and they had some degree of control over the pace of their work.

The ideal notion of wage work during the nineteenth century was that it was a temporary condition. The general belief, as late as the 1860s in fact, was that any penniless White male could eventually become at least a small capitalist. Within this context, wage work was seen as merely the start of that process. It was felt that through wage labor the worker would save and eventually buy tools or land. After that point, he would work for himself while saving more money. After working and saving in this manner, the formerly penniless worker was supposed to be able to hire another penniless worker for wages. The process was to continue in this fashion ad infinitum. Wage work was thus viewed during this period as the plight of the penniless, and permanent wage work was viewed as a form of punishment (Ware, 1974). The rise of industrial capitalism in the form of the factory system thus flew in the face of the above ideal of worker independence. Wage labor was, in fact, being transformed from a temporary stage of existence to a permanent state of being.

The response of skilled craftsmen to the rise of permanent wage labor was to attempt to preserve that ideal notion through migration westward and through unions. The early unions were designed to protect the control of skilled workers over their relatively privileged conditions of labor. Despite the fact that by the 1830s they were being driven into small shops and in some instances were being paid wages, the division of labor in shops had not moved to the point where skilled workers could be replaced by unskilled workers.

Journeymen cordwainers, printers, carpenters, and tailors formed local societies of protection during the early nineteenth century. Their struggles focused upon gaining a ten-hour day, abolishing the evils of apprenticeship, and establishing a minimum wage for skilled workers. Those demands were accompanied by strikes, but with little success (Commons, Phillips, Gilmore, Sumner, and Andrews, 1958, Volume III).

One problem facing these early organizations was their lack of national unity. Journeymen of a specific craft in each city joined together without contacting similar groups elsewhere. This, along with other factors beyond their control, contributed to the failure of such organizations in preventing the erosion of the position of skilled workers during the nineteenth century. But attempts at organizing skilled laborers continued despite defeats.

The major problem faced by skilled workers during the early nineteenth century was in fact the ability of merchants and capitalists to obtain the support of the national government in attacking labor organizations. Labor organizations had begun to take direct action against employers during a time of severe competition among employers as well as workers. Employers attempted to meet this situation by hiring cheaper and less-skilled workers, by trying to gain support for easier immigration regulations, and by introducing laborsaving mechanical devices. Skilled workers responded by continuing the attempt at unionizing. Employers, in turn, sought help from the state in order to blunt the strategy of the workers. Commons and coauthors (1958, Volume I: iii–iv) state:

After the close of the Revolution, and particularly after the new national government under the Federal Constitution went into effect, the factory system expanded and the custom of "bespoke" work in various fields, such as shoemaking, was being supplanted by wholesale order work for an outside market. To meet new and severe competition, employers introduced "green hands" or cheap and less skilled labor, sought to keep open their labor supply and to keep down the costs of production, including wages. . . . To meet this formidable threat the skilled craftsmen turned to the trade union. As the trade union movement spread employers in city after city looked to the courts to choke its growth.

The power of the skilled workers had to be contained before unskilled laborers could be brought into the factories on a large scale. During the 1820s, the industrial capitalists tried to use the courts to contain the skilled workers. But that did not totally silence the skilled laborers. During the 1830s, they were still attempting to organize to protect their interests. The Depression of 1837 to 1843, however, eventually weakened and destroyed most of these early skilled unions. Massive unemployment made unity and resistance more and more difficult on the shop floor as well as in the courts.

The destruction of unions during the 1840s was a sign of a far greater change in the economic conditions of skilled workers in the United States. The shift of investments from commercial to industrial ventures also was taking place at a great pace. The factory was becoming a common sight in the Northern landscape, the demand for cheap unskilled labor grew, and the power of skilled workers over the production process diminished. Aronowitz (1973:147) states: "The replacement of skilled by unskilled and semiskilled labor in the industries that constituted the economic matrix of the country transformed the social position of skilled workers. They were no longer the core of productive labor."

The relationship of native-born laborers to immigrant laborers during the nineteenth century can now be seen more clearly. The resistance of native-born workers to the influx of immigrants took on an antiethnic, antireligious tone. But that resistance was basically another round in their losing battle against the rise of unskilled labor and the domination of the factory system. The influx of immigrants following the crushing of craft unions provided the type of labor force desired by the industrial capitalist. The new immigrants who went into the factories were unskilled, willing to work cheaply (or starve), and, most significantly for the owners, had not been formerly involved in work conditions where unionization was common (Aronowitz, 1973).

Therefore, not only did the rise of the factory system result in a division of labor between skilled, unskilled, and semiskilled, it also gave rise to an ethnic division of labor. The process began when relatively large numbers of unskilled workers were needed in the factories. In writing about the textile mills of New England, Gitelman (1967) states: "The technology employed at the Waltham mill required relatively large numbers of unskilled workers, yet unskilled labor was at a premium in the United States." The crushing of the skilled unions during the early nineteenth-century depression did not supply enough workers for the factories and led to the early tendency to involve native-born unmarried women as well as children as the dominant labor force in the factory system. Women and children were used because they could be hired more cheaply than men (Gitelman, 1967:238). This native-born group was later to be distinguished from the Irish immigrants to the factories.[11]

Labor in general was made subordinate to capital as the factory system spread during the nineteenth century. But the division of labor along skill lines needed in the factories created the conditions for conflict within the work force itself. The division of labor was part of the organization of the factory, hence it was structural. The placement of laborers within that organizational structure reflected the ability of other segments of the population to resist being assigned as unskilled laborers, however. The native-born workers had some skills, knew the language, had some experience or at least knowledge of organizing, had some access to the West, and thus had more power than the Irish immigrant workers. The Irish workers, on the whole, were starving, had no capital or skills to take advantage of in the West, and had no history of union activity. They thus were a pliable labor force for capitalist and a hostile one for more skilled laborers.

This early stratification along ethnic lines had long-term consequences for U.S. society. Once the native-born workers were able to dominate the skilled and white-collar jobs, the unions that later arose protected their positions within the job market. This led to a process by which groups of people from specific regions of the world and from specific structural positions within those regions were assigned to similar structural slots in the U.S. labor force. Without a sense of how the original structure was built, it is logical to assume that ethnic differences and capacities led to their different positions within that labor force.[12]

According to Aronowitz (1973), the industrial labor force of the United States was divided along these lines by 1850:

1. Native-born skilled workers who had occupied the critical positions within the handicraft industries remained at the top of the labor force under the rising factory system.
2. A relatively small number of young farmers came to the cities and towns in the 1830s and 1840s instead of going West. When they did not become skilled workers, they moved into the factories as unskilled workers. In the long run, they became managers and foremen.
3. German, French, Scotch-Irish, English, and Welsh immigrants came to the society with definite industrial skills, usually in textiles, iron, and mining. They were able to earn good wages.
4. Irish peasants emigrated from southern Ireland during the potato famine. They and the Chinese (on the West Coast) were the first U.S. proletarians. They had no property and they had no skills with which to bargain in the rising industrial system.

The stratification of new immigrants within the industrial system was the structural equivalent of the stratification system that arose along racial lines during the late seventeenth century. In both instances, economic transformations called for large numbers of laborers who were not sufficiently available within the country. In both instances, the social value of specific groups was determined by the slot in which they were assigned, although stereotypes enforce the notion that their social value was inherent to their prior racial and ethnic identities.

Furthermore, in both instances a stratum of laborers was created between the new group and those who controlled the methods of production. In the seventeenth century, it was the free White laborer. In the nineteenth century, it was the native-born/Protestant/Northern European worker. The important marks of vertical classification in this context were religion, geographical origin, and language. It was therefore the needs of the new system, rather than the attitudes of the existing native-born laborers, that ultimately determined the creation of the new structural position in which Irish immigrants were placed.[13] But conditions within Ireland and the European world economy at large determined that a sector of the Irish population would be made available for placement in that slot. We now turn to Ireland to look at the processes that made a segment of that society available as a cheap unskilled labor force in the United States during the nineteenth century. One result of that process was that a segment of Irish society became identified as *the Irish* in the United States.

9   Ireland in the periphery

If we were to start our discussion of how some people from Ireland were made available as the cheap unskilled labor force for the U.S. economy by concentrating on the period of the famine (mid-nineteenth century), our understanding of that process would be severely limited. If we look at their assignment to the low structural slot in the free/White sector of the nineteenth-century U.S. labor force in relation to Irish history between the seventeenth and nineteenth centuries, however, our understanding of their assignment in the United States and the negative social value that they initially acquired there will be broadened. There are two factors that are crucial to this discussion. At the most abstract level they provide additional insights into the relationship of identity construction to macrosocial systems.

The first factor is that Ireland became a peripheral region of the European world capitalist system during the seventeenth century. Within the context of that vertically stratified system, Ireland's assignment to its low structural position was carried out most graphically through the military invasions known as the Cromwellian and Williamite Settlements during the middle and late seventeenth century. This process was not fully completed, however, until Ireland was formally consolidated with England under the Act of Union at the beginning of the nineteenth century. An important impact of the assignment of Ireland to the periphery was the inability of those in control of the state structure to act consistently on the behalf of Irish interests. English core interests took precedence because of England's greater military, economic, and political power. With the domination of Ireland, it is then not surprising that the English referred to Ireland in terms such as child, weak, female, which had negative social value. In turn, the Irish people were perceived as being hopelessly disunited and incapable of self-government (Curtis, 1968:6).

During the period of the peripheralization of Ireland, Protestants from England and Scotland became the dominant economic, political, and social groups within the society. They controlled the land and dominated trade and the few manufacturing industries in Ireland. Despite the presence of this Protestant group within Ireland, however, fundamental conflicts between so-called Irish and so-called English interests were constantly in evidence. These conflicts were based upon economic competition rather than upon racial or religious differences.[1]

The second factor that influences our perception of those from Ireland who were assigned to the lower structural slot as free but cheap

101

unskilled labor during the nineteenth century is that those who became available for migration were in the lower structural position within a society that was in the periphery of the European world system. Their life chances were thus strongly affected by the fact that the upper group in Ireland was confined to an increasingly peripheral status within the European world economy.

Because Irish Catholics were generally dominated by Protestants by the end of the seventeenth century and because Ireland was dominated by England, the conflict between the ruling group in Ireland and the ruling group in England had a very real effect upon the Catholic population. Irish Catholics were affected as the Protestants in Ireland made adjustments to the actions of the Protestant ruling group in England. A lack of power and the indirect impact of English domination therefore largely accounted for the inability of the Catholic majority to protect itself from the full force of the conflicts between the two ruling groups. In addition, the ruling group in Ireland was able to pass down the losses it faced to the dominated Catholic group. On the whole, the Catholic group was at the bottom of the social structure and therefore was powerless to pass down losses to any other group. However, the Catholic category was itself stratified, and some within that classification passed down losses to the less powerful.

The conflict between England and Ireland can then be seen as a conflict among specific social, economic, and political interest groups of those societies. The conflict between Catholics and Protestants within Ireland and within the Catholic group in Ireland can be similarly understood. For example, those who monopolized the major land holdings, the large trading businesses, and the industrial sector of the society were Protestants. Those who were relegated to being medium and small traders, small holders of land, occupiers of the land, tenants, and laborers were Catholics.[2] As a group, they were the producers in the society. The use of racial, national, and religious labels does not negate the historical truth of these facts.

The peripheralization of Ireland during the seventeenth century

The domination of the people and land of Ireland by Protestants as a result of the Cromwellian Wars (1641 to 1652) was the critical act in the peripheralization of the region. Cromwell initially intended to make Ireland into a direct extension of England. The Cromwellian Settlement called for the removal of the native Irish population from the three eastern provinces and their concentration in Connaught, the westernmost province of Ireland. There Connaught was conceived of as a reserve for what was assumed to be a surplus population. It was further assumed that the gap created by the removal of the native population would be filled by English settlers, specifically capitalist farmers and their English laborers.

The response of English farmers and agricultural laborers to the Cromwellian Settlement was not as vigorous as was expected, however. Agricultural conditions in Ireland were not as good as in England, and with the exception of Ulster, the plan for settlement was a failure. Nonetheless, English Protestants gained control over most of the land of Ireland. As a result, sectors of the native population were forced into becoming tenants and laborers on holdings that were transferred to the Protestants. Thus, most of the population on the land remained Catholic, while the ownership of the land shifted into Protestant hands.[3]

Because the Irish population remained on the land outside of Ulster, profits were extracted from the land by means different from what had been planned. English settlers were to become laborers as well as capitalists. Because there was little migration of free laborers from England, however, the relationship between the owners and the occupiers of the land became more closely feudal than capitalist.

The actual relations did indeed stem from the fact that the native population, rather than laborers from England, occupied the land. But the difference between the intended and the actual relations was not determined by the desire of the Protestant landowners to treat Irish Catholic laborers more harshly than English Protestant tenants. The difference in treatment resulted from two factors having little to do with religion or nationality. First, the Irish population was totally defeated by the Cromwellian and Williamite invasions of the seventeenth century. Second, prior to being dominated by England, production relations in Irish agriculture were vastly different from those in England (Pendergast, 1922:19).

Because Ireland had not gone through a feudal stage, as had the rest of Northern Europe, before the Cromwellian and Williamite invasions, most of the land was common property during the seventeenth century. In that social system, all members of the clans had access to land. There was some stratification within sectors of the Irish population before the invasions, however. Although they were slight, those differences were to become significant. The chief families of Ireland had portions of land appropriated to them in perpetuity. This led to the development of a form of inheritance not strictly consistent with communal social relations. Other members of the society and their families, such as the bards and physicians of the tribes, also enjoyed hereditary land rights (Pendergast, 1922:13).

This slight degree of stratification embodied in communal Irish law can be contrasted with what happened when English law was applied to Irish lands during the seventeenth century. According to English law, for instance, all Irish lands held under feudal tenure belonged to the English king and his royal tenants. In fact, the lands outside of the areas that were fully dominated by the English were hybrids. Clarke (1976:170) states: "Both traditional native and authentic feudal arrangements survived in many places in various stages of modification. It was neither unusual for land to be held in common without partition in the Irish manner, nor uncommon for it to be held according to the most elaborate stipulations of feudal overlordship." The differences between the native and English uses of Irish land were not nearly as great as those between the native use of Irish land and the use of land in England, however.

In seventeenth-century England, land ownership had moved far beyond the feudal relations that were being developed in Ireland. For example, the enclosure movement continued to operate as more and more lands were being utilized for sheep raising and the intensive raising of cereal and animal feed. In addition, small farms had become consolidated and the small farmers were being driven from the land to become agricultural wage laborers or wandering peasants. The new farmers (or the yeomanry) were essentially capitalist farmers who rented land from the large landowners and used the newly expropriated population as their wage laborers. These yeomen and wage laborers had been expected to migrate to Ireland through the Cromwellian Settlement. Thus, there were major differences between the group that would have occupied the land if the migration scheme of the settlement had worked and that group had occupied the land. The treatment of the Irish population was thus conditioned by military domination and the differences between the social structures of Ireland and England.

One indication of the peripheral status of seventeenth-century Ireland was the transfer of land ownership from Catholics to Protestants. The relationship between the Irish Parliament and the English Parliament was another. When the Cromwellian Settlement was threatened by the Civil War in England, the Williamite Settlement and the restoration of Protestant rule in England at the end of the seventeenth century were used to secure the lands to those who had gained them as the result of the earlier Cromwellian wars. By the end of the seventeenth century Irish land and the Irish Parliament were both dominated by Protestant landlords.[4]

The Catholic population was largely excluded from Ulster, hence the Protestants in that region were in the majority. In the rest of Ireland, however, the Catholic population remained in the majority and Protestant landowners were open to military attack by Catholics who were being forced to give up their legal and property rights. Thus, Protestants in Ireland tolerated their subordinate status to England partially because it provided the large landowning group with English military protection.

This early period resulted in Catholic exclusion from and English domination of Irish affairs, rather than the control over Irish affairs by the Protestant colonists who owned most of the land. In 1652, Ireland was placed under commissioners appointed by the English Parliament. This seemed logical to the new landowners, who saw Ireland as an insecure country because of its armed Catholic majority. Among other things, the commissioners rewrote the deeds to the Irish lands to enhance the conditions of the new landowners as well as to provide a legal basis for the destruction of the old system of Irish land ownership (Pendergast, 1922:32).

By 1691, after the signing of the Treaty of Limerick, the implications of the English and Anglo-Irish domination of Ireland became clearer. Although that treaty was designed to protect the civil and property rights of the Catholic gentry, those rights were violated as the Irish Parliament, now wholly reflecting the Protestant landlords' interests, tried to rule the country with the force of the English military behind it. But the Irish Parliament was very weak. It did not control the army in Ireland or Irish financial policy. Under Poynings Law (1694), for instance, all legislation suggested by the Irish Parliament had to be approved by the English Privy Council in London. In this sense, Ireland was ruled in the colonial style – directly from England. This was clearly evident by the fact that the lord lieutenant, the representative of the English government in Dublin, could dissolve the Irish Parliament at any time.

Therefore, despite the correctness of the assertion by the Catholic gentry that the Irish Parliament did not represent Catholic interests, the larger reality was that the Irish Parliament of the late seventeenth century did not even completely represent Protestant interests in Ireland (Fisher, 1911:4). Anglo-Irish Protestants were represented in the British Parliament, but there they were a minority. Irish Protestants of Ireland faced an ambivalent situation, and their awareness of their disadvantage led to a two-way struggle. On the one hand, they attempted to gain legislative and financial freedom from England. On the other hand, they began to make economic changes involving the use of Irish land to protect their investments. The latter changes led to the struggle between Protestant landlords and Catholic peasants.

The peripheralization of Ireland is also evident from legislation passed by the British Parliament and was manifested through changes in the economic position of Ireland in the world economy. The Protestant-dominated, although largely ineffectual, Irish Parliament was not unmindful of this fact. MacCurtain (1972:196) states:

William Moyneux, a member of the House of Commons (Ireland) in 1698 published a pamphlet, THE CASE OF IRELAND'S BEING BOUND BY ACTS OF PARLIAMENT IN ENGLAND STATED, in which he examined – in relation to the commercial interests of his own class – the constitutional straight jacket which circumscribed the free functioning of the Irish Parliament. His book was ordered to be burnt publicly.

Concern by the British Parliament over the possible damage to Protestant economic interests in Ireland did not come out of thin air. In 1660, for instance, the British Parliament passed an act that prohibited the exportation of raw wool from England, Wales, and Ireland to world markets. But the surface equality of the restriction did not manifest itself equally in the three countries. For example, before 1660 Ireland was able to export its raw wool to any market in the world. After the act, Irish raw wool could only be exported to England and then only with special license from the lord lieutenant. English wool manufacturers were thus able to obtain raw wool for their industry and the finished products could then be sold anywhere by merchants in England.

In 1660, while the Irish wool industry was still a home industry, another act was passed that restricted the entrance of Irish manufactured wool products as well as other finished specialized textile goods into England through the imposition of duties on such goods. This act severely hurt the growth of the Irish wool industry by cutting off access to markets other than the small Irish home market. On the other hand, there were no restrictions placed upon the export of finished goods from England to Ireland. Such activities were in fact given an almost unlimited range for expansion. As a result of these acts, the Protestant-dominated Irish wool industry, which had expanded to meet the needs of the home market by the end of the seventeenth century, could grow no further. This is another indication that this conflict was not between English Protestants and Irish Catholics per se.

The passage of acts restricting the Irish wool market at the end of the seventeenth century stands in stark contrast to other actions taken at the same time as well as only a few years earlier, however. For instance, the duke of Ormonde, an English representative in Ireland, encouraged the development of the wool trade in 1666. He invited Protestant refugees involved in wool production to settle in Ireland during that period. Plantations were set up for them, and out of it the Irish wool industry became dominated by Protestants (Murray, 1907:99).

Because of its late start and the limitations of the home market, Irish wool manufacturers were generally smaller than their English counterparts. Their development was aided, however, by an act of the Irish Parliament that decreased the exportation of Irish wool as well as the importation of English manufactured wool products. Murray (1907:101) states: "During these years [the reign of Charles II] there was a great rise in Irish revenue, and this was generally attributed by both English and

Irish to the progress of the woollen manufacturers." By 1698, in fact, it was estimated that 12,000 Protestant families in Dublin and 30,000 in the rest of Ireland worked in the woolen industry. Many Catholics were also beginning to enter the industry by the end of the century as laborers.[5]

With the success of the wool industry in Ireland, however, protests began to be heard in England. In 1697, for instance, petitions were sent to the English Parliament by English merchants and manufacturers asserting that there was a connection between the decline of the wool industry in England and the inexpensive products from Ireland (Murray, 1907:53). The manufacturers, mostly located in western England, greatly feared the access Irish manufacturers had to the English market as well as the movement of skilled workers from England to Ireland. Later, merchants from Bristol and Exeter joined the clothiers from the west in complaining bitterly about what they considered to be the advantages of the Irish manufacturers and traders (Cullen, 1972:134–5).

Action came swiftly from the English Parliament. A petition by those concerned about the wool industry in England was recommended to the commissioners of trade and plantations in 1697. A report was then sent to the lords justices in Ireland in early 1698. The report asserted that it was impossible for both Ireland and England to have healthy wool industries. It then stated that the industry in Ireland should be restricted to producing finished woolen goods (with the exception of frieze, which could be imported into England) for the Irish market. At the same time, however, the report recommended that raw wool be exported from Ireland to England without the imposition of a tariff. This essentially meant that Irish access to the world market would be restricted to the provision of raw materials.[6]

A commission report in 1697 stated that another industry should be started in Ireland to compensate the economy that would be affected by the decline of the wool industry. Despite the gesture, it is clear, given the impetus of the action and its subsequent results, that interests in England were perfectly willing to destroy the Irish wool industry despite the fact that both industries were dominated by Protestants. Indeed, by January 3, 1698, a bill incorporating the recommendations of the commission was sent to the Irish House of Commons. That house attempted to stall the bill, but despite that attempt, in June 1698 the English Parliament recommended to King William that the Irish wool trade be suppressed and that the linen industry be encouraged in its place. The recommendation was accepted with the justification that the wool industry was the staple industry of England, while its linen industry was small and stagnant (Murray, 1907:55).[7]

After 1698, heavy tariffs were imposed upon all manufactured wool products exported out of Ireland.[8] As was the case with the English recommendation, the encouragement of the linen industry was used to justify this action. A major problem with this scheme to shift from wool to linen, however, was that wool production was possible throughout Ireland, while linen production was possible only in limited areas of the country. The shift from wool to linen therefore restricted the possibilities of generating employment in most areas of the country. By 1699, the English Parliament had acted to restrict the trade of goods made of or mixed with wool between Ireland and the rest of the world. Such goods had to go to England first, but only with the permission of the commissioners of the revenue and after high duties were paid. Such actions finally destroyed the Irish wool trades as a legal activity.

It is significant that the decline of the wool industry in Ireland also led to a decline in wage labor employment. Because most wage laborers were Protestants, however, they were hit the hardest by the decline. As a result, workers who could afford to do so emigrated to other parts of Europe and to the United States at the end of the seventeenth century.[9] Other groups were also affected by this decline, however. Landlords found it hard to collect rents; merchants were affected by the decline of trade; shopkeepers found it hard to obtain sales for their small items. The net result was that Ireland in general was in a state of decline because of the actions of the British Parliament.

A significant result of the economic depression in Ireland was that land that was once used for pasture was shifted to grain production. Although the agricultural, industrial, and trading interests in Ireland usually survived the attacks of their English counterparts by shifting capital from declining ventures to more profitable ones, their ability to expand was severely hampered. Irish peasants and laborers were also affected by the shifting investments in Ireland in order to accommodate English economic interests. Unlike the agricultural, industrial, and trading elites, however, the laborers were not able to shift to or create new fields of employment. Thus, as the range of profitable investments available in Ireland was systematically decreased, the prospects of the peasant and laboring population decreased at an even greater rate.

Poverty and the emigration of Protestant workers resulted directly from the response of the Protestant capitalists in Ireland to English domination, because the Protestant colonists were not able to resist the impact of the English Act of 1699. They were unable to gain their economic and political freedom and instead had to shift their investments to nonrestricted areas. In so doing they passed their economic loses down to the workers and tenants (i.e., primarily Catholics). These actions and reactions were clearly conditioned by economic issues. When we analyze the social structural conditions in Ireland during the nineteenth century with its complex cast of characters, we must be careful not to shift the analysis from these economic conflicts to religious and ethnic conflicts merely because the actors in the drama were using such concepts to justify their actions.

Before the Cromwellian Settlement, a large export trade in livestock, specifically cattle and sheep, had been established by the Old English in Ireland.[10] In 1620 alone, 100,000 head of cattle were sent from Ireland to England (Murray, 1907:20). Early in the seventeenth century, large areas of land were used as pasture rather than for agricultural production. This was a viable economic strategy for the Old English because pasturage required few laborers; they therefore did not have to depend totally upon the native Irish to work their estates.

By 1663, however, the trade in Irish livestock was dominated by the Protestant soldiers and adventurers who had invested in the Cromwellian wars and received Irish lands as interest. They began livestock breeding on a larger scale than had been undertaken by the Old English. Specifically, in 1663 the export of sheep, oxen, butter, and beef were up one-third from the beginning of the Cromwellian wars in 1641, when the basis for the shift from Catholic to Protestant domination of the land took place.

As was the case with the wool trade, however, successful business in Ireland resulted in concern in England about the unfair advantage that livestock breeders in Ireland had over their English counterparts. Murray (1907:24) states: "The breeders complained that land in Ireland was so plentiful and cheap that cattle and sheep could be bred practically for nothing, and that in consequence English cattle, which could only be bred at great expense, were being undersold." Not surprisingly, the English Parliament passed a bill in 1663 prohibiting the importation of Irish cattle into England between July 1 and December 20 of that year. Attempts made in Ireland to prevent the enactment of the bill were not successful.

Political leaders in Ireland resorted to using a Council of Trade to convey to the English Parliament the effects of the bill restricting Irish cattle exports upon that industry. In November 1664, the council reported that the export of livestock from Ireland had almost completely ceased. The council added that Protestant tenants were giving up leases, taxes were falling, and additionally, military and civil expenses were becoming difficult to meet. The English Parliament was unmoved by these pleas. In fact, by October 1665, breeders from the northern counties of England had petitioned Parliament to call for the complete cessation of livestock importation from Ireland. That petition became the Cattle Act in 1666.

The Cattle Act of 1666 initially had a destructive effect upon Ireland's economy. At its height, the cattle trade to England made up three-quarters of Ireland's trade. Although the destruction of the wool industry was detrimental to Ireland's economy, it was not the dominant source of revenue for the economy. Livestock was the most important trade item for the Irish economy. The decline of that trade, although temporary, resulted in the increased indebtedness of the Irish treasury to the English treasury. The livestock traders in Ireland responded by shifting to the provision trade, which only temporarily supported the economy, because the shift kept the Irish economy dependent upon foreign trade. This dependence would eventually facilitate the expropriation of the Irish peasantry from the land as well as force Irish landlords to shift production to adjust to changes in the world market.

The creation of a dependent population

During the seventeenth century, fundamental transformations in Ireland created the conditions that made a labor force available for the cheap unskilled labor slot in the United States during the nineteenth century. Eighteenth-century Irish history reflects a continuation of forces put in place during the previous century. It is thus possible to pay less attention to social conditions during the eighteenth century to explain these transformations.

The economy of late-eighteenth and early-nineteenth-century Ireland was overwhelmingly agricultural. No less than 90 percent of its population was connected with agriculture (Adams, 1932:6). The agrarian classes were divided between large landlords, middlemen who traded in land, small farmers, cotters, and day laborers. The large landlords were generally absentees living in England (Robinson, 1962; Large, 1966). The middlemen leased large areas of land from the head landlords, but did not use it for production. Instead, they made their profits from rents by subletting small parcels of land at high rents to small farmers who then became undertenants. Small farmers usually owned from five to fifteen acres of land, not including land rented from the middlemen.

Most small farmers relied upon the labor of their immediate family. There were some small farmers, however, who employed either cotters or day laborers. Cotters did not receive payment in money; they instead were provided a hut and a plot of land (one-quarter to one-half acre) on which to grow potatoes. The day laborers occupied a lower level in the social system. They were forced to rent land on a yearly basis rather than having it provided for them by the farmers as payment for labor. This system was know as the conacre system. Both labor systems relied on labor to pay the rent (Pomfret, 1930; Woodham-Smith, 1962; Gairnes, 1967:165). The lack of money of the society was a significant factor in the use of this method of payment.[11]

During the Napoleonic Wars (1793 to 1815), major economic and political shifts pushed Ireland into a more dependent (peripheral) relationship to England and the European world economy, despite positive signs in the Irish economy during that period. One impact of the wars was the increased demand for grains and provisions (largely beef products) from Ireland. Farmers large and small profited from the high price of these exports (Hueckel, 1976).[12] In addition, the rise in the price for corn as well as pastoral commodities resulted in an increased demand for laborers. McNeill (1947:141) asserts that this demand for labor resulted in the movement of Irish peasants from relying upon the potato patch to cultivating grain. This resulted in increased competition for land and increased rents during the war years.

In addition, an increase in the subletting of lands resulted from the wars due to the increased demand for land by small farmers who were also hoping to profit from the war boom. Increased subletting also occurred because labor was paid in land use rather than in money. Thus, the increased demand for labor led to a further subdivision of land. An additional impact of the Napoleonic Wars on Ireland was that the import of capital goods increased more rapidly than the import of consumer goods. Cullen (1972:100–1) states:

During the war years, the Royal and Grand canals, the most capital-intensive projects undertaken in Ireland, were completed. New factory investment was also at a high level, and the building of flour mills reached a new peak. . . . Town growth was very rapid . . . the major expansion of Irish towns and urban buildings being crowded into the years 1790–1815.

During the same period, bank circulation expanded greatly, further reflecting the increased level of economic development in Ireland.

From the growth of capital investments, there also was an increase of nonagricultural labor in Ireland. The building of towns, canals, roads, and factories all required such a labor force. For example, approximately 8,000 laborers constructed the Dublin-Drogheda railway and the harbor improvements at Dundalk. Once construction was completed, their functioning required a type of labor force distinct from the traditional agricultural laborer (Freeman, 1957:20).[13]

The Napoleonic Wars were, in many respects, clearly a period of boom for the Irish economy. At the national level during that period the volume of exports rose sharply, reaching 4 million pounds, four times the size of the late eighteenth-century surplus. But despite this economic boom and the shifts in labor, most Irish laborers were still agricultural. Even further, that labor force depended upon the small plot and the potato for survival. Therefore, despite the fact that the Irish economy generally flourished, the conditions of the peasantry, although improved, remained tenuous (Cullen, 1972:100).[14] The end of the wars revealed the extent to which the growth of the Irish economy at the end of the eighteenth century was as tenuous as were the conditions of the Irish peasantry. With the coming of peace, there was an immediate decrease in the demand for goods that resulted in a worldwide drop in agricultural prices.

In reference to that period of Irish history, Donnelly (1975:45) states: "The soaring prices and windfall profits of the Napoleonic Wars ended with the arrival of peace in 1815, and a long, painful period of deflation followed. The deflation lasted until about 1836 and caused Irish farmers severe difficulty and loss." From this we can see that the impact of the end of the wars on the Irish economy was initially not significantly different from its impact on the U.S. economy. During the wars, both had grown because of the role of merchant capital and hence both suffered from the decreased demand for foreign goods after the wars were over.

There was a significant distinction between the U.S. economy and the Irish economy during this period, however. The U.S. economy received some protection from the strength of its state structure, but such was not the case in Ireland. The possibilities for an independent Irish state and economy were stopped during the Napoleonic Wars by the failure of the rebellion of 1798, and they were destroyed entirely by the Act of Union that went into effect in 1801.

The Act of Union was designed, on its face, to prevent the possibility of Ireland becoming a supporter of England's Catholic enemies, France and Spain. The fundamental result of the act, however, was the elimination of the Irish Parliament and the annexation of the Irish economy to England. This meant that all representative government and economic decisions for Ireland would now be explicitly made in England. Here we can clearly see that English political and economic control over issues concerned with Ireland, which began in the seventeenth century, intensified between then and the early nineteenth century.

As was true in the earlier case, the tendency has been to view the relations between England and Ireland as one of Protestants versus Catholics. From the end of the seventeenth century, however, Protestants in Ireland were most directly affected by the moves in the English Parliament to redirect the interaction of the Irish economy with the larger world market. Indeed, Catholics were also affected by those changes, but that resulted from their structural position in the society rather than their religion. The overwhelmingly Catholic peasantry was placed in an even greater position of dependence by the actions of the English Parliament *and* by the attempts of large landowners, merchants, and industrialists in Ireland (who were overwhelmingly Protestant) to adjust to the social, economic, and political reality that was being dictated to both from England. Thus Ireland, as a dependent society, was a reactive society. Without a clear sense of its social structure, we lose sight of social factors other than religion that greatly influenced group behavior during this period of Irish history.

After the Napoleonic Wars, the economic challenge from English goods on the Irish market increased primarily because English merchants had greater access to the internal markets of Ireland as the result of the infrastructural changes that were accomplished during the war, such as the new canals and roads that made transportation easier and less costly. In addition, the removal of protective duties on English goods entering Ireland, as stipulated in the Act of Union, made those goods very cheap compared with goods produced less efficiently in Ireland. Within this context, commodities produced in Ireland were faced with a declining share of an already small market (O'Brien and Thomas, 1972:526).[15] The great irony is that the growth of investments in canals and roads during the war period was a major factor in facilitating the transportation of English commodities within Ireland.

Therefore, despite the fact that conditions were created to develop an industrial sector in the Irish economy, the results for those at the top and the bottom of the Irish social structure were negative, which is clearly indicated by the dramatic decreases in the number of textile industries and wage earners. In addition, the number of wool manufactures in Dublin dropped from ninety-one to twelve. Even more dramatic, the number of people employed in that industry in Dublin dropped from 4,918 to 602; the carpet industry in Dublin was entirely destroyed, silk-loom weavers receiving wages dropped from 2,500 in 1800 to 250 in 1840. Similar dramatic shifts can be seen in the textile industries of Kilkenny, Balbriggan, Wicklow, and Cork during this period (Marx, 1974, Volume I:131–2).

In the Irish industrial sphere there was thus a dual movement in progress during the nineteenth century. On the one hand, home spinners and weavers were being forced into factories, while Irish industries were facing competition from larger and more efficient English factories. On the other hand, those weavers and spinners found themselves being required to live on extremely low wages (Black, 1960:102). Increasingly, laborers were forced to supplement their income with a small plot of land upon which they could grow potatoes. Underemployment due to the competition of English commodities resulted in large numbers of individuals flooding the rural areas, seeking land and employment and thus further driving down the price of labor and increasing the demand for small parcels of land (Freeman, 1957:41).[16]

But contradictory forces were also operating in the rural areas. For example, the existence of labor rent was prevalent during the eighteenth century because of the lack of money circulating in the economy. By the end of the Napoleonic Wars, however, the demand was for the payment of rent in money. Workers were still generally paid for their labor with the right to use land, but as tenants they were forced to pay their land rent in cash (O'Brien and Thomas, 1972:10). In this context the migration process became integral to Irish society.

The essential point is that Irish tenants were forced to become migrant laborers within the society as well as in Scotland and England because of the necessity of providing the rent in money demanded by landlords. The curious fact here is that the lack of money in circulation led the landlords to exchange land for labor, but at the same time it forced them to demand money from their tenants. The lack of wage labor in the economy meant, however, that there were few ways tenants could obtain money without migrating to an economy that had made a more fundamental transition to wage labor (Willcox, 1931; Handley, 1945; McNeill, 1947:132).[17] Wage labor could most readily be obtained by Irish laborers in Northern Ireland, Scotland, and England.

The demand for money rents had a twofold impact in the world economy. On the one hand, those regions of Northern Ireland, Scotland, and England that were able to utilize wage laborers now had a relatively cheap labor source. On the other hand, the landlords of regions of Ireland in which the granting of land under lease remained the dominant form of payment to laborers benefited as the returning laborers paid their rent in money. Thus, Irish landlords were able to gain some degree of liquidity. The peasants, now transformed into temporary wage laborers, were able to gain the experience of travel and wage work, but little else, because they usually returned home with enough money merely to pay their rent.

The consolidation of small farms was another factor that decisively affected the agrarian classes of Ireland (O'Brien and Thomas, 1972:52). There were two basic methods of consolidating lands. The first was the reclamation of marshlands. This was both expensive and time-consuming. The second was simply to dispossess small holders whose leases were up or whose rents were in arrears. The end of the Napoleonic Wars and the fall of commodity prices placed many farmers, as well as middlemen, in arrears. This latter type of consolidation, of course, had the greatest impact upon the small holders. But the elimination of the small holders was the easiest method of consolidating land (O'Brien and Thomas, 1972).

If we recall that the war years (1798 to 1815) led to increased subletting and subdivisions as well as increased utilization of agricultural labor, it becomes very easy to envision the extent to which consolidation disrupted the lives of the Irish rural poor. In addition, the end of efforts toward investing in infrastructure sent laborers back to the land at a time when soldiers were also returning home and looking for jobs. The expansion of the pastoral and tillage industries was also responsible for bringing about a massive problem in the rural economy of Ireland. The pastoral industry required a smaller percentage of labor in relation to land than did tillage, while technical improvements in agriculture also decreased the demand for labor. The postwar agricultural expansion of production for export, therefore, left a large number of the Irish rural population without land as well as without employment (Connell, 1950).[18]

The economic pressures that were pushing tenants off the land were soon supported by political power as a result of the passage of the Ejectment Act and the Land Code by Parliament in 1816. Pomfret 1930:14) states that:

The harshness of this code stands out by contrast with the law in England during this period. There an action could not be completed in less than a year and the cost was 18 pounds. The landlord was not allowed to seize growing crops and was not permitted to sell distrained goods. In other words, parliament had given the Irish landlord power to evict in cases in which he was not entitled to this remedy by contract or by common law.

Those parliamentary actions, along with the larger profits to be had from pastoral rather than tillage farming, strongly support the conclusion that landowners did indeed desire and attempt land consolidation immediately after the Napoleonic Wars. Forces moving in the other direction, such as the violence of the rural poor and the lack of capital in Ireland, were largely mitigated by landlord-supported emigration and the use of local and county military and police forces to secure evictions. In addition, problems for the rural poor were compounded by their increased dependence upon the potato after 1800 (Cullen, 1972:21).[19]

The fundamental result of this period was that the Irish economy entirely depended on its links to England and thus the European world economy. The peasantry's great difficulties were finding ways to stay on the land and finding alternative local sources of employment, which were scarce. Those factors provided clear signs of the impending Great Famine that triggered the mass migration to North America during the mid-nineteenth century. In the next chapter, we explore the failed intellectual, political, and economic responses to the signs of famine and the famine's impact upon the various sectors of society.

10 The Great Famine and forced emigration

During the nineteenth century, the people in the lower structural position of Irish society faced a dire and rapidly declining predicament. Numerous speeches, articles, and commission reports identified their plight, and all of the assertions that disaster was inevitable came true in the form of the Great Famine.

In 1822, the Irish Poor Law Commission reported that the situation in Ireland was dire, and 300,000 English pounds were spent that year in the attempt to relieve the distress of the population. Nicholls (1967:42) summarizes the committee's report in this manner:

In the districts where the distress chiefly prevailed, the potato constituted the principal food of the peasantry, and *the potato crop had failed; but there was not deficiency in the other crops,* and the prices of corn and oatmeal were moderate. Indeed the exports of grain from ports within the distressed districts, the committee observed, presented the remarkable example of possessing a surplus of food, whilst the inhabitants were suffering from actual want! *The calamity of 1822 may therefore be said to have proceeded less from want of food in the country than from the people's want of the means to purchase it.* Or in other words, from their want of profitable employment [emphasis added].

It is significant that this report states that there was food in Ireland! This finding alone gives us a sense of the stratification in Irish society during the nineteenth century. In fact the Calamity of 1822 was a small version of the disaster that would occur approximately a quarter century later. The problem was not that there was not enough food in the society, but that the lower strata of society were not able to afford the food that was available.

Most of the rural-based Irish population (a peasantry in transition perhaps, but clearly a surplus labor force) could not afford to buy food. They were day laborers, tenants, and seasonal migrant workers or some combination of these types. The distinction between this composite group and a permanent wage-labor force comes from the fact that with the exception of the seasonal migrant workers, they were paid with the use of land rather than with money.

Those who were in want of employment–who needed to be paid in money–in the early nineteenth century were pushed off the land without having alternative means to provide for their subsistence. Thus, while the

116

terms "lack of employment" and "lack of capital" imply the existence of a fully developed capitalist economy, in reality, that was precisely what was lacking in Ireland. Within this context, it is extremely interesting that the commission report did not look at the possibilities of providing land to the rural population. The commission members assumed that there was only one direction in which the economy could move. This position represented the economic and political interests of the landlords, merchants, and industrialists. They entirely ignored the economic and political interests of the segment of the population that needed immediate help.

By 1830, conditions within Ireland remained serious for those who had no access to money. The Select Committee of Commons, To Take Into Consideration the State of the Poorer Classes in Ireland, And the Best Means of Improving Their Lot reported that:

A very considerable portion of the population is considered to be out of employment. The number is, they say, estimated differently; by some one-fifth, by others at one-fourth, and this want of demand for labor necessarily causes distress among the laboring classes, which combined with the consequences of an altered system of managing land, is said to produce misery and suffering. (Nicholls, 1967:95)

This report added some historical details that give us a broader picture of the conditions in Ireland during the third decade of the nineteenth century. It states that increased prices during the Napoleonic Wars had led to an expansion of agricultural production. This resulted in a greater demand for labor, an increase in land value, the subdivision of land, and the rise of a class of middlemen who merely leased land for profit. The end of the wars and the resulting decrease of agricultural prices brought forth the opposite results. The middlemen were destroyed, because the occupying tenants were unable to pay their rents. As the middlemen defaulted and their leases were terminated, the landlords were able to consolidate most of the small rented pieces of land and change the structure of agricultural production in Ireland.

Relying upon the process of consolidation, the 1830 report concretely stated how the rural population was being driven into poverty:

It is said that the consolidation of farms would lead to better husbandry, to a certainty of crop, to the providing-buildings and more comfortable habitations, and to an increase in the quantity and improvement in the quality of the produce. These are all important considerations, and if the landlords and the tenants who continued in possession were alone to be regarded, the change would appear an unmixed good. But there is another class, the ejected tenants, whose condition, it is said, necessarily becomes most deplorable (Nicholls, 1967:99).

This report thus recognized that the problem was not merely the lack of wage labor.

Expropriation occurred in Ireland at the same time that conditions for a transition to a more fully developed home market were destroyed. Once again the rural population was being pushed off of the land, while the conditions for wage labor were being eroded. Thus, a surplus labor force was being generated in Ireland, largely because land was seen primarily in terms of its ability to generate profits in the world market. At the same time, the upper group in Ireland had little or no ability to protect local industries in order to develop a home market. The 1830 report, in recognition of problems other than employment, recommended government-sponsored emigration as a way out of the coming disaster.[1]

There was no unity on the subject of emigration, however. Although landlords in Ireland and workers in England would have benefited from the migration of the rural Irish population out of Europe, the large capitalist farmers in England, who were dependent on the cheap seasonal labor from Ireland, would not have benefited. Kerr (1968) argues that an increased demand for seasonal rather than permanent laborers in English agriculture was rooted in a partial transformation of the system of agricultural production. She states that:

Among other innovations on the farm was the threshing machine which was in common use by 1830. Through this invention the disproportion between summer and winter work became greater, as the winter occupation of threshing could now, with the aid of machinery, be done in a short time immediately after the harvest. No invention, however, had yet rendered possible any reduction in the numbers of the harvesters; so at certain seasons the regular laborers had to be supplemented by outside workers. At such times, the prospective employer had two alternatives; he could employ the village paupers, whose work was notoriously slipshod and unreliable, or he could obtain his extra workers from further afield. (1968:366)

Those extra workers from further afield often came from Ireland. Within this context, emigration was not in the interest of the English capitalist farmers.

From the beginning, the question of whether public funds would be provided for the emigration of segments of the Irish population revolved around economic and political (structural) interests. The final decision was political, but it reflected the differential power of specific interest groups. In England, the struggle over this question reflected the larger struggle for domination of the state between the landed interests and industrial interests.

Views on emigration

An indication of the connection between poverty in Ireland and economic classes can be gleaned from the writings of the classical economists during the prefamine days. For example, Malthus (1872:465) looked at these facts on Ireland and proposed "moral restraint" as the only long-term solution to "over-population." Emigration, he felt, was a temporary solution for the Irish case, because ultimately it would never be able to forestall the "famine" and "pestilence" that would result from a population that was too large. He also rejected the implementation of poor laws and other methods to improve the conditions of the poor of Ireland, because he was convinced that those actions would only delay the natural checks upon the population increase and thereby cause greater pain to the laborers of Ireland in the future (Malthus, 1872).

Ricardo (Sraffa, ed., 1951) and Torrens (Robbins, 1958) found fault with the rigid concept of "moral restraint" with which Malthus approached the problems facing the laboring population of Great Britain between the Napoleonic Wars and the famine in Ireland. They rejected Malthus's approach as too subjective and instead attempted to solve Ireland's poverty by utilizing the model of the developing English capitalist economy.

Torrens, in particular, thought that the major problem in Ireland was the existence of a surplus labor force. He recommended that emigration of the surplus population to areas of the world where there was a surplus of land that could be combined with capital should be encouraged. He suggested the British colonies in North America (basically Canada during this period), South Africa, and Australia as good candidates for settlements. Not moral restraint but removal of the population, he felt, was the best method of reducing the poor rates and the pressures of population. Torrens's larger assumption was that emigration would set the stage for the development of capitalism in Ireland and at the same time eliminate the possibilities of famine for the laboring population (Robbins, 1958:289).[2]

The call for emigration resulted from the recognition that the movement of Irish laborers into the English and Scottish markets would increase competition for unskilled work while decreasing the wages of the English and Scottish workers. This movement, in turn, would put additional strain upon the poor rates of England and Scotland. Thus, Torrens's purposes would not have been served by seasonal or permanent migration from Ireland to other parts of Great Britain.[3]

Torrens believed that removing the surplus labor force from Ireland would also encourage the flow of surplus capital to Ireland. In a speech on emigration he stated:

Ireland, exchanging her raw produce for the wrought goods of England may extensively adopt the improved system [relying upon land consolidation] of farming long before her native manufactures becomes so flourishing as to give employment to the hands no longer required upon the soil. In this case, unless timely and energetic measures of precaution be adopted [i.e., emigration], Ireland, in advancing towards wealth and prosperity, must necessarily pass through a period of the most aggravated and intolerable distress. (Robbins, 1958:151)[4]

Torrens felt that Ireland, like England, would develop economically if labor and capital were brought into line with each other. For him, land consolidation would have checked the Irish population during the 1820s. He felt that a program of emigration and consolidation would ultimately bring the population in line with the level of subsistence.[5]

Along with Torrens, Wheatly, Nassau Senior, Horton, and Wakefield saw emigration as the fundamental solution to the problem of Irish "over-population" and poverty (Johnston, 1972:170–1). The basic distinction between their position and that of Malthus was Malthus's concern with maintaining a society dominated by landed interests and keeping down the birth rate. The others were concerned with the rise of an industrial capitalist-dominated society and the utilization of the surplus population for further capitalist development in the British colonies. In both instances, however, the elimination of a segment of the poor from Ireland was deemed crucial.

Ricardo and McCulloch opposed emigration and colonization, but they were not strong supporters of moral restraint either. Ricardo, in particular, felt that emigration and colonization would diminish the level of productivity of Ireland without providing any comparable benefits. Like Malthus, McCulloch felt that emigration would only lead to an increase in wages and an eventual increase in marriage and population, thereby filling the vacuum created by emigration. Both Ricardo and McCulloch felt, however, that it would be more realistic to be concerned with the conditions that would introduce capital and how its security could be achieved in Ireland. They felt that the introduction of capital would lead to capital accumulation, and then Ireland, like England, would develop a capitalist system of production (Black, 1960:19).

For them, the introduction of capital was premised upon making capital investments in Ireland safe from attacks by the rural poor. In addition, the consolidation of small holdings was important to furthering technological improvements. Their ideal was that the redundant population would be employed in the industrial sector, thereby producing the nonsubsistence goods demanded by laborers as their tastes for luxury goods increased. The basic premise was that national capitalist development was open to all nations.

There were others, such as John S. Mill and John Bright, who supported peasant proprietorship as the solution to the Irish problem (Black, 1960). Their views were expressed after the Great Famine, however, when it had become obvious that solutions involving full employment through migration either were not going to be implemented or had already failed. They nonetheless still held onto some basic assumptions from the prefamine days. What is significant in that regard was the belief that the problem rested within Ireland and was independent of its links to the European world system.

The failure of theoretical solutions

Until the 1830s, most Protestant workers migrated permanently from Ireland. Poor law commission reports discussed migration as a solution to the increasing problem of poverty in Ireland, but never became actively involved in emigration. In addition, the commission's recommendations that were implemented (even the implementation of a poor law for Ireland) did not effectively address the problem. In the case of the classical economists, discussions of emigration were concerned with methods that could transform Ireland into a fully capitalist economy without creating a massive famine. Partly because their ideas were at odds with those of the powerful English industrial capitalists, however, they were not carried out.

The eventual famine and emigration, therefore, did not come as a complete shock to all in Ireland and England. As early as 1829, for example, Mr. Villiers Stuart crystallized general thinking in a speech to the House of Commons:

The evil of the Irish system namely the potato-minimum did not stop here; for the potato, though a very productive esculent, was liable to blight and frost in the winter, and always fell off in the spring season. You could not preserve it by an exertion for more than a year; and if there happened to be a failure in the new crop, where then were the stores for the subsistence of the poor? The granary might be full to overflowing; but of what advantage was it to them: Their labour was paid for in the potato, and they were therefore unable to purchase bread (Hansard's Parliamentary Debates, 1829:1127–8).

The contradiction between the potato as the basis of payment for laborers and the need for money to pay for items other than the potato is here clearly stated. It vividly demonstrates the existence of a social system that was caught between noncapitalist and capitalist methods of production.

The Great Famine in Ireland began with the destruction of at least half of the potato crop in 1845 and the total destruction of the crop in 1846. The *potato blight,* as it was called, came with the heavy rains of September. A fungus first destroyed the leaves, then the body of the potato. But Ireland was neither the only nor the first country to be hit by the blight. In fact, during the 1840s potatoes were destroyed in the western parts of the United States. In 1841, the blight appeared in Germany. By 1842, it hit the potato crop in Belgium. In 1844, there were reports of the destruction of the potato crop in Canada. In 1845, the blight appeared in England, Scotland, and Ireland. Of all the reported instances, the potato blight in Ireland wreaked the most devastation (O'Rourke, 1875:48). The Eighth Report of the Irish Poor Law states:

Although the potato had thus failed, not only in Ireland, but in England and Scotland, and throughout the greater portion of Europe, *the grain crops were generally abundant,* and would in a great degree supply the deficiency caused by such failure, except where the potato constituted the chief or nearly sole article of subsistence, as was the case in many parts of Ireland [emphasis added]. (Nicholls, 1967:308)

Thus, the problem for the Irish poor (the cotters and laborers) resulted from their great dependence on the potato and not on the blight.[6]

It should also be kept in mind that although the movement of people out of Ireland clearly increased as a result of the destruction of potato crops in 1845 and 1846, the rise in emigration from Ireland had begun already (Figure 4). Thus, we would be acting hastily to conclude that the migration out of Ireland during the 1840s only resulted from the potato blight.[7]

The use of Irish lands for the production of livestock, provisions, and corn for export made the Irish economy totally dependent upon fluctuations in the world market. The use of land as payment for labor created an additional problem, however. Because laborers were producing their own means of subsistence, the diminished demand for labor would then naturally diminish the access of laborers to land. As their access to land diminished, they were forced to find alternative sources of subsistence or starve. The lack of industry in Ireland (partly a result of actions taken in the English Parliament) and the lack of land and agricultural employment left the rural population of Ireland without the means of obtaining alternative sources of subsistence after they were driven from the land.

Once pushed off the land, the rural population became a full-blown surplus (redundant) labor force. The initial response of that population was to seek employment as seasonal or permanent laborers in England and Scotland. This was the start of the massive movement out of Ireland. It was a movement born of necessity. The four economic crises (1818 to 1819, 1825 to 1826, 1837 to 1839, and 1846 to 1847) in the European capitalist world market had an immediate impact upon the surplus labor force of Ireland. These crises resulted in the massive unemployment of English and Scottish workers, who were then forced to seek employment in lower-paying areas they had formerly rejected and left to Irish laborers. Many of those jobs that had formerly been rejected were

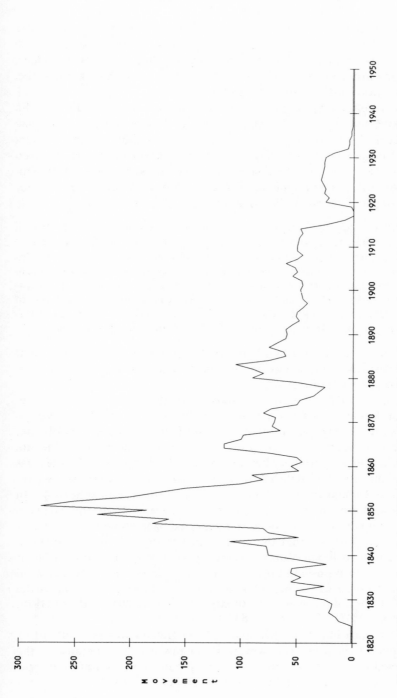

Figure 4. *Migration from Ireland (1820 to 1950). Source: N. H. Carrier and J. R. Jeffery (eds.), External Migration: A Survey of the Available Statistics. London: Her Majesty's Stationery Office, 1953.*

in the areas of the economy such as agriculture that did not require skilled laborers. It was precisely in those areas that the seasonal as well as the few permanent laborers from Ireland had found employment. Workers from England and Scotland were therefore thrown into direct competition with workers from Ireland.

The results were not good for workers from Ireland because they did not have the support of a state structure. Within the context of the hierarchical structure of the European world capitalist system, workers from Ireland were structurally lower than workers from England.[8] Even before the famine, the English viewed Irish workers as lazy, dirty, violent, dishonest, and impulsive. These attitudes provided the context for the struggles over work. Woodham-Smith (1962:281) states:

Earlier than this [the famine period], the Irish were detested by the British workingman; a large Irish immigration had already taken place, and the part played by the Irish in 19th century industrial Britain had not been happy. No regulation of wages then existed, trade unions were still struggling to establish themselves and the Irish were a source of cheap labour. On at least two occasions, at Newton Heath and Preston, owners of mills brought over bands of immigrants from Ireland for the purpose of strike-breaking. As a result, it was frequently impossible to get English and Irish labourers to work together.

The conflicts between English and Irish laborers was the meeting point of the vertically stratified world capitalist system with the vertically stratified social system of Ireland.

By spring 1847, tens of thousands of destitute individuals from Ireland suffering from fever spread over England, Scotland, and Wales. They were moving away from the ports for fear of being sent back home. At this time the power of the core state structure in determining the fate of workers in the periphery became explicit. During May 1847, a bill was rushed through the English Parliament making it legal to round up paupers from Ireland and send them back home without formal hearings. In Glasgow during that year, beggars and vagrants from Ireland were rounded up daily by the police and deported back home. The net result of these actions was that the poor from Ireland were forced to try to survive in their home country during a period of severe economic crisis that was in turn pushing them out of their country. This only increased the devastation of people who were already facing starvation as the result of the potato blight (Woodham-Smith, 1962:281; Redford, 1926; Handley, 1945).

The potato blight of 1846 and 1847 in Ireland was not without its immediate beneficiaries, however. Merchants benefited because of the increased price of foods other than the potato. One indication of how they benefited can be found in the Poor Relief Bill of 1846. The body of the bill provided outdoor relief and established soup kitchens for the poor. Prior to this bill, Clause 41 of the 1838 Irish Poor Law stipulated that relief was to be granted only to individuals who were in workhouses (government-organized units essentially like the late-twentieth-century homeless shelters). Preference for positions in the workhouses was to go to the aged, those with physical handicaps, and destitute children. The 1846 bill eased those restrictions because they were no longer, if ever, enforceable. Approximately 2,385,000 able-bodied poor swarmed toward the cities of Ireland after the destruction of the potato (Woodham-Smith, 1962:165). The workhouses were incapable of containing such large numbers.

During this period, the price of food on the open market had risen so substantially after the blight of 1845 that the government could no longer establish public works that could pay well enough so that people would not starve. In adddition, too many people were applying for the impossibly low paying jobs, massive corruption created other problems, and the public works projects usually ended up being an indirect subsidy for Irish merchants. Woodham-Smith (1962:167) states:

Throughout December of 1846, prices rocketed, and speculators made fortunes out of Indian corn. Mr. Heweston, at Cork, wrote on December 30 that 40,000 and 80,000 pounds were spoken of as having been made by merchants in Cork, and he wished government would do something to check the exorbitant prices, but supposed they were according to the spirit of trade and therefore legitimate.

Ending the public works and setting up soup kitchens was viewed by some as a way of feeding the poor as well as ending the government subsidy of the merchants. It was clear, however, that things were very much out of control.

Within the chaos, however, the two quarter-acre clauses to the Poor Relief Bill of 1846 significantly benefited the large landlords of Ireland.[9] The first clause stated that tenants whose rents were valued at less than five pounds and who gave up their land to their landlord would be assisted by the guardians of the poor law union to emigrate. The landlord would, in turn, agree not to press for back rents and would also pay two-thirds of the "fair and reasonable" cost of emigration of the tenants and his family. In addition, the poor law guardians were stipulated to pay the tenants any amount up to half of what any landlord contributed. This clause was designed to rid the very small tenants from the land and allow landlords to further the process of land consolidation. We can see the results of this process in the dramatic decline in the number of smaller holdings (one to fifteen acres) and the increase in the number of larger holdings (fifteen to thirty acres and over) between 1841 and 1851 as reflected in Table 2. [10]

Table 2. *Number and percentage of holdings above one acre in Ireland (1841–1901)*

Year	Total holdings[a]	1–5 acres		5–15 acres		15–30 acres		Over 30 Acres	
		No. of Holdings	%	No. of Holdings	%	No. of Holdings	%	No. of Holdings	%
1841	691,114[b]	310,436	44.9	252,799	36.6	79,342	11.5	48,625	7.0
1851	608,066	88,083	15.5	191,854	33.6	141,311	24.8	149,090	26.1
1861	610,045	85,469	15.0	183,931	32.4	141,251	24.8	157,833	27.8
1871	592,590	74,809	13.7	171,383	31.5	138,647	25.5	159,303	29.3
1881	577,739	67,071	12.7	164,045	31.1	135,793	25.8	159,834	30.4
1891	572,640	63,464	12.3	156,661	30.3	133,947	25.9	162,940	31.5
1901	590,175	62,855	12.2	154,418	29.9	134,091	26.0	164,483	31.9

[a]Includes holdings of less than one acre.
[b]Does not include holdings of less than one acre.

Source: Agricultural Statistics of Ireland, with Detailed Report for the Year 1901, p. 15 [Cd. 1170], H.C. 1902, cxvi – Part I.

The second clause literally forced the poor to choose between giving up all claim to the land and starving. It stated:

And be it further enacted, that no person who shall be in the occupation, whether under lease or agreement, or as tenant at will, or from year to year, or in any other manner whatever, of any land of greater extent than the quarter of a statute acre, shall be deemed and taken to be a destitute poor person under the provisions of this Act, or of any former Act of Parliament. Nor shall it be lawful for any Board of Guardians to grant any relief whatever, in or out of the workhouse, to any such occupier, his wife or children. And if any person, having been such occupier as aforesaid, shall apply to any Board of Guardians for relief as a destitute poor person, it shall not be lawful for such Guardians to grant such relief, until they shall be satisfied that such person has *bona fide,* and without collusion, absolutely parted with and surrendered any right or title which he may have had to the occupation of any land over and above such extent as aforesaid, of one quarter of a statute acre. (O'Rourke, 1875:331)

Those who owned or occupied more than one-quarter of an acre of land could not receive state aid. This exclusion not only applied to the owners and occupiers, but also to their spouses and children. Even further, if those in need no longer possessed more than one-quarter of an acre of land, documentation to that effect had to be established before aid could be granted.

Given the usual difficulties of obtaining legal documents in nineteenth-century Ireland, to say nothing of the tremendous amount of chaos existing in the country during the potato blight, the insistence upon documents can easily lead to the conclusion that the greatest concern of the drafters of the clauses was with clearing the land while diminishing the possibility of future legal entanglements. Both clauses took advantage of the inability of the rural population to resist; thus, the law effectively cleared the land. In addition, landlords benefited from the land clearings without having to resort to military force and without even having to pay full value for the removal of tenants. Within this context, the potato blight, with the resulting deaths and emigration, enriched the landlords and merchants of Ireland.

Some landlords did, however, take the initiative to support fully the emigration of their tenants, even while the quarter-acre clauses were in effect. Thus, some were being humane even in the face of the benefits to be gained from the government's action to consolidate the land. But others remained concerned only with the fact that the poor, without work and without land, might turn upon the landlord class and the landlord's property. Both reasons motivated some landlords to supply ships to bring tenants to North America. The Honorable Mr. Wandesford from Kilkenny, a Colonel Wyndham from Clare, and a Mr. Spraight from Limerick were among the landlords who took that action early in

1846. Still others only gave their tenants the small fare required to get to Liverpool. By June 1847, 300,000 persons had emigrated to Liverpool alone (Woodham-Smith, 1962:214,276).

Partly because of the mass migration and deaths from starvation and fever, the population of Ireland decreased from 8,175,124 to 6,552,385 between 1841 and 1851. However, using Ireland's previous ratio of births to deaths, we see that its population should have increased to 9,028,799 during that period. The difference between the actual population for 1851 and the projected population was 2,476,414. Of that decrease, approximately 1,436,862 people migrated and therefore approximately 1,039,552 died of starvation, disease, or were not born. This upheaval led to large-scale migration from Ireland to the United States. But clearly this final convulsion was fundamentally rooted in the relationship of Ireland to the European world economy and the relationship of the rural population in Ireland to the landlord classes in both Ireland and England (O'Rourke, 1875).

Why the Irish migrated to the United States

It is significant that those leaving Ireland during the 1840s crisis in the world economy were of a particular class (landless peasants, seasonal migrants, some urban workers) rather than the Irish in general. It is also significant that most of those leaving Ireland came to the United States when there was an increased demand for unskilled laborers. What I have not specifically addressed, however, is why they came to the United States rather than going elsewhere. The tendency has been to place networks in the forefront of the explanation of why sectors of the Irish population came to the United States. The reasoning generally has been that those who came before pulled those who came later. Although that reasoning is correct on the surface, it does not explain the migration from mid-nineteenth century Ireland. The explanation rests more readily on an understanding of the structural transformations within the European capitalist world economy and of the nature of the capitalist method of production.

The question of why the migrants from Ireland went to the United States (another part of the European world capitalist system) rather than to a society that did not have a capitalist method of production thus becomes important. A surplus labor force from a capitalist system can migrate to regions without a capitalist system of production only if that group can make its livelihood through agricultural production. In the case of the population from Ireland, migration to a noncapitalist region would have required that they obtain land and the means by which to provide for themselves during the initial period that the land was being brought under cultivation. In other words, they would have needed a reserve in the form of cash or goods to provide for themselves for a period of time. Neither were available to the population of Ireland that was being cleared from the land. They had been driven from the land with little more than their clothes. They therefore were generally without a reserve of any kind (Woodham-Smith, 1962).

The migrants from Ireland moved quickly toward sectors of the U.S. economy that provided quick access to a means of survival (i.e., wage labor). From that movement we know why the migrants from Ireland came to the United States rather than to the Urals, for example. In their situation, time was of the essence. In any economic system other than one that utilized cheap unskilled laborers (i.e., workers who required little or no time to train to get on the job and on the payroll), people from Ireland who had been pushed from the land during the nineteenth century would have died on a scale that was larger than they did.

During the period of the mass migration from Ireland, the routes to wage work in England and Scotland were closed. The movement of the United States from a trading and agricultural society to one that combined trading and agriculture with industrial production provided the ideal and perhaps the only place where a population that had so long been trapped between feudalism and capitalism could have survived. The movement to the United States was thus conditioned by the availability of the means of survival with the least delay. We can only assume that the immigrants would have moved to any region that could have provided them with the means of survival.[11] The expanding industrial economy in the United States provided jobs, while the contracting industrial economy of England generated hostility, unemployment, poverty, migration, and death. There was thus little choice about where to go.

Therefore, when explaining the movement of the primarily rural population from Ireland to the United States during the nineteenth century, we have to look at various processes. First, we must examine how the means of subsistence were generated in regions without wage labor. Second, we have to look at how the means of subsistence were generated in regions that had capitalist production relations. Regions that had capitalist production relations also have to be examined within the context of the European world capitalist system. Secular and cyclical trends within that system resulted in different labor needs in the distinct political regions of the system. Those who left Ireland were therefore pushed from access to their lands and from England and Scotland and pulled toward the cheap, unskilled labor market in the United States.

It should therefore not be surprising that the social value of the sector of the Irish population that migrated to the United States during the famine period was negative. They were, after all, a population that was forced from the lowest rung in Ireland into the lowest rung (in the free/ White labor system) in the United States. It is also here that we can begin to understand why those who were leaving Ireland for the United States did not remain a race unto themselves, but instead became an ethnic group in the White race (Knobel, 1986).

The situation faced in the United States was quite different from that faced by those who went to England. In England, the population from Ireland has been identified as a distinct minority race with much lower social value than those who came to the United States (Curtis, 1968; Lees, 1979; Douglas, 1982; Knobel, 1986). As is consistent with my general position, migrants from Ireland have generally occupied lower structural positions in England than in the United States. In the litera- ture on race and ethnicity, however, the tendency has been to lump that population of Irish descent together with all Whites/Europeans and thereby explain their social value based upon their skin pigment. This position is not able to utilize the same explanation for the social value of the population of Irish descent in both England and the United States, however. The net result is that the ad hoc feature of explanations about the social value of people of Irish descent is camouflaged by treating distinct situations as instances of a primordial group.

But by looking more widely at how marks of vertical classification operate (i.e., different marks in different social structural contexts in different historical periods), we can devise a theoretically justifiable understanding of the creation of racial and ethnic identities. Racial and ethnic identities cannot therefore be justifiably treated as the basis of primordial group identities that can be analyzed in isolation from their social construction within specific social systems (Weber, 1978:385).

11 Racial and ethnic social values – the formation of identities

The labor category in which individuals are located provides the basis for their economic and political power in a specific social structure. The social value given to the common characteristics of those occupying a specific labor category, however, becomes the generally accepted explanation of their place in that labor category. The specific identifying characteristics are marks that provide relatively clear contrasts between those at the top of the social structure and those at its bottom. The fact that the characteristics chosen have to provide contrasts between all members at the very top and all members at the very bottom does not mean, however, that those in the intermediate positions are not identified by one of the two labeled categories. This is precisely the object of utilizing biological and natural marks as the basis for identification. They obscure the social content of group structuring while stressing its natural aspects. By reducing the emphasis on the use of power to assign individuals to specific labor categories, while enhancing the role of biologically based marks, certain social categories get transformed into race and ethnicity and thus acquire the air of natural categories.

It was in this manner that all Africans were labeled as heathens who were only capable of being slaves. It has not been sufficiently acknowledged during or after the abolition of slavery that there were people within societies in Africa who had logical economic, political, and social reasons for exchanging humans for goods. This admission would have implied recognizing structural differences within that population that were similar to those in Europe, rather than maintaining the notion that all Africans were the same, based purely upon their skin pigmentation.[1]

The slave, a labor category and a structural position within a society, has never been the same as the African. Some people of African descent have been slaves, but African and slave are not synonymous. To assume that they are would imply that there has never been and could never be a slave who is not of African descent. That would clearly be historically inaccurate. Slavery is merely one of the most brutal methods by which some humans utilize power to force others to produce for them.

Slave labor, like other labor categories, carries specific values and hence elicits specific responses from those who are not slaves. Thus, regardless of who the occupants of that labor category are or have been,

131

the manner in which they are viewed and valued within the society will be similar (Davis, 1966).[2] The equating of African with slave in the consciousness of the U.S. population therefore camouflages the link between structural position and the social values that become attached to groups. This indicates that social values are independently attached to the slave structural slot, but not to groups occupying that slot. This understanding has important implications for our sense of the role of social structures in the creation and transformation of group identities.[3] Equally important is that as Africa became merged with slavery as dark, dumb, nonhumans and contrasted with the merger of European and free laborers as light, smart, humans, the hierarchical structure of U.S. society became less apparent and social value was read from skin pigments as well as from structural slots. But responses to structural slots common to all human beings became secondary, while skin pigmentation became a primary sign. It was as a result of this transformation that the United States became a racially defined society.

Social scientists have accepted this transformation, thereby assuming that race is a natural category that can legitimately be utilized to explain social inequality. As long as race and ethnicity are used within the social sciences in this manner, the impact of stratification (inequality) in the United States is obscured. This occurs whenever the classification of a population is assumed to be primordial rather than based upon their structural position within a social system. Such a disjuncture provides the basis for the notion that any sample of individuals that carries the primordial mark reflects the totality of that population.

The process by which primordial marks become dominant can abstractly be characterized as the transformation of the part into the whole (Marx, 1974; Weber, 1978).[4] The part has also been expanded into the whole in the case of European ethnic groups. For example, the expulsion of a portion of the peasantry from Ireland has become the "Irish migration" and this has allowed social scientists to contrast the Irish with native Protestant Americans.[5] The social inequalities within Ireland that resulted in the expulsion of one sector of the society are thus ignored in such an analysis. Likewise, social inequality within the United States is dismissed when a homogenous native Protestant population is characterized as structurally above the homogenous Irish population.

In the context of the movement of Europeans to the United States, the historical basis of their migration also becomes obscured when the part is transformed into the whole. The possibility of developing sociological theories that are truly social is thus at risk. By truly social I mean theories that are concerned with how similar social structures produce similar responses among different classifications of human beings. Instead, the conceptual shift discussed above has resulted in the generation of theories that are assumed to be concerned with the responses to different primordial groups of humans to each other. This latter approach emphasizes marks as natural, thus ignoring their use by a society as forms of classification that assign people to specific slots within the society. In this approach, what needs to be explained is precisely taken for granted as the point of departure of theory development.

The same logic stands behind the idea that the mass movements of people from all European countries was a voluntary migration. The Irish case, however, clearly demonstrates that such a characterization is not accurate.[6] The movement of immigrants from Ireland during the nineteenth century was not involuntary in the same way that the trade in people from Africa was. It was, nevertheless, involuntary because economic forces generated conditions that confronted many people from the lower social group in Ireland with the prospect of starving to death. Those forces simultaneously gave those who were able to stay the opportunity to acquire land. Economic forces could not have pushed people out of Africa from the seventeenth to the early nineteenth century because during that period the region was not dominated by a capitalist system. As a result, the upper group could not use economic force to increase its economic and political power by shipping out the surplus labor force. As long as the general population had access to the land, they were protected against economic, although not military, coercion.

Economic coercion worked in Ireland during the nineteenth century because most of the native Irish had not owned land since the beginning of the eighteenth century. As the new owners of the land found themselves being moved toward a peripheral capitalist society, the rural population became increasingly vulnerable to forms of economic sanctions. Large landowners were even able to take access to the land away from the poor native Irish population. These sanctions were exercised in cycles. When profits were to be had from granting laborers access to the land, it was given to them. On the other hand, when utilizing the land for cattle and sheep was more profitable, people were pushed from the land.

After the Act of Union (1800) and even more so after the end of the Napoleonic Wars in 1815, there were increased expulsions of the poor native Irish from the land. Famine resulted from the combination of such expulsions, a decrease in wage labor opportunities in Ireland, and the economic downturn in England and the world economy at large. These factors provided the large landlords with the opportunity to expel the peasantry from Ireland.

Historical evidence suggests that the famine could have been contained and thus the extent of the migration could have been limited. Indeed, public actions could have been taken to meet the needs of that sector of the Irish population that was affected by the potato blight. The

English Parliament could have provided emergency relief for those in need without the passage of the Quarter Acre Act. After emergency relief was granted, land could have been redistributed to expand the tiny plots that were only capable of supplying potatoes, thus providing a more diversified food base for the rural poor.

There also could have been efforts to expand the economy so that more jobs could have been made available for the poor. All of these actions were possible, but they were not probable, because the general public would have had to pay for the measures through taxes. In addition, these measures were not in the interest of the large landlords and merchants who were the dominant forces in English and Irish politics. It is thus not surprising to find few indications that those who migrated did so as a first choice. They were clearly forced to migrate by economic and political factions that were stronger than they were.

Thus, our notions of voluntary and involuntary migration have to be reassessed. The best way to do so is by looking at the mass movements of people to the United States within the context of the world capitalist system. The migration from Ireland appears voluntary only if compared to the specific military form of the trade in people from Africa. The economic character of the movement of people out of Ireland during the nineteenth century depended on the peripheral status of Ireland within the capitalist system of surplus extraction and thus affected a specific population. Similarly, the military character of the movement of people out of Africa depended on the link between the capitalist system of surplus extraction in Europe and the long-distance trade and tribute-paying system of surplus extraction in Africa. In both cases the mass movement of people out of their societies was involuntary, one by military force, the other by economic force. The two reflect the different methods by which surplus was extracted within the societies from which the migrants came.[7]

We live in a world composed of people who look different from each other. Different societies may have different methods of organizing production and extracting surplus for the maintenance of the upper groups. As the capitalist method of production has expanded, it has linked up with and transformed all other methods of production, creating a world capitalist system. An offshoot of that system has been the creation of societies, such as the United States, composed of the diverse peoples of the world.

The previous analysis suggests the conceptual problems associated with the utilization of racial and ethnic classifications as independent units of analysis to explain social relations within the United States. Such an approach ignores the class origins and hierarchical structure that exist in U.S. society. It also ignores the fact that the mass movement of people to the United States occurred in waves consisting of individuals with similar physical features (skin pigment in particular), but most important, with similar economic, political, and social power. Why similar physical and cultural types occupy specific labor categories within the society must then be explained by considering the fact that the logic of the groups with economic and political power in the societies from which the migrants came led them to expel members of the weaker groups on a mass basis. To this we must add the need for large numbers of laborers in the United States.

Focusing upon similarities of physical type has led social scientists, as much as laypersons, to believe that physical and cultural features are the bases by which people become available as specific types of laborers. This easily leads to the further assumption that those features are the bases for social interactions within societies where race and ethnicity are accepted forms of identification. The racial/ethnic approach has thus generally obscured the importance of analyzing the social structures out of which people have come as well as the social structures to which they have moved. This incomplete approach can be rectified by studying the creation of specific social structures to understand the attitudes that are attached to specific physical and cultural features. Furthermore, such an analysis must be done both at national and international levels.

Studying the development of racial and ethnic attitudes about Africans and the Irish in the United States will help us understand the relationship between negative attitudes and slot assignment. It is significant that those attitudes were developed about all Africans and all Irish whether or not they were in the United States. A distinction has not been made between individuals from Africa and Ireland who were pushed and pulled to this society and those in Africa and Ireland who benefited from it. In the same way, developing differences within those populations that became a part of U.S. society have not been integrated into the mind set of the culture.

In a sense, racial and ethnic attitudes have legitimated forms of power and domination by emphasizing pigmentation, religion, and culture, all of which can obscure the existence of the social structure that provides social value to its members. We see this in the process by which labor categories (class position and structural position), once transformed into racial and ethnic categories, have developed over the history of this society. The following sections will illustrate this process as it applies to people of African descent and people of Irish descent in the United States by looking at the changing attitudes toward them within a historical perspective.

Changing attitudes toward African-Americans in the United States

There are three basic and interconnected assumptions (reflecting the period of slavery to the present) underlying the negative attitudes that exist toward African-Americans in the United States. First is the assumption that people of African descent are a homogenous, natural group (a race) that is inferior to the homogenous, natural European group (another race). As such, those of African descent are not quite members of the human group. Slavery could be justified through this assumption. The next assumption is that the inferiority of those of African descent remains, but their humanity (as a distinct racial group) is granted. Within this frame of reference, the inferior population is only qualified for poorly compensated jobs and the resulting poor quality of life that comes with it. The third and most recently developed assumption does not even rest upon inherent inferiority. There is the notion that people of African descent (as a race and like other races) should be eligible for good jobs and a good quality of life. But this modern view rests upon the assumption that those of African descent (as a race) are less qualified for good jobs than are those of European descent (as a race). It is these racially based assumptions that have been used to justify the unequal treatment of African-Americans in U. S. society.

Critical to these assumptions is the notion that people of African descent are a primordial group with homogenous intellectual, emotional, and physical traits. The same is assumed to be true for Europeans when they are compared with Africans (Weber, 1978, Volume 1: 385). Once this notion became fully developed and was incorporated into the collective consciousness, the mechanism of reallocating specific people to specific structural slots within the society was fully legitimated. Such a homogenizing/lumping process has resulted in one of the most fundamental distortions of the human reality in contemporary society.

During the Colonial period, the use of sectors of the African population as slaves was sometimes justified by reference to the Bible (Ruchames, 1969:56). One such defense was taken from Leviticus 25:44 of the Old Testament, which states: "Both thy bond men, and thy bond maids which thou shalt have shall be of the Heathen, that are round about you: of them shall you buy bond men and bond maids" (Harper, 1968:16). The key word in the above quote is *Heathen*. Even though there is no overt reference to race, Native Americans and later Africans became equated with Heathen. In fact, the word was used in the early charters given to the English settlers to justify taking land from the native population and later to justify slavery.

The general logic implied that as long as a group could be viewed as fundamentally different from the dominant group, any acts could be committed against them. The essential premise was that physical and cultural differences create different types and levels of human beings. This lumping process, which still persists, shifts our attention away from the existence of diversity in humanity as a whole and toward the classification of groups in similar structural positions in a society.

The use of the assertion that Africans were subhuman to defend slavery became more specific during the period leading up to and including the Revolutionary War. This occurred at the same time that slavery replaced indentured servitude as the dominant form of unfree labor. During this period, there was a shift in emphasis away from oblique passages in the Bible (which did not include explicit references to Africans) to specific assertions about conditions in Africa, suggesting that slavery was a form of advancement for all Africans. One such defense was written in 1773 by Richard Nisbet, a former slave owner from the West Indies. He asserted that one need only look at the physical differences between Africans and slaves in the United States to see the value provided by slavery for those enslaved (Ruchames, 1969:144).[8]

The argument claimed that Africans were being rescued from the misery and brutality of their societies. It was felt that slavery, even though harsh, served a positive function because it helped make Africans human. The justification of the exclusive use of Africans as slaves therefore necessitated the creation of an image that presented all African societies and individuals as identical, as uncivilized, and as experiencing an earlier stage of human development when compared to European societies and people.[9]

These ideas can be illustrated in the classic notion of the duality of good and bad. Good was light, human, and Christian, while bad was dark, uncivilized, and heathen. When these notions were applied to society, there was no sense of social structures influencing position or values, only idealized images. Those idealized images supposedly interacted with each other based upon their innate human capacities so that the good, high, and light group would naturally win over the bad, low, and dark group. This type of mystification parallels the glorification of domination in terms that cleanse the actions of real human beings. Its ultimate result is the creation of racial and ethnic identities (Weber, 1978).

Between the 1830s and the Civil War, the justifications for slavery took two directions. The idea that Africans had been rescued from the savagery of Africa continued, while a new notion developed suggesting that free Africans in the United States were worse off than those who were slaves. This again was viewed as proof of the value of slavery (Ruchames, 1969:390). This later development can be seen through the words of Henry Clay, who relied upon statistics from the 1840 census to support his assertion that the mental and physical conditions of slaves were better than those of free Black men and women. Even though these statistics were later shown to be grossly incorrect, the notion that slavery was good for Africans in the United States remained a common one (Ruchames, 1969:393–400).

Once the legal structure made slavery an inheritable condition based upon skin pigmentation, there was a clear need to keep individuals of African descent out of mainstream society. After all, if there were visible Africans who were successful, either intellectually or economically, the good (successful), civilized, light image versus the bad (unsuccessful), uncivilized, dark image would not be effective in justifying the exclusive use of Africans as slaves. The rise of the antislavery movement made that exclusion and its defense even more vital for slaveholders. Given an ideology that justified the peopling of the slave slot by the uncivilized state of Africans, evidence of their ability to function in *civilized* society became an important argument for those who were against slavery.

The antislavery movement began its major push during the 1830s. Along with the increasing conflict between Western farm and Northern industrial interests on the one hand and Southern farm and merchant interests on the other, the movement forced the defenders of slavery to justify the utilization of Africans in that labor slot in ways different from the argument that "things are better in America than in Africa." Therefore, during this period we find assertions that Black laborers should not compete with White laborers. This implied that there should always be some mechanism to exclude African-Americans from the general labor force. The most rigid form of this discourse crystallized in the notion that "slavery is the Negro system of labor."[10]

After the Civil War the defense of slavery was replaced by the defense of segregation, the separation of the races. We can see that this shift was a method of continuing those benefits to the more powerful economic and political group in the United States that had been earlier derived from the prevention of competition between Black and White labor.[11] The strength of the new image was rooted upon the interests of the Southern landowners who still needed a cheap agricultural labor force. It should be kept in mind that this image was supported by many European immigrants who, as small farmers and laborers, feared the potential competition that the freed slaves might bring. By insisting upon the exclusive use of African-Americans in certain sectors of the society the implication was that European-Americans had unlimited access to the other areas.

The attitude that African-Americans were only capable of being slaves and that they benefited from the civilizing process of slavery gave way to the more straightforward assertion that those identified as Whites should be able to monopolize all well-paying jobs in the society. This was clearly an economic issue. White laborers were supported in monopolizing the well-paying jobs in return for supporting White landowners in their continuing monopoly over the labor force of those who were excluded from the wage labor system. Exclusion based upon skin pigmentation was thus, in this instance, the exercise of power in the distribution of societal resources rather than another manifestation of *primordial race reactions*.

The period between the end of the Civil War and the end of World War I was characterized by the use of pseudoscientific justifications for the segregation of the African-American population. The major shift in the discourse was from the assertion that African-Americans were not human toward the assertion that African-Americans as a race were human but of an inferior caliber when compared to the White race. This notion followed the movement of most African-Americans out of slavery, while at the same time many were confined to forms of labor not far removed from it (Du Bois, 1977). In this manner the continued exclusion of African-Americans from social, political, and economic equality in the society was justified. It is interesting, however, that the economic, social, and political benefits gained from this exclusion by some sectors of the society are rarely mentioned in historical or sociological accounts of race and ethnic relations. Instead, the emphasis is placed on the psychological consequences of exclusion for Blacks.[12]

Belief in the physical and mental inferiority of the African-American population, along with the resulting social aversion to that population, were the dominant attitudes after the legal ending of slavery (Bean, 1975:46; Shaler, 1968:54). This was primarily a period of segregation with serious attempts by the landowners to keep the African-American population on the land in the South. In addition, rights that were granted immediately after the end of the Civil War were taken away from African-Americans. The historian Hubert Bancroft (1968:83) justified that treatment by stating:

As a laborer, bond or free, the Negro is of economic value only in certain localities and under certain conditions. The labors must be agricultural and upon a large scale, so that he can be worked in gang under the eye of an overseer. The cotton and tobacco field of the south alone meet his requirements. In the plantation life alone he finds happiness. . . . He depends upon the white man to do his mental work, his thinking and managing for him, preferring himself only to serve. He is by nature and habit a servant, not alone because of his long period of enslavement, but because of his mental inferiority.

In the above statement, there is a willingness to grant "freedom" to "Negroes" in the United States, but their place is defined by self-serving notions about where they would be most happy.[13]

Concern for the well-being of the African-American was always asserted, but with a clear insistence upon the need for a definite (i.e., limited) place for all people of African descent. Thus, there was absolutely no place for diversity within this group. There was no room for the many who had creative, scientific, and artistic skills. There was no room for those whose desires transcended performing backbreaking work that only benefited others. Nonetheless, this notion was accepted as fundamentally valid. Once again race hid the specific interests of those occupying the upper structural slots of the stratified social system.[14]

The Jim Crow laws and the separate but equal accommodations put in place at the end of the nineteenth and the beginning of the twentieth centuries were legal efforts to reestablish the economic, political, and social boundaries that were disrupted during Reconstruction. Park insightfully characterized the stabilization of such boundaries as a process of accommodation. As such, he was clear that accommodation would be manifested as the negation of competition (Park, 1950). The fact that race was the basis of this effort after Reconstruction is related to the fact that race had earlier been established as the mechanism used to legitimate the monopoly over those areas of society.

The striking down of the separate but equal laws during the 1950s and 1960s occurred when the African-American population was leaving agricultural and nonwage labor jobs to become urban wage laborers. As they moved into the urban areas, primarily as cheap unskilled workers, their status finally (but approximately one hundred years later) became similar to that of the European ethnics who migrated to the United States during the nineteenth and early twentieth centuries.

Similar, however, only refers to their common structural position as cheap unskilled workers. Indeed, because of the time difference, there were fundamental differences between the two groups. Chief among them are the different stage of development of the U.S. economy and the world economy and the fact that the latter period had a more rigidly structured labor force for newcomers to compete within. Not only was the U.S. economy growing at a slower rate during the 1950s and 1960s, but there were more impediments to obtaining work because of the rise of labor unions. By the 1950s, unions acted as monopoly institutions protecting those racial and ethnic groups with seniority and denying access to those without it.

Structural characteristics such as the existence of seniority lists and a slowly expanding economy have not had sufficient impact upon popular thought or the social analysis of race relations and social mobility. Instead, the more popular notion is that the European ethnics provided the permanent technique by which to move up the socioeconomic ladder of society. The ability of the ethnics to work their way up has been given stronger weight because the African-American population has been in the society for a longer period of time (Greeley, 1971). In any legitimate analysis, however, we cannot compare African-Americans and European immigrants and their descendants without taking the late arrival of most African-Americans as urban wage laborers into account. Late arrival into the wage labor category was in fact more significant for life chances than was late arrival into the society itself.[15]

As they became a cheap wage-labor force, justifications for the treatment of African-Americans in the United States also changed. The assertions that they were not human, that there existed natural prejudice, or that social aversions made segregation necessary gave way to an emphasis upon ability and motivation as determinants of differential rates of social mobility (Light, 1972). Indeed, after the 1960s, the passage of federal statutes to address inequality in all walks of life was met with the assertion that African-Americans were not willing to pull themselves up by their bootstraps. Those opposed to the new laws have continued to assert that African-Americans have been receiving special treatment from the federal government.

Many arguments against Affirmative Action programs revolve around the notion that the unqualified are being given positions at the expense of the more qualified. This approach is a continuation of the tendency toward linking past and present structural positions with the attributes of those who occupy them rather than recognizing the connections between attitudes and the structural positions.

Changing attitudes toward the Irish in the United States

The negative attitudes expressed toward African-Americans between the 1960s and the present were, with slight variations, similar to those expressed toward the Irish when they arrived as cheap unskilled laborers nearly one hundred years earlier.[16] Wittke (1968:7) summarized the prevalent attitude toward the Irish expressed before the Civil War in this manner: "The Irish image was that of a noisy, ill-mannered, uneducated, hard drinking, rioting individual, who was good-natured but reckless, and thriftless and priest-ridden." Advertisements for help frequently stated, "No Irish need apply," and homeowners in non-Catholic areas would systematically refuse to sell to the Irish-Americans because of the commonly held belief that their presence would have a depressing impact on the value of real estate. Thus, while they remained the dominant urban unskilled labor force, they were viewed as: "People who were hopelessly quarrelsome, verging on social dereliction, and both incapable and undesirous of self improvement" (Wittke, 1968:7).[17] This was the response to the people of Irish descent in the United States during the middle of the nineteenth century. It is interesting to see how their structural position and the attitudes toward them changed over time.

That segment of the Irish population that came to the United States during what has been called the famine migration did not move into the rural areas of the U.S. society in significant numbers. Most of them crowded into the urban areas of the northeastern United States primarily because they did not have the resources to acquire land especially during the closing of the frontier.

The mid-nineteenth-century immigrant population from Ireland was largely relegated to work at unskilled jobs in and around the urban and industrializing areas of the northeastern United States. They initially became the porters, waiters, street cleaners, unskilled construction workers, factory workers, chambermaids, domestic servants, bartenders, and longshoremen in that region. They did the work that required strong backs and brawny arms (Wittke, 1964; Johnson, 1966; Knobel, 1986).

Social scientists who study "native" attitudes toward the immigrant population tend to take these attitudes at face value. Their approach is based on the assumption of the permanent existence of ethnic groups and the attitudes toward them. An indication of how those assumptions about the immigrants from Ireland operated can be seen in historical discussions of the New England textile industry, which was a major source of employment for them.

Using ethnic terms, Ware (1966) asserts that although the *Yankee* population was not willing to accept the terms of employment within the factory, the Irish were. Despite the basic truth of her argument (workers from Ireland did replace native workers), it does not convey the entire situation. That immigrants from Ireland worked in textiles does not explain why that population moved into the textile industry with its declining work conditions. Explanations of why *native workers* moved out of the textile industry must also be scrutinized.[18]

What is missing from Ware's argument is an analysis of the possibilities that existed for those who moved into the factories and for those who moved out. Of vital importance is that those who moved in did not find the kinds of alternatives to factory work that the native group did. Therefore, the alternative positions available to the native population and the lack of such positions for the immigrants from Ireland more fully explains how each reacted to factory work and to each other.[19]

Another generally held belief about interactions between immigrants and natives during the nineteenth century was that the native factory workers were unwilling to work next to those from Ireland (Hansen, 1940). This goes hand in hand with the idea that stresses the centrality of ethnic difference as an explanation for group behavior. For example, Gitelman (1967:253) states: "They [the immigrants from Ireland of the 1850s] were not homogeneous additions to the population. They lacked a shared sense of values with the community at large. They were despised and feared." Were they "despised and feared" because they were from Ireland or because they were a population with few skills for survival in an industrial capitalist society? As long as that question is not asked, as long as ethnic labels and cultural values are used and labor categories are not, it is easy to assume that natives reacted toward the immigrants merely because the latter came from Ireland.

It was certainly true that much of the hostility toward the new immigrants from Ireland came from native workers, but there are structural explanations for that hostility (Bagenal, 1882). One native group was organized into the Know-Nothing Party during the 1850s. The Know-Nothings called for restrictions on immigration, were hostile to the Catholic Church, and wanted Catholics barred from public life. Their ultimate aim was to prevent the immigration of cheap workers who would compete with native workers. But those workers from Ireland who entered the society at the bottom of the free/White structural slot not only had to face the hostility of native workers, they also faced the reality of entering an industrial labor force that was stratified so that they were stuck at the bottom (Aronowitz, 1973:146).

The above instances provide important information about structural positions and attitudes. The antagonism of native workers toward unskilled workers (who came primarily from Ireland during the mid-nineteenth century) took an anti-Irish form, but it was clearly oriented toward protecting economic interests. If those coming into the society had been Protestants from Northern Europe with skills similar to those who came from Ireland, they would most likely have encountered a similar response. This is based upon the assumption that the conflict between the natives and the newcomers was generated by struggles over jobs, rather than by a primordial negative response by one group toward another.

Conflicts over structural positions can easily be transformed into ethnic conflicts because the individuals in competition have been socialized to identify themselves as ethnics rather than as occupants of a specific structural position within a stratified social system. Thus, the confinement of the new immigrants to the lower rungs of the labor market could legitimate the notion that the Irish were willing to work cheap because they had no desire to improve their condition. Again, structural impediments are ignored, whereas the final results are explained by factors specific to the group under discussion.

Toward the end of the nineteenth century, the expansion of the U.S. economy resulted in the movement of a new wave of immigrants to the east coast. Such expansion also provided opportunities for the social mobility of people of Irish descent who had arrived earlier (Thomas, 1954; Aronowitz, 1973).[20] Along with their social mobility, attitudes toward them also changed. The shift in attitudes, however, did not entirely dislodge the Protestants' assumptions that there was something inferior about the people of Irish descent and Irish culture (Knobel, 1986).

We also can observe the continued tendency toward ignoring the links between structural positions and attitudes in the fact that the upward mobility of immigrants from Ireland was assumed to be linked to the ability of that population to assimilate Anglo-Saxon values. The upward movement by Irish immigrants and their descendants was attributed to their replacement of negative values with values that were more conducive to economic, political, and social mobility (Gossett, 1975:138). As attitudes toward the Irish changed, however, the qualities that had formerly been attributed to them were passed along to the new immigrants. Gossett (1975:289) documents the fact that "racial" characteristics that were later attributed to the Italians and other immigrants from southern and eastern Europe were first expressed toward the Irish.

In addition, having made the connections between the Irish on the east coast and the Chinese on the west coast, Gossett (1975:292) asserts that the feelings expressed toward the Chinese were also expressed toward Italians, Jews, Poles, Serbs, Hungarians, Greeks, and other non-Teutonic peoples from Europe who filled those low structural slots that the Irish had earlier filled. He then states: "Frequently the temptation was irresistible at this point to add the bald statement that the immigrant was often defective because of his race and thus he could not be assimilated into American civilization without having a bad effect upon it." It can be concluded, then, that attitudes are often expressed in the form of ethnic and racial tones that imply biological permanence, even though attitudes toward a specific group are subject to change, with some time lag after the structural position of the group changes. The sense of permanence about racial and ethnic attitudes is therefore a social myth rather than an historical reality (Grant and Davison, 1930; Grant, 1916; Morse, 1969).[21]

Conclusion

I have argued here for an exploration of the idea that the development and peopling of structural slots led to the creation of racial and ethnic identity (social value) in the United States. Toward that end I have used as examples two populations who came early to the United States in large numbers and were not landowners or skilled workers. Both instances have helped to show that neither *race* nor *ethnicity* can account for the creation of a surplus labor force in Africa and Ireland nor for the need for labor within the developing United States. As identity categories in the United States, *Black* as well as *Irish,* are sociohistorical creations within the structure of the society rather than natural groups that were transplanted from Africa and Ireland to the United States. The range of social classes encompassed under the identity category Irish in Ireland was much broader than was the group that initially became identified as the Irish in the United States during the nineteenth century. Likewise, the range of social classes encompassed under what became the identity category Black in Africa was broader than was the group that initially became the "Negro" in the United States. More strongly, their creation as identity groups (social values) came, first, as a result of the structural position into which they were placed and, second, only as a result of their pigmentation, or religion, or place of geographical origin.

Because social scientists have paid insufficient attention to the peopling process of the United States, our knowledge of the interactions of groups within the society is distorted. It is not possible to observe clearly the processes by which the movements of people to the United States have taken place without looking at the social structure of the countries of origin of these migrants. Similarly, without looking at the social structure of the United States, we cannot understand the reactions of natives to immigrants upon their arrival or during their movement through the society.

By and large, the literature on race and ethnicity has taken for granted the notion that some Africans were moved to the New World because Europeans needed slave labor, thus resulting in Europeans capturing Africans and transporting them to North America. In parallel fashion, it assumes that the movement of people from Europe to the United States was rooted solely in their voluntary desire to leave their countries of origin because of the possibilities for better conditions of work and life in this country. I have here illustrated that there are indeed some conceptual limitations of this involuntary/voluntary approach to the understanding of the peopling of this country.

I am not, however, trying to negate the valuable contributions to our thinking that have been made by the race and ethnicity literature. On the contrary, the study of how people in the United States at present view themselves and others along racial and ethnic lines has generally been insightful. However, that approach does not clarify the basis of those racial and ethnic attitudes that exist within contemporary America. I have taken for granted that those attitudes are indeed real (i.e., they exist within the current population), but I assert that they result from the negation of the history of the populations that compose the society and hence result from a distortion of the history of the society itself.

The racial and ethnic identities (social values) that we presently feel so strongly in our daily lives are legitimations of, rather than the causes of, specific forms of inequality within the society. This position is distinct from merely asserting that racism is used by the capitalist class as a mechanism to maintain its rule. Racial and ethnic identities are here seen as reflections of the manner in which inequality is socially marked in hierarchically stratified social systems, regardless of whether the social system is capitalist. Therefore, I have stressed the role of hierarchical social systems in Europe, North America, and West Africa. Capitalism is hierarchical, but it is not the only form of hierarchical social relations.

Even further, race and ethnicity have not been taken for granted in this work as exclusively resulting from the domination of one group that can timelessly and universally be physically distinguished from their dominators. Instead, I have proposed that race and ethnicity are the creations of stratified social systems, whether or not there initially were obvious physical distinctions between the dominant and dominated groups. Physical distinctions (social marks) have been seen as historically rooted in the fact that specific individuals populate and function in specific unequal structural slots. In this sense race and ethnicity are instances of that more inclusive form – status categories – that unify sectors of hierarchically stratified societies across class boundaries (Weber, 1978).

The exclusive attention to racial and ethnic identities as presocial realities ignores the domination of one segment of hierarchical social systems by another. Thus, the historical basis for the exploitation of groups that have been classified by physical features can easily appear to be rooted in the attitudes of one *race* or *ethnic* group toward another. This exclusive attention dismisses the analysis of why people who are physically and culturally different from each other ever become involved in the same social structure. Most fundamentally, it ignores the way in which labor is used in society. This results when people – classified by their skin pigmentation and culture – are seen as independent from production and from the competition for resources, whereas their social classification becomes all-important.

In the last analysis, my ideas do not provide a practical solution to contemporary racial and ethnic problems, and indeed that has not been my intent. The possibilities for social change will remain the same with or without these ideas, precisely because they are social facts that are rooted in the hierarchical structure of the existing society. This work does indicate, however, that we can only be frustrated in attempting to think about changes in racial and ethnic attitudes independently of changes in the structural inequality of social systems. This work attempts to move in that direction by providing insight into the basis of racial and ethnic identities and attitudes. By indicating that the pervasiveness of racial and ethnic antagonisms result from how human beings have structured social systems and are not instinctive or innate, we can move away from the sense of hopelessness on the one hand and idealism on the other about social problems. There are solutions; the real difficulty is in our ability as a society to carry them out. However, first there must be conceptual clarity.

Rather than seeing racial and ethnic identities (social values) as primordial, a priori categories, this work has taken the position put forth by Durkheim, following Kant, that our categories of reality are not just in the world, but rather they are "collective representations." It moves one step further by attempting to provide a social basis for those "collective representations." As such, race and ethnicity are cultural reflections of the peopling of hierarchically stratified international and national social systems (Lukes, 1985).

Ultimately, this work is a call for an end to the complicity of social scientists in the reproduction of racial and ethnic identities (social values) that occurs when they are treated as primordial categories, as if their existence is devoid of historical and social structural influences. This approach, at the most abstract level, is directed toward opening up our thinking about how dualistic thinking (good/bad, sacred/profane) becomes manifested as daily realities for human beings.

Notes

1 A critical feature of this discussion relates to the issue of point of view. From whose perspective are good and bad being recorded? The views are basic societal assumptions. But although not all members of a particular society will hold the basic assumptions about a particular group, most will, especially if no time constraints are placed upon these basic societal assumptions. This study starts from the premise that there are fluctuations in the extent to which a specific group is considered good or bad, although the existence of good and bad slots within hierarchically arranged social systems is fixed.

This premise provides us with two conceptual units of analysis. One centers around those individual entities that collectively constitute the whole social system in question. The other centers around structural divisions within the whole social system. In the former case, the entities can fluctuate between being defined as having good and bad social value. The why and how are for the moment being held in abeyance. In the latter case good and bad structural positions are fixed features of the social system. The relationship between the two positions is such that the social value to the entities can fluctuate as the entities move between the fixed features of the social system. The value of the entities is thus assumed to depend upon their place in the social system.

2 Skin pigmentation is shorthand for some combination of skin pigmentation and other physical features generally linked to the head (e.g., hair color and texture).

3 This can be seen in the shift of the Irish from a race to an ethnic group between the nineteenth and twentieth centuries in England and the United States.

4 This assumption also exists within the sociological literature, even among those who are comfortable with the notion of race as a social construct. This will be taken up more fully later in this chapter.

5 The basic idea rests with the definition of race/ethnicity utilized by Cox (1948) and Van den Berghe (1967). Although coming from different perspectives, both assert that race indicates the existence of inequality. Cox more explicitly states that this is an indication of inequality built into the social system. I stress Cox's position, with the added feature that race as we know it is merely one historical manifestation of inequality in society.

6 The important point here is that the literature on stratification basically concentrates upon White subjects and hence there is little discussion of race or ethnicity when stratification in general is being investigated. Investigations of race, ethnicity, and gender are seen as separate categories within that literature.

7 Kardnier's *The Mark of Oppression* provides the appropriate notion here.

My point is that it is difficult for us to see the extent to which *any mark* could be used as the sign of oppression.

8 This type of boundary making creates discontinuity in a continuous world. In this case not only are possible connections among races lost, but the links between ethnicity and race are also lost. Thus it becomes logically possible to analyze each as independent of the other.

9 This is currently the more popular perspective.

10 Although this approach sees race and ethnicity as social constructs of vertically classified social systems, it stresses the process by which such social systems create race and ethnicity.

11 Height, eye color, hair color, and length of fingers, are some of those categories. All could readily be used as marks of race and ethnicity (i.e., as marks by which to place individuals in a hierarchically stratified social system).

12 Thus, this area is relegated to the secondary regions of the discipline. Its status, interestingly, is similar to that accorded to the profane side of discussions of ethnic and racial groups in the society at large.

13 It was commonly accepted that the governor of the State of New York, Mario Cuomo, was a serious contender for nomination as the Democratic National Candidate in 1988. He was an articulate, personable, and seasoned politican who knew the issues. It is not uncommon, however, to have read and heard that being Italian would have hurt his chances of actually winning the presidency if he had been nominated. Similar notions surrounded Jesse Jackson's attempt to be recognized as a serious presidential contender because he is Black. Even the eventual nominee, Michael Dukakis, was seen as having the ethnic liability of his Greek heritage.

14 Despite the position taken by Jordan (1968), even if it is accepted that Europeans as a monolithic group tended to view Africans as a monolithic group, as inferior, the historical evidence indicates that such a view did not immediately result in the domination of Africans by Europeans.

15 Later dominant marks of human value do not necessarily replace earlier marks. It is just as likely that they accumulate. However, there will always be a dominant mark.

16 Commercials for changing eye color, plastic surgery, and growing hair, for example, are very common in all media in the United States.

17 Douglas (1982:67) makes this same point when she states: "The style appropriate to any message will co-ordinate all the channels along which it is given." Channel congruence is also achieved through the process by which attributes that correlate with a specific mark obtain the same social value as the mark. Hence, skin pigmentation and texture of hair are correlated in their social value. This serves to reinforce the notion that race and ethnicity are natural phenomena.

18 It cannot be the case, however, that there will be the same response to a mark in every context. Even in the most rigidly segregated social system, there are moments when the polarities get transformed. When those carrying the negative mark are alone with each other there is no reason to believe that the mark will be viewed in exactly the same manner as it is viewed by those with the positive mark.

19 However, foot size could be made to have social consequences and skin pigmentation could lose its social consequences.

20 When distinguishing features take on a natural tone, the tendency will be to ignore the essentially comparative nature of social value and slip into the view that social value is attributed to marks independently of a measuring process. The issue of *passing* also can be discussed here. Although passing has meant that an individual is acting in a duplicitous manner, it in fact occurs when an individual is acting upon the social definition of human value. Those who pass are in fact exposing the flaws in a system of social values based upon the assumption of natural marks.

CHAPTER 2

1 The central focus for Wallerstein is the European modern world system.

2 This is an instance of how vertical classification is manifested. Power is clearly a critical component in how it is generated.

3 It is worth speculating that surplus flows are functional for the existence of all vertically classified social systems. I do not wish to defend this statement here, however.

4 This division of social systems into two levels is clearly simplistic. It is surely the case that within each of those levels there are many divisions. The basic point that those above will tend to have similar social values while those below will tend to have similar social values still holds, however. In addition, although social systems clearly do not have a point of view, there are indeed individuals and groups within all social systems who do have a degree of control (e.g., through the media) over social perceptions.

5 Keep in mind that it is not being argued that the emergence of the European world system laid the basis for the creation of hierarchical stratification. Rather, the point is that it greatly expanded the size of an already stratified social system.

6 As we will see, however, the impact was far from uniform across all social groups within any particular region, despite the impression given by the use of status group labels such as nationality and race.

7 This statement is similar to the assertion that racial and ethnic groups are interdependent rather than independent categories.

8 They were also producing their own means of subsistence on less and less land. The squeeze was on to use as little land as possible for subsistence production.

9 It was therefore not surprising to find the new elite taking a nationalist position that sounds very much like one that would have been taken by the newly dominated groups in the periphery. Similar terminology (or ideology) does not necessarily mean similar interests, however. The nationalists struggles in Irish history (Catholic, Protestant, secular) clearly illustrates this point (Garvin, 1981; Boyce, 1982).

10 The elite becomes more interested in maintaining links to the world market.

11   The existence of different skin pigments in the world will provide a twist to the straightforward link of structural position in the world system and moral value. However, if there were no skin pigment differences, there would still be vertical classification as long as there are hierarchical social groups.

12   There were plans to push the peasantry of Ireland toward the west coast of the island ("to Connaught or hell") to clear the land for plantations, but this plan was not successful.

13   The existing native populations on the east coast of North America were almost entirely destroyed as their lands were put into production with a world market focus. Those who were not destroyed were isolated on reservations and basically not fully integrated into the national economy. Ironically, the native populations were extremely significant in aiding the survival of the European population, as well as in being one of the poles of a moral (civilized versus heathen) classification that was utilized to build a common European identity (Morgan, 1975).

14   Although the initial plan during the settlement of North America was to look for precious metals, once it was determined that such metals were not available farming became the focus of the settlement.

15   Fundamental to those conceptions is how a group is constituted. Does similar skin pigmentation constitute a group in some a priori sense? This certainly has come to be the meaning derived from the mark of skin pigment. However, this notion, which is premised upon the idea that any common attribute makes a group, is not carried to its logical extension. Do differences, for example, exists among people with the same skin pigmentation? No doubt there are many. Why then were those attributes not agreed upon as the mark by which to divide humanity? Ridley (1986:3), in addressing this issue in regard to biological classification, shows us clearly that decisions about attributes are far from absolutely objective even in a scientific field.

16   The stress upon a sector is important. It will be explored further when we discuss who was made available for enslavement and who was susceptible to be moved out of Ireland during the famine.

17   The issue of different outcomes for African and European elites is certainly important, but that should not stand in the way of an understanding of the process by which the transfer of people occurred. We can, in fact, legitimately separate the transfer process from the outcome. This is so primarily because the process benefited the African elite. They indeed were acting out of self-interest. The fact that they lost out in the long run because of their actions does not then legitimate ignoring their participation in the process of enslavement.

18   This fact may appear trivial, but it actually is a fundamental blow to those who would assert that "races" – not skin color – are natural groups.

19   The point here is not that skin pigment classification is negative and destructive, while other forms of vertical classification are not. It is that people have created hierarchies and can therefore change them.

20   Assignment here presupposes the existence of hierarchically stratified social systems with specific moral value attached to the unequal, but interconnected, strata. It also presupposes the existence of groups with unequal access to

power. In addition, the issue of power is crucial in shifting our focus away from the mark of vertical classification and toward the existence of vertical classification itself.

CHAPTER 3

1 There is much discussion about how differently the two groups were treated, but their legal status is more telling. Some Africans were able to gain their freedom through the legal system, even during the seventeenth century (Smith, 1965).

2 In addition to historical distortions, there was the constant personal problem of where to place those who were the product of a Black/White union. The creation of the mulatto category was the solution. Such a residual category deserves more conceptual investigation than it has received to date. The point is that it resulted from the practical necessity of fitting reality into a rigidly dualistic world view. The placement of Asians and Native Americans was also a problem.

3 It is now generally accepted by scholars that there were African indentured servants in early Colonial America (Alpert, 1987).

4 In reference to indentured servants, Smith (1965:278) states: "They bought and sold them, sued each other for possession of them, and set up engines of law for the protection of their rights in them."

5 See Craven (1971) and Morgan (1975) for additional supporting evidence of such instances.

6 This position is a variation on the enslave-the-different-looking-people argument. It is not entirely without merit, however. Nonetheless, it does ignore the issue that the transfer of people from West Africa on a mass scale required a greater organization than could be implemented by European traders alone.

7 The series of acts during the sixteenth century by the English Crown that rejected Catholicism, then accepted it, then rejected it again were important to the desire of the English for access to the new lands.

8 The impact of the Crown's protection of the wool industry was felt throughout English society. On the one hand, merchants and industrialists gained in wealth. On the other, emphasis upon the production of wool cloth resulted in sheep replacing people on the common lands.

9 Halifax, Nova Scotia, is near that northern latitude.

10 According to Brown (1890, Volume II:15): "John Cabot was sent to America, and charters for discovery and colonizations were granted to him and his sons, and also to Richard Warde, Thomas Ashurst, Hugh Eliot, Nicholas Thorna the elder, and others; but these charters, in order to be 'without prejudice to Spain and Portugal, were above 44 degrees latitude.' "

11 Neither the earlier aim of exploiting the native lands and labor nor the later one of producing commodities for profit is consistent with the emphasis in the present society upon viewing the beginning of English expansion into North America as rooted in obtaining a haven for oppressed religious groups (Morgan, 1975).

12 Although the extraction of precious metals required using unfree labor, a

different system developed to supply commodities for the world market. The first utilized an existing population as unfree labor, whereas the second required the importation of people to fill an unfree labor slot. The persistence of the use of unfree labor does indicate, however, that such a labor form may have been a structural requirement of such systems rather than merely personal desires on the part of Europeans.

13 Connected to this is the fact that the image of English organizational expansion in North America is of a homogenous social structure of small farmers and craftsmen, all on a fairly equal social footing. We will see that this was certainly not the case with the first colony in Virginia, whose structure was highly stratified.

14 People were classified by specific marks, but the underlying function of the marks was to provide a fairly rigid mechanism in order to place people in the different slots within the stratified system.

15 This no doubt also accounts for the mention of gold in Newport's letter. It is therefore interesting that the reports generally circulated in England at the time did not mention that gold was found. These accounts turned out to be correct. Neither gold nor silver were found (Neill, 1968:17–18; Brown, 1890, Volume I:110–13; Osgood, 1958, Volume I:53).

16 This situation in part resulted from the failure of English wheat and other crops to take to the environment. The seeds of fruit and vegetables fared better, but they were not sufficient for subsistence (Osgood, Volume I 1958:39).

CHAPTER 4

1 It should be kept in mind that even after the establishment of a free/unfree dichotomy based on the skin pigmentation mark, those who constituted the free labor slot were not homogeneous in all aspects of their lives. This was especially the case in regard to social, economic, and political factors. The free group thus became homogeneous as a result of the differences in skin pigmentation between the Europeans and the Africans. Other factors that caused inequality within the free group were ignored.

2 See also M. I. Finley, *Ancient Slavery and Modern Ideology* (New York: Pelican, 1980) and Orlando Patterson, *Slavery and Social Death* (Cambridge: Harvard University Press, 1982).

3 Although the lines to the powerful and the high structural slot are not always made clear, their existence is implicit in the notion of low/high and powerful/powerless as interdependent (relational) rather than independent concepts.

4 Once implemented, such land grants were used not only to obtain capital, but also to obtain laborers for the colony.

5 According to Diamond (1958:467):

The full code of military discipline was not worked out until the arrival of Captain Thomas Dale. . . . Dale supplemented the usual list of religious offenses and crimes against the state and the person with a series of enactments designed to protect the company's interests. Slander against the company, its officers, or any of its publications, unauthorized trading with the Indians, escaping to the Indians, theft, the killing of any domestic animal without consent, false accounting by any keeper of supplies – all were punishable by service in the galleys or death.

6   The natives were also to be encouraged to bring all items used in trade to the settlement, thus reducing the settler's work load (Kingsbury, 1933, Volume I:20–2).

7   Tobacco became the first commodity to function as a profitable trade product between England and the colony.

8   The significance of the labor slot in new settlements can be seen vividly if we envision what would have happened in seventeenth-century Virginia (where there was lots of land but few laborers) if sources of labor were not found. At best there would have been subsistence production. More likely, however, there would have been no production and the colony would have failed as it had in the sixteenth century. A vivid image of this possibility is presented by Williams (1966), recounting Wakefield's discussion of Australia. There a planter brought over laborers for his fields. Upon landing, however, the laborers found so much land available that they decide to strike out on their own rather than work for the planter. Thus we can see that there were at least two clearly defined and connected pressures that demanded attention in the developing United States early in the seventeenth century. On the one hand, land had to be utilized to produce commodities and labor had to be assigned to the land. Solutions in both areas were crucial to the survival of the social structure in which skin color became the basis of assigning individuals to the top (free) or bottom (unfree) positions within socity.

9   The assertion that labor was available will be discussed in more detail later in this chapter. It is valuable to keep in mind, however, the fact that such laborers were surplus (i.e., unemployed and underemployed in the English economy).

10   The issue here will also be discussed more fully later in this chapter. With large tracts of unoccupied lands, however, it would have been difficult to prevent laborers from finding and working on their own land.

11   According to Perkins (1980:20): "From a struggling settlement on the verge of starvation and abandonment, Virginia's economy boomed in the early 1620s when the price of tobacco temporarily skyrocketed."

12   Main here uses "White" in its present sense. That was not the case at this moment in history, however. A more accurate term would be "all lower-class European." To the extent that the term "White" existed during this period, it was as in contrast to the native population (Main, 1982:106; Alpert, 1987).

13   In justifying the lack of attention paid to indentured servitude in the United States, it can also be argued that indentured servitude was in fact not as dehumanizing as slavery. Those who were bounded laborers, after all, were only temporarily forced to labor and thus should not be confused with a permanent commodity (Craven, 1971).

This argument certainly has merit. The two forms should not be viewed as the same, and certainly there should be no debate about which was worse. My point goes beyond that issue. It stresses the point that although the two labor forms are distinct, we should not ignore what is fundamentally similar about them. Indentured servitude and slavery are unfree labor forms. This is a significant point within the context of the development of all of the staple-producing colonies. The fact that labor was tied to the land *is* significant, not the degree of degradation involved in the particular type of labor. The reliance upon labor that was tied to the land stands out as an important social relationship for exploration.

14 Not only was the Virginia colony hierarchically structured internally, but it was part of an even larger hierarchically stratified social system, the European world system. This forces us into a set of considerations that are different from those that arise in nonstratified social systems (Wallterstein, 1974).

15 Planters sometimes paid directly for the transport of an individual and obtained land and the use of their labor for seven years. They also bought the contracts of such individuals from a trader in servants. Such traders became influential in the Virginia colony and in some instances later transferred their "talents" to the trade in people from Africa (Smith, 1934–1935; Kingsbury, 1933, Volume III).

16 This point enables us to see the close connecton between indentured servitude and slavery. The existence of a labor contract marked a shift from servants being treated in the English manner to their treatment as property. Galenson (1981:8–9) states: "An important difference between the colonial indenture system and English service in husbandry was that colonial masters were free to sell their servants for the remaining term of their contracts whenever they pleased." Davis (1966:32) adds: "As laws governing chattel property evolved from the earliest civilizations, it was almost universally agreed that a slave could be bought, sold, traded, leased, mortgaged, bequested, presented as a gift, pledged for a debt, included in a dowry, or seized in a bankrupty."

17 The existence of some people in England who could afford to pay for transportation, of other people who were willing to subject themselves to the dangers of ocean travel, disease, and being bonded for between four and seven years indicates that people were moving from one hierarchically stratified system to another.

18 After the shift away from discovering precious metals, the colonial social structure was directly transplanted from England. Therefore, the need to set rigid conceptual lines of demarcation was not great. The need to keep the lower group in its place as laborers remained necessary, however, and was worked out through the legal form of indentured servitude.

19 Women and children are not included in this classification scheme.

20 He continues by describing the similarity between them and the African slaves.

21 According to Coleman (1956:284): "in Stuart England between a quarter and a half of the entire population were chronically below what contemporaries regarded as the official poverty line."

22 This is another instance of a situation in which a systemic need for labor created a social and structural slot that had to be peopled if the society was to survive. These structural slots are at the bottom of the social system. Using the

logic of Schwartz (1981), we have been concerned with the slots characterized as down/bad, not those characterized as up/good.

23 They did not remain important as laborers, but their lands remained critical to the development of the United States. Two centuries later (i.e., the nineteenth century), natives in the plains and the West of the developed United States again served as sources of social cohesion.

24 Stone and Stone (1984:397) stated that the mark of classification within this class context is related to "the privilege of birth." Wrighton (1982:22) saw it as based not only upon birth, but also upon socially produced phenomena such as "conferred title," "wealth," and "legal status." Wrighton's position more accurately reflects the basis of the entire social system in that some social mobility was possible. The mark stressed by the Stones, as they intend, more accurately reflected the mark that distinguished between the true elite and the rest of the society.

25 The notion of the poor as "voiceless" and to be "ruled" did not suddenly disappear as people came from England to the colonies. Hill (1961) pointed out how problematic was the voluntary basis of the migration of the poor: "The poor were treated as utterly rightless. In 1618 a hundred young boys and girls that lay starving in the streets of London were shipped to Virginia."

CHAPTER 5

1 The issue of the shift from indentured servitude to slavery should not blind us to the fact that indentured servitude was an unfree labor slot and that Africans, in addition to Europeans, were assigned to that labor category prior to being assigned to the slave slot. In addition, although the slave labor slot did not immediately eradicate the indentured servant labor slot, such was the case in the long run. We can then legitimately argue that the slave slot reflects a transformation of the indentured servant slot. This is true especially when we see that the type of work done by those assigned to both slots was essentially the same (see Hurd, 1968:220).

In addition to the individual laboring for life, the children of slaves also became slaves. This is certainly not to be ignored. The significant point here, however, is that from the perspective of the landowners who utilized the laborers, the shift from indentured servitude to slavery extended the amount of time individuals were under their absolute control. This perspective is important because we have to keep in mind that the landowners were the actors in this context who were making decisions about labor needs. At this level, there is little if any room for sentiment.

2 This cannot be exclusively the case, however, because the people who filled either slot could be from inside or outside of that social structure.

3 The use of the term *structural compulsion* does not imply that human actors with specific desires were not central here. Its use is important as an indication that actors "act" through existing structures rather than merely out of personal desires.

4 That is to say, this position assumes that there is no need to concern

ourselves much with the social structure of Africa because the power of Europeans, in combination with their attitudes toward Africans, made any positions that the latter group had irrelevant.

5 Winthrop Jordan (1968) represents this viewpoint. He asserts that Europeans already had a negative image of Africans and, therefore, it was "natural" that Africans became the Europeans' slaves. This view is perhaps extreme, but it reflects a common opinion that the assignment of the African to the slave slot was determined solely by Europeans. In more general terms, it denies the necessity of a world system perspective.

6 This easily results from ignoring the possibility of skin pigment as one of a wide range of marks of vertical classification. That is, it ignores the relationship between hierarchically organized social systems and the systematic peopling of the stratified slots of such a system.

7 Though the figures vary greatly, it is safe to assert that between 2 and 12 million individuals were taken out of Africa between the late seventeenth and the mid-nineteenth centuries. Although our present concerns are with those who came to the North American colonies during the seventeenth century, the larger numbers are significant (Williams, 1966; Curtin, 1975).

8 See Chapter 9 for discussions of the Cromwellian settlement that resulted in the indenturing as well as enslavement of Irish patriots. But the need for the labor of the native Irish around the end of the seventeenth century curtailed their widespread use as unfree laborers outside of Ireland.

9 Wallerstein (1974) characterizes a peripheral region as one in which the production of lower-ranking goods occurs. These goods are less rewarded than those produced in core or semiperipheral areas, but are nonetheless deemed important for daily use in the core. External regions, on the other hand, are "those other world-systems with which a given world-economy has some kind of trade relationship, based primarily on the exchange of preciosities, what was sometimes called the rich trades" (p. 302). Although these definitions are too rigid, they do set some parameters for distinguishing between the two. For my purposes, it is best to characterize the difference as one between regions that produce primarily for the core and those regions within which only surplus production moves toward the core. It is in this context that rich trades can be seen as a *specific* instance of surplus exchange, rather than its *only* form.

10 Although notions of labor organization and surplus appropriation are more abstract means of identifying the structure of social systems, they can still provide some connections between structural positions and moral values within social systems. We therefore have not moved away from our concentration upon identity formation and the marks that represent it.

11 Discussions of the relationship between the types of social structures that existed in Africa during the rise of the trade in people also vary in regard to the relevant unit of analysis. Middleton (1966) takes the position that the unit of analysis is regional. He argues specifically for small-scale studies because they are most relevant to precolonial Africa. Anthropologists generally focus upon this level. Amin (1976) takes for granted a large-scale unit of analysis. Meillassaoux (1971) stresses the large scale in his focus upon long-

distance trade. Lovejoy (1979) takes a unit in between the small-scale and the large-scale units for granted.

12   We will see that trading people as commodities became more profitable for the upper group than did allowing traditional forms of production and tribute paying to function as the basis of surplus extraction. Such a shift gave more power to the upper group in relationship to the traditional producers.

The military-political force that was eventually used to trade people as commodities during periods of crisis, in the precapitalist social system, functions in a manner similar to the economic force used to generate the mobility of people to sell their labor power, in a capitalist social system. This has already been touched upon concerning the generation of indentured servants for the North American colonies.

13   We have already seen that this form was tried by the settlers in Virginia with the native population. The term tribute was even used in the "Instructions" of 1609.

14   Again, we can see some similarities between what occurred in West Africa during this time and what occurred later in the Virginia colony. A fundamental difference is that the West African context was between groups with the same skin pigment, whereas the Virginia case involved groups with distinct skin pigment. It is therefore of interest for us to look at how this distinction influenced the mark that was utilized as the mechanism for assigning people to slots.

15   This is not to indicate that individuals who were owned did not work in the household. Rather, the point here is to focus upon the role of slave labor in generating goods rather than providing personal services. Goods can more easily be exchanged than services. The production of goods is therefore important in the development of interactions between communities.

16   There are three reasons why the slave-owning labor form in Africa is not more generally discussed. First, it was submerged by other dominant labor forms and is not always apparent. Second, those attempting to find a singular labor form dismiss it as insignificant. And third, those attempting to view the Atlantic slave trade in a moral light feel that their position is weakened if slavery is acknowledged to have existed in West Africa prior to its link with European traders.

17   See the next chapter for a detailed discussion of the empires of West Africa that were significant to this point.

18   Coquery-Vidnovitch (1976a) distinguishes between direct control in the new states and control by independent merchants over the trade of the old empires.

CHAPTER 6

1   Its ability to influence production and to develop a unified bureaucracy within which revenue was efficiently generated made the Songhai empire attractive as a source of revenue to the Moroccan empire, which was in dire need of resources. The need for resources, ironically, was largely the result of the Moroccan king's successful defense of his empire against the Portuguese toward the

end of the sixteenth century. That defense was achieved at the expense of the royal treasury, however. The attack and defeat of the Songhai empire, between 1591 and 1595, was thus a desperate act on the part of Morocco.

2 The Atlantic route did not require the extensive expenditures necessary for the desert link to European trade. This shift made it easier for smaller state structures to act as power brokers in the Atlantic trade than was the case in the Saharan trade.

3 It also, of course, led to the decline of societies toward the Sahara region.

4 They were based upon military, political, and religious domination. They encompassed classless societies as well as societies that produced commodities for the market. They thus represented that organizational form within which the administrative unit has separated itself from the direct producers (the period during which an upper class develops), but has not yet totally subjugated the direct producers.

5 We have already seen that there had been a continual movement on the part of ruling groups to gain more independence from the direct producers. The most dramatic example of this process was the development of royal estates that utilized slave labor to produce goods directly for the ruling group. Sale of the direct producers was indeed an ad hoc response to a situation in which old forms of trade were disrupted, warfare was rife, and there were decreased possibilities for the development of stable bureaucratic systems. Of course, the arrival of Europeans with demands for various products on the Atlantic coast was also accidental at that historical moment. From the perspective of the ruling groups in West Africa, this process got them out of having to wait for goods to be produced as well as having to rely upon the direct producers for an accurate accounting of tribute.

6 According to an account reported by Donnan (1965:47): "The voyage made by M. John Hawkins esquire, and afterwards Knight, Captaine of the 'Jesus' of Lubek, one of her Majesties shippes, and generally of the 'Salomon', and other two borkes going in his Companie, to the Coast of Guinea, and the Indies of Nova Hispanic, begun in Am. Dom. 1564."

7 Despite the fact that it was a novel, *Roots* has served as a contemporary reinforcer of the notion of the Hawkins-based process of enslavement as the basic form of enslavement.

8 Warfare took the form of traditional battles across groups as well as the taking of individuals without overt military links. War is thus here used generally as the use of force to take individuals against their will.

9 This system of ransom was clearly another means of generating revenue within a situation that was socially unstable. In addition, it was a mechanism by which to again gain some independence from the tribute-paying system proper.

10 Alford's work, entitled *Prince Among Slaves: The True Story of An African Prince Sold into Slavery in the American South* (1977), is an example of how status distinctions operated even after a ruling group member was actually placed in the slave labor slot. It is the story of a West African prince who was freed after 40 years of enslavement. His freedom was brought about by President John Quincy Adams. This story is truly remarkable, but primarily because

it indicates the extreme differences in treatment of distinct status groups from West Africa.

11   This is a very important point. It indicates that making people available for the unfree labor slot in North America was not determined, at its source, by skin pigment. Any argument relying upon skin pigment differences as the explanation for the use of Africans in the unfree labor slot has to take this fact into account.

12   Differences between the English and West African economic structures during the sixteenth and seventeenth centuries tend to lead us away from this important point.

13   Structural similarities between the European and the West African social systems are clear here. Without a demand for labor, the ruling group in West Africa would not have needed to sell the direct producers. On the other hand, if people in West Africa were not expendable (from the perspective of the ruling group), there would not have been a supply of labor available for shipment.

CHAPTER 7

1   World view here means more than an attitude toward organizing land and labor. It also encompassed the actual methods by which the group gained its economic, political, and social status in the European world economy.

2   The significance of this point is that marks of classification are derived from features of those who are assigned to structural slots, but the social value of the marks are determined by the preexisting social value of the slot. Whether the mark will be skin pigmentation or hair color or a tattoo is thus conceptually less important than is the value of hierarchically structural slots in relationship to each other.

3   The antifeudal side of the Puritans and the insistence of the Cavaliers upon feudal relations point to an important aspect of the conflict that would result in the English Civil War (1642 to 1648) and the defeat of the Cavaliers during that period. Despite the contrast between Puritans and Cavaliers in regard to land, however, Puritans (given their support of the monarchy) were moderates in the Civil War. The non-Conformists, under the leadership of Oliver Cromwell, wanted to abolish feudalism and monarchy. As we shall see, the initial success and later failure of the non-Conformists affected the fates of the Puritans as well as the Cavaliers in the Virginia colony.

4   The additional element that transformed that possibility into a reality was the existence of surplus laborers who could be economically transported to the colony. This aspect of the creation of an unfree labor slot can never be ignored.

5   In 1660, Sir William Berkeley returned to office not merely as governor, but as governor in the name of the Cavaliers.

6   This was in contrast to what was possible under the small export-orientated Puritan organizations that had developed previously in the colony.

7   As has been pointed out in the two previous chapters, the use of Africans to fill that permanent unfree labor slot developed for many reasons. It is thus

important to see that the creation of a demand for labor of a particular type can be seen as separate from the availability of the people to fill that demand.

8 This is clearly absurd. If individuals from Africa had not been brought into the colony in the first place, they clearly could not have been able to generate fear. To assert that fear provided the basis for slavery thus clearly ignores more fundamental historical facts.

9 It is interesting, although not surprising, that indentured servitude as well as the Puritan-Cavalier struggles are submerged in our historical thinking.

10 In addition, people from Africa have been excluded from the indentured servitude labor category, and the indentured servitude labor category has been all but lost to our national consciousness.

11 Bacon's Rebellion was an attempt by small landowners and potential landowners to make more land accessible to the commoner population. It took the form of attacks against the Cavalier-dominated council as well as against the Native American population. It ultimately was an attack against the feudal land policies of the Cavaliers. The land policies of the Puritans were more acceptable to the rebels. In this situation, a shift from indentured servitude to the enslavement of sectors of the African population (i.e., the use of sectors of the African population as unfree laborers based upon skin pigmentation) would indeed deflect the rebels away from the Puritan position. Nevertheless, the structural conditions for slavery (regardless of skin pigmentation) were put in place by the Cavaliers. In addition, the large landowners in Virginia could not control the fact that English laborers were becoming less available and that people from Africa were becoming more available as laborers. Nevertheless, the availability of some Africans was crucial to the fact that skin pigment ultimately determined who occupied the slave labor slot in North America.

12 The critical point is that the use of Africans as slaves (despite its prior existence in the West Indies) was hardly a natural process.

13 The Native American population was also enslaved.

14 However, the categories that seemingly define life chances also hide the extent of stratification within the White category.

15 Although these labor forces were legally prevented from competing with each other, their activities had important influences upon each other (Du Bois, 1965). The legal monopoly of free labor by those of European descent led to the development of the sense that there existed White and Black work. This distinction is quite similar to the notion of English and Irish work that has existed in England.

16 The unfree labor system persisted legally until the 1860s. The increasing stratification – reflected in the importation of large numbers of people from different parts of the world, but mainly Europe – of the free labor category was not matched by significant changes in the unfree system. Once slavery was declared illegal and those in the two labor forms were theoretically put into competition with each other, those who were already in the free system had more economic, political, and social power than those who were formerly in the unfree system. During that time the mark of vertical classification became skin pigment throughout the society as those groups with the same skin pig-

ment as the U.S. upper class utilized their economic, political, and social position to battle for social mobility within the free/White category (Knobel, 1986).

CHAPTER 8

1 This assertion can easily take readers by surprise, partly because it goes counter to the notion of European migration as having been voluntary and the movement of people from Africa as involuntary. The important point here, however, is that there were similar processes at the level of U.S. society as well as at the level of the European world system that are lost when global notions such as voluntary/European and involuntary/African are utilized as analytical categories. In both cases, there was a need for labor in the United States. In addition (as we will see more fully later in the example of the Irish), conditions within both sending societies have to be taken into account more fully before we can understand how these particular groups of people became available to fill a labor slot created in the United States. The larger point, however, is that the social value attributed to people characterized as Irish has been created in a manner similar to the social value of people characterized as Black. Both are reflections of the structural slots to which they have been assigned and from which they have been excluded.

2 The distinction used here between peripheral and semiperipheral regions of the European world economy is taken from Wallerstein (1974). In his second chapter, Wallerstein characterizes a peripheral region as one within a world economy that tends toward a monoculture, concentrates on export, and uses forced labor. It is clear that the Virginia colony of the seventeenth century, in particular, is an example of a peripheral region. Wallerstein characterizes semiperipheral regions as those with some complexity of production, where production is for internal consumption as well as for export.

Wallerstein's conception of semiperipheral regions is based upon the European context, in which sharecropping was the characteristic labor form during the seventeenth century. In reference to the United States during the mid-nineteenth century, one can concentrate less upon the dominant labor force and more upon the tensions between those capitalists who were attempting to develop a strong state structure by expanding the home market and those who were concerned with extracting profits from external structures through trade. This conflict was largely resolved by the Civil War.

3 The West during the early 1800s included what are now the states of Wisconsin, Illinois, Minnesota, Missouri, and parts of the Nebraska and Kansas (Lippincott, 1973).

4 Because there were greater technological advancements in England than in the United States, English goods were cheaper than U.S. made products. The English, needless to say, were extremely concerned that access to the latest technology remain in their hands to prevent competition from elsewhere in the world.

5 Alexander Hamilton saw three things that stood in the way of industrial

production in the United States during the late eighteenth century. The first was a scarcity of lands. The other two were the "dearness of labor" and the "want of capital." Under a section entitled, "As to the Additional Employment of Classes of the Community not Originally Engaged in the Particular Business," he states, "in general, women and children are rendered more useful; and the latter more easily useful, by manufacturing establishments, than they would otherwise be" (Cole, 1968:259). It can be clearly seen that the issues of land, capital, and labor, which were critical to the shaping of the actions of groups in seventeenth-century Virginia, remained highly significant – although in a different form – in the United States, even during the late eighteenth century.

6   A similar decrease in the market position of Irish agriculture occurred during the same period and for the same reason; British capital returned to dominate those markets that had been left to investors in the United States and Ireland while it was at war with France.

7   In addition, English industrialists eventually invested heavily in the development of the U.S. infrastructure (e.g., railroads), which greatly facilitated the industrial development of the United States.

8   Homespun production was merely one in a series of tasks performed by the members of a household. Production and consumption on this scale was virtually the antithesis of capitalist production. The means of production as well as the labor power used to make the goods were the property of the family unit. This type of production arose out of the existence of isolated households. It was closely associated with agricultural production; the separation of industry from agriculture had not yet occurred. Such production, therefore, tended to persist where markets were scarce and gave way to other forms of production as the population became concentrated and technological advancements increased.

9   According to Aronowitz (1973), the slave population was 30 percent of the labor force of the United States prior to the Civil War.

10   If we look at Ireland and the United States as being part of the same world system during this period, it would then be possible to assert that indeed the labor force was homegrown.

11   Gitelman (1967:238) makes the point that the use of Irish immigrants as unskilled laborers was also premised upon the ability to exploit that labor force without fear of evoking a great public outcry. Such an outcry, he implies, would have been expected from the exploitation of the native-born workers. Although there is indeed evidence of such outcries on a sporadic basis, it was not as systematic as he implies.

12   Speaking of a later period, Aronowitz (1973:151) states:

The consolidation of labor stratification meant that most southern and eastern European immigrants remained at the unskilled and semiskilled levels. In most cases, their native born children did not become skilled workers, professionals, or proprietors. Instead, first-generation workers from these nationality groups re-entered the mills as unskilled or semiskilled labor or became workers in service industries and the public sector. . . . Entrance into skilled occupations was restricted as trade unions established mechanisms, such as separate seniority lists, that distinguished between crafts and the rest of the labor force. Unskilled and semiskilled workers were to remain barred from skilled jobs even when they accumulated seniority.

13 Native-born workers did not determine the creation of the unskilled labor slot, but they were certainly influential in generating an image of immigrants from Ireland that justified their exploitation and the negative social value/identity attached to them during the nineteenth century.

CHAPTER 9

1 The conflicts were often formulated in racial and religious terms. It is curious, however, that the frequency with which such formulations transcended those differences. Premising conflict upon racial and religious differences also does not account for the fluctuations in conflict.

2 Their position as traders allowed some Catholics to gain wealth through illegal activities. This situation created a strain within the society around the social mobility of the descendants of this group. See, for instance, *The Correspondence of Daniel O'Connell,* ed. by Maurice O'Connell, New York: Barnes and Noble, 1973.

3 The ownership of land is the key variable here; it was the source of military and political power, and was obtained by the use of Protestant military and political power.

4 The Catholic majority was excluded from parliamentary representation by the Penal laws of 1695.

5. Again we are faced with the necessity of keeping in mind the fact that the relations between these religious groups are largely determined by their different structural positions within the society.

6 We should recall here the position England held as the exporter of raw wool to Europe at the end of the sixteenth century. In that position it was economically obvious to its merchants and manufacturers that the major profits in the industry were in providing finished goods for the world market, rather than as the providers of raw wool to the manufacturers.

7 The fact that the wool industry was also important to the Irish economy does not seem to have mattered.

8 According to Murray (1907:57): "This Act of 1698 imposed an additional duty of 4 shillings for every 20 shillings in value on broadcloth exported out of Ireland, and 2 shillings for every 20 shillings in value on all manufacturers of new drapery, friezes only excepted, to be imposed from the 25th of March, 1699, to the 25 of June, 1702." Despite the limit on the tariffs, it was clear that they would greatly restrict the wool industry in Ireland.

9 It is here that we begin to see signs of migration from Ireland to the United States. It is too often the case, however, that no distinction is made between this population and those who came after the famine; all were characterized as Irish.

10 Old English here refers to Catholics who left England for Ireland prior to the English Civil War.

11 The situation and its intent are well described by Cairnes (1967):

In the early and rude state of society, the expedient used by landed proprietors to get rid of the task of raising food for their laborers is as follows: They set aside for their [the laborers] use a portion of their estate, and leave them to extract their own subsistence from it at their own risk; and they [the landlords] exact as a rent for the land thus abandoned, a certain quantity of labor to be employed upon the remaining portion of the estate (1967:165).

Woodham-Smith (1962:82) adds: "The potato, not money, was the basic factor by which the value of labor was determined."

12   Hueckel (1976) notes that the price of corn and other provisions (i.e., beef, mutton, pork, and butter) rose significantly during the Napoleonic Wars.

13   Fewer workers were needed to operate them than to construct them. This fact became significant later in the nineteenth century.

14   Cullen (1972:100) states that "the years from 1793 to 1815 were the culminating phase of a long wave of expansion going back to the 1740s."

15   O'Brien and Thomas (1972:526) state: "In the early years of the 19th century, the need for a circulation medium was so little felt by a great part of the people that practically no currency circulated in the country districts of Ireland. The vast majority of the population consisted of the families of cottiers and very small farmers, and such families were for the most part self-supporting."

16   Freeman notes (1957:41): "Four-fifth of the population in 1841 lived outside towns or villages and were in theory supporting themselves on the land, as farmers or labourers."

17   McNeill (1947) states: "A heavier initial population and a more limited natural wealth combined to bring the population [of Connaught] to the margin of subsistence sooner than in other parts of Ireland."

18   Despite the debate concerning the extent of consolidation, all agree that there was indeed an increase in consolidation after 1815. The debaters tend to see land subdivision and consolidation as mutually exclusive. Both the Poor Inquiry of Ireland (1836) and the Devon Commission (1845) reported an increase in subdivisions as well as consolidation, but stress was put upon the continuation of subdivision. Connell (1950:192) states that unemployment and unfavorable landholding arrangements (e.g., tenancy at will, yearly tenancy, etc.) increased as competition for the little remaining land increased.

19   Cullen (1972:21) states:

The potato diet appeared first among cottiers and labourers, and never came to dominate the diet of farmers in any part of Ireland. Again, the tenant farmer did well from rising prices. The cottier or labourer, on the other hand, often had to pay a competitive rent for his plot without in many instances the compensation of higher money wages or more regular employment.

CHAPTER 10

1   There were many debates in the British Parliament on this subject before as well as after the Act of Union went into effect. See *Hansard's Parliamentary Debates,* 2nd series, 1798 to 1850 passim.

2   Hamilton's cry for laborers in the United States came during this same period. The conditions for the import and use of wage laborers in the society were not yet in place, however (see Chapter 8). It should also be clear that the situation facing the rural population in Ireland during this period was similar

to the situation faced by the rural population in England during the late six-teenth and early seventeenth century. One significant reason for the differ-ences of outcome is that until manufacturing could be developed the upper groups of England were able to utilize colonies as an outlet for their surplus populations.

3 Torrens did not think that the seasonal migration of Irish laborers to England and Scotland was sufficient to meet the needs of Ireland or England. He felt that permanent migration from Ireland would solve the problem and that such a permanent migration should not be to England, which did not meet his surplus land criterion.

4 General reports of hostilities by Scottish and English laborers toward Irish laborers on the grounds of competition do not become prevalent until the later 1820s and early 1830s (Freeman, 1957:45). But it was well known that the poor rates decreased wages, while population growth and military demobiliza-tion worsened unemployment and underemployment after the Battle of Water-loo. Torrens's presentation of labor conditions therefore has ample grounding (Hobsbawm and Rudé, 1968).

5 "Substance of a Speech Delivered by Col. Torrens in the House of Com-mons: 15th of February 1827, on the Motion of the Rt. Hon. Robert Wilmont Horton, for the Reappointment of a Select Committee on Emigration from the United Kingdom" (Robbins, 1958:151).

6 According to Robbins (1958:289): "In Ireland, a main cause of excessive population is excessive subdivision." This point ultimately, though unintention-ally, fits into the general Malthusian notion that subdivision, by providing a plot of land and a hut for the children of the Irish poor, leads to early marriage and thus to a lack of moral restraint.

7 O'Rourke (1875:487) states:

Within the decade of years comprised between 1831 and 1841, emigration was at its minimum in 1838, the number that left our shores [Ireland] in that year being only 14,700; it rose to its maximum in 1841, namely 71,392. It rose still higher in 1842, the emigrants of that year being set down at 89,686. The year 1843 was named by O'Connell the Repeal Year; the people were filled with the hope of soon seeing a parliament in College Green, and to this fact may probably be attributed the great falling off in emigration; the number of that year being only 37,509. It increased in 1844 to 54,288; and in 1845 – the eve of the famine, to 74,969 persons. In the year 1846, as might be expected, emigration from Ireland reached a height which it had never attained before in a single year; the number as estimated by the Emigration Commissioners, being 105,955.

There are some differences in absolute numbers between Figure 4 and O'Rourke's statement, but the orders of magnitude are the same.

8 As early as 1829, the Duke of Hamilton (a member of Parliament from Scotland) supported a Poor Law for Ireland for these reasons: "It was a great hardship that the poor of one part of the empire should be thrown for support on another. Scotland in particular groaned under the effects of that system; for there was an immense influx of the poor of Ireland into several parts of that country." In 1830, the Committee on the Condition of the Irish Poor recom-mended emigration as a method of decreasing the number of Irish workers in the

British market (Hansard Parliamentary Debates, 21, second series, March 31 to June 24, 1829:404).

9 We can see that the choice of one-quarter of an acre was not an arbitrary figure when we remember that laborers were generally paid by being given a lease to a quarter of an acre of land to grow potatoes.

10 Between 1841 and 1851, the number of smaller holdings decreased from 81.5 percent of all holdings to 49.1 percent of all holdings. The number of larger holdings correspondingly rose from 18.5 percent of all holdings to 50.1 percent of all holdings. The data are for holdings of one acre and above, but it nonetheless makes the point that large landowners benefited during this period. This dramatic shift certainly parallels the shift in land ownership from the native population to those who came as a result of the Cromwellian and Williamite settlements during the seventeenth century.

11 Many Irishmen joined the British Army during the nineteenth century to survive economically. They were provided with work and food, despite the fact that England was clearing the population from the land.

CHAPTER 11

1 Such an acknowledgment would have made the legitimation of slavery very difficult if not impossible. This does not mean, however, that there would not have been slavery. It does mean that for slavery to exist within any society there have to be mechanisms that justify the notion that those who are enslaved are less than human.

2 Davis points out the connections throughout human history between slavery and the negative attitudes attributed to the people who occupy that structural position. In the United States, the separation between the labor category slave and the African people has not yet occurred.

3 This difficulty in distinguishing between slavery and Africans has been partially responsible for some of the numbness on the part of the American public to instances of slavery during this century in Europe and other parts of the world. It has also resulted in idealizing Greek and Roman slavery.

4 Marx discusses this transformation within the context of the small ruling group, asserting that it rules in the name of the majority. Weber discusses it in regard to status groups. He points out that status groups can encompass various classes. He further states that class identifications become significant during conflict and crisis, while status identifications are significant during periods of social stability. The shift toward race and ethnicity as the significant forms of social identity is therefore not unique to the United States. What is significant here is the form they took. It clearly also means that race and ethnicity are social facts. However, class is also a social fact.

5 A similar phenomenon occurred when the later wave of immigrants from southern and eastern Europe came to the United States. The shift of all European immigrants into the Whites category is another phase of the same process.

6 Some of the immigration from Scotland, Italy, Poland, Germany, and Russia also was clearly not voluntary.

7 This approach not only forces us to shift our understanding of voluntary and involuntary migration, it also makes a significant theoretical point. Because of the separation of involuntary migrants from Africa and involuntary migrants from Ireland, we have been kept from looking completely at the historical data upon which theories of racial and ethnic interactions have been based. Even further, this approach suggests that the tendency to utilize data only about Europeans in the building of sociological theory (non-Europeans are relegated to the race/ethnic area) is extremely problematic. In addition, it reinforces the notion that there are fundamental distinctions between the physically diverse types of human beings.

8 The same idea was expressed by a Harvard student in 1773. His feelings were as follows:

On the whole, since it is evident beyond all controversy, that the removal of the Africans from the state of brutality, wretchedness, and misery in which they are at home so deeply involved to this land of light, humanity, and Christian knowledge, is to them so great a blessing, however, faulty an individual may have been in point of unnecessary cruelty, practiced in this business; yet, whether the general state of subordination here, which is a necessary consequence of their removal, be agreeable to the law of nature, can by no means longer remain a question. (Ruchames, 1969:156).

9 Chapter 2 includes a reference to an attempt made to justify schemes to utilize the labor of Native Americans during the early Colonial period.

10 George Fitzhugh (Ruchames, 1969) states: "Negro slavery would be changed immediately to some form of peonage, serfdom or villienage, if the Negroes were sufficiently intelligent and provident to manage a farm." The implication is clear here; some Africans were enslaved only because they were not capable of performing any other type of labor. Despite the limited freedoms connected with the alternative forms listed above, all rely upon a relative degree of independence in regard to the occupation of land. Yet Fitzhugh insists that the only impediment to these alternative forms was the capacity of Africans.

11 This defense of White labor was one way of connecting the white upper class and the White lower class. In this manner there was the sense that all Whites had the same interests.

12 Weber points out the manner in which forms of economic and social exclusion are justified through so-called natural factors. His insights are vital to the construction of a theory of race and ethnicity.

13 James Bardin (1968:23), for instance, asserts: "First and foremost, the southern man is interested in raising the economic value of the Negro. To accomplish this various means have been adopted, all designed to train the Negro in things of practical usefulness."

14 This ongoing defense of the exclusion of people of African descent from free access to the economic, social, and political arenas of the United States was also implicitly supported by social scientists, based upon the assumptions that Europeans were socially adverse to Africans and had innate race prejudice against them (Odum, 1968:63; Bruce, 1968:70).

15 The point is that the groups can be compared only after they have been on an equal economic footing. The fact that some Africans arrived early has to

take a secondary position to the fact that on the whole that population was excluded from the economic, political, and social arena. Certainly European ethnics were also excluded, but there is undeniably a fundamental distinction between slavery and cheap unskilled wage work. In this regard, attitudes toward the Irish of the 1850s and 1860s could more logically be compared with attitudes toward African-Americans during the 1950s and 1960s. There is the additional issue of slavery in the United States, of course. The lingering effects of slavery were clearly stronger than the effects of migration on those from Ireland who came to the United States.

16   See note 15 above.

17   The similarity in the attitudes toward the immigrants from Ireland before the Civil War and the attitudes toward them in England during the same period has led some to assume that the former was primarily an import from the latter (Knobel, 1986). It needs to be kept in mind, however, that both populations were in the lower structural slot of the societies under discussion. As a result they were subject to the negative social values attached to the slot (cf., Curtis, 1968).

18   Weber (1978) points out that behavior is not necessarily an indication of desire.

19   Steinberg (1982) provides insightful examples of this important point.

20   The Irish moved upward as the Italians and Poles came into the urban areas as cheap unskilled wage laborers. The Irish did not leap over the other northern European groups who were above them in the labor hierarchy, however. They were able to move up, but they remained in the same relative structural position to those who were above them.

21   McCaffrey adds to the notion that ethnic and racial attitudes are passed along. He (1976:6) states that the Irish experience in the urban ghetto was a preview of the experience of almost all other minority groups that followed them into the cities of the United States. The notion that changes in attitudes are related to the greater enlightenment of the population is popular, but problematic, because of the tendency for negative attitudes to be shifted to the new group entering the low structural slot. By concentrating upon specific groups while ignoring the persistence of negative attitudes, we lose sight of what is theoretically important.

Bibliography

Adams, William F. *Ireland and Irish Emigration to the New World*. New Haven: Yale University Press, 1932.

Ajayi, J. F. Ade and Ian Espie (eds.). *A Thousand Years of West African History*. New York: Humanities Press, 1972.

Alford, Terry. *Prince Among Slaves: The True Story of an African Prince Sold into Slavery in the American South*. New York: Oxford University Press, 1977.

Alpert, Jonathan. "The Origin of Slavery in the United States–the Maryland Precedent." In Kermit Hall (ed.), *U.S. Constitutional and Legal History: The Law of American Slavery*. New York: Garland, 1987.

Amin, Samir. *Unequal Development*. New York: M. R. Press, 1976.

Anderson, Perry. *Passages from Antiquity to Feudalism*. London: New Left Books, 1974.

Lineages of the Absolutist State. London: New Left Books, 1979.

Andreano, Ralph (ed.). *New Views on American Economic Development*. Cambridge, Mass.: Schenkman Publishing, 1965.

Andrews, Charles M. (ed.). *Narratives of the Insurrections: 1675–1690*. New York: Barnes and Noble, 1952.

The Colonial Period of American History. 4 volumes. New Haven: Yale University Press, 1964.

Aronowitz, Stanley. *False Promises: The Shaping of American Working Class Consciousness*. New York: McGraw-Hill, 1973.

Auster, Ellen and Howard Aldrich. "Small Business Vulnerability, Ethnic Enclaves and Ethnic Enterprises." In R. Ward and R. Jenkins (eds.), *Ethnic Communities in Business*. Cambridge: Cambridge University Press, 1984.

Bagenal, Philip. *The American Irish*. Boston: Roberts Brothers, 1882.

Bancroft, H. H. "A Historian's View of the Negro." In I. A. Newby (ed.), *The Development of Segregational Thought*. Homewood, Ill.: The Dorsey Press, 1968.

Banton, Michael. "Race as a Social Category." *Race,* 8(1), July, 1966.

Bardin, James. "Science and the Negro Problem." In I. A. Newby (ed.), *The Development of Segregational Thought*. Homewood, Ill.: The Dorsey Press, 1968.

Baron, James. "Organizational Perspectives on Stratification." In *The Annual Review of Stratification*. Volume 10. Palo Alto, Calif.: Annual Reviews, 1984.

Bean, Richard N. *The British Trans-Atlantic Slave Trade, 1650–1775*. New York: Arno Press, 1975.

Bent, James T. (ed) *Early Voyages and Travels in the Levant*. New York: B. Franklin, 1963.

Berger, Peter and Thomas Luckmann. *The Social Construction of Reality.* New York: Anchor Books, 1967.

Berry, Brewton. *Race Relations: The Interaction of Ethnic and Racial Groups.* Boston: Houghton Mifflin, 1951.

Bimba, Anthony. *The History of the American Working Class.* New York: International, 1936.

Black, R. D. Collison. *Economic Thought and the Irish Question, 1817–1870.* Cambridge: At the University Press, 1960.

Blau, Peter and O. D. Duncan. *The American Occupational Structure.* New York: Free Press, 1967.

Boahen, Adu. *Topics in West African History.* London: Longman, 1966.

Bolino, August C. *The Development of the American Economy.* Columbus, Ohio: Merrill, 1961.

Bonacich, Edna. "A Theory of Middle Man Minorities." *American Sociological Review,* 38(5), 1973.

The Economic Basis of Ethnic Solidarity: Small Business in the Japanese American Community. Berkeley: University of California Press, 1980.

Bottigheimer, Karl S. *English Money and Irish Land.* Oxford: At the University Press, 1971.

Bourne, Henry R. *English Merchants: Memories in Illustration of the Progress of British Commerce.* New York: Krovs Reprint, 1969.

Bowen, Frank C. *The Sea: Its History and Romance,* 3 Volumes. London: Halton and Truscot Smith, 1961.

Boyce, David. *Nationalism in Ireland.* Baltimore, Md.: Johns Hopkins University Press, 1982.

Braudel, Fernand. *The Mediterranean.* 2 volumes. New York: Harper Torchbooks, 1976.

Brown, Alexander. *The Genesis of the United States.* 2 volumes. Boston: Houghton Mifflin, 1890.

Bruce, Philip A. *Economic History of Virginia in the 17th Century.* New York: P. Smith, 1935.

"In Defense of Southern Race Policies." In I. A. Newby (ed.), *The Development of Segregational Thought.* Homewood, Ill.: The Dorsey Press, 1968.

Bucher, Carl. *Industrial Evolution.* Translated by S. Morley Wickett. New York: Henry Holt, 1912.

Cairnes, John. *Political Essays.* New York: A.M. Kelley, 1967.

Carmichael, Stokley and Charles Hamilton. *Black Power: The Politics of Liberation in America.* New York: Random House, 1967.

Carrier, N. H. and J. R. Jeffery (eds.). *External Migration: A Survey of the Available Statistics, 1815–1950.* London: Her Majesty's Stationery Office, 1953.

Catlin, Warren B. *The Labor Problem in the United States and Great Britain.* New York: Harper and Brothers, 1926.

Cipolla, Carlo M. (ed). *The Economic Decline of Empires.* London: Methuen, 1970.

Clark, Dennis. *The Irish in Philadelphia.* Philadelphia: Temple University Press, 1973.

Clark, Victor S. *History of Manufacturers in the United States, Vol. I, 1607–1860.* New York: Peter Smith, 1949.

172   Bibliography

Clarke, Aidan. *The Old English in Ireland*. Ithaca: Cornell University Press, 1966.
   In T. William Moody, F. X. Martin, and F. S. Byrne (eds.). *A New History of Ireland, Volume III*. Oxford: Clarendon Press, 1976.
Cochran, Thomas C. and William Miller. *The Age of Enterprises: A Social History of Industrial America*. New York: Harper Torchbooks, 1961.
Cole, Arthur H. (ed.). *Industrial and Commercial Correspondence of Alexander Hamilton*. Reprints of Economic Classics. New York: A.M. Kelley, 1968.
Coleman, D. C. "Labour in the English Economy of the 17th Century." *Economic History Review*, 8(3), 1956.
Collins, Randall. *Conflict Sociology*. New York: Academic Press, 1975.
Collins, Robert (ed.). *Problems in African History*. Englewood Cliffs, N.J.: Prentice-Hall, 1968.
Commons, John R., U. B. Phillips, E. Gilmore, H. Sumner, and J. Andrews. *A Documentary History of American Industrial Society*. 4 volumes. New York: Russell and Russell, 1958.
Connell, K. H. *The Population of Ireland: 1750–1845*. Oxford: Clarendon Press, 1950.
Coquery-Vidnovitch, Catherine. "The Political Economy of the African Peasants and Modes of Production." In I. Gutkind and I. Wallerstein (eds.), *The Political Economy of Contemporary Africa*. Beverly Hills: Sage, 1976b.
   "Research on the African Mode of Production." In I. Gutkind and I. Wallerstein (eds.), *The Political Economy of Contemporary Africa*. Beverly Hills: Sage, 1976b.
Cox, O. C. *Caste, Class and Race*. New York: M.R. Press, 1948.
Craven, Wesley Frank. *Dissolution of the Virginia Company*. New York: Oxford University Press, 1932.
   The Southern Colonies in the 17th Century. Baton Rouge: Louisiana State University Press, 1949.
   White, Red, and Black: The 17th Century Virginian. Charlottesville: The University Press of Virginia, 1971.
Cullen, L. M. (ed.). *The Formation of the Irish Economy*. Cork: Mercier Press, 1969.
   An Economic History of Ireland Since 1660. London: B.T. Batsford, 1972.
Curtin, Philip. "The Atlantic Slave Trade, 1600–1800." In J. F. A. Ajayi and Michael Crowder (eds.), *History of West Africa*. New York: Columbia University Press, 1975.
   Economic Change in Pre-Colonial Africa. Madison: University of Wisconsin Press, 1976.
Curtis, L. P. *Anglo-Saxons and Celts*. Bridgeport, Ct.: University of Bridgeport Press, 1968.
Daaku, Kwame. *Trade and Politics on the Gold Coast, 1600–1720*. Oxford: Clarendon Press, 1970.
Davenant, C. *On the Plantation Trade*. Farnborough: Gregg, 1968.
Davidson, Basil. *The African Slave Trade*. Boston: Atlantic Monthly, 1961.
Davies, Kenneth Gordon. *The Royal African Company*. New York: Octagon Books, 1975.
Davis, David B. *The Problem of Slavery in Western Culture*. 2 volumes. Ithaca: Cornell University Press, 1966.

Davis, R. "English Foreign Trade, 1660–1700." *Economic History Review,* 2nd series, 7(2) 2, 1954.

"Merchant Shipping in the Economy of the Late 17th Century." *Economic History Reivew,* 2nd series, 9(1), 1956.

Davitt, Michael. *The Fall of Feudalism in Ireland.* Shannon: Irish University Press, 1970.

Diamond, Sigmund. "From Organization to Society: Virginia in the 17th Century." *American Journal of Sociology,* 63(5), 1958.

Donnan, Elizabeth. *Documents of the History of the Slave Trade to America, Volume 1:1441–1700.* New York: Octagon Books, 1965.

Donnelly, James S., Jr. *The Land and the People of 19th Century Cork.* London: Routledge and Kegan Paul, 1975.

Douglas, Mary. *Natural Symbols.* New York: Pantheon Books, 1982.

Du Bois, W. E. B. *The Suppression of the African Slave Trade to the United States of America, 1638–1870.* New York: Russell and Russell, 1965.

Black Reconstruction. New York: Atheneum, 1977.

Durkheim, Emile and Marcel Mauss. *Primitive Classification.* Chicago: University of Chicago Press, 1963.

Edwards, Robert D. and T. D. Williams (eds.). *The Great Famine: Studies in Irish History, 1845–1852.* Dublin: Browne and Nolan, 1956.

Engels, Friedrich. *The Condition of the Working Class in England.* Stanford: Stanford University Press, 1968.

Ergood, Bruce and Bruce Kuhre. *Appalachia.* Dubuque, Iowa: Kendall/Hunt, 1983.

Ernst, Robert. "The Economic Status of the New York City Negroes, 1850–1863." *Negro History Bulletin,* 12(6), 1949.

Farley, Reynolds. *Blacks and Whites: Narrowing the Gap?* Cambridge: Harvard University Press, 1984.

and Walter Allen. *The Color Line and the Quality of Life in America.* New York: Russell Sage Foundation, 1987.

Finley, M. I. *Ancient Slavery and Modern Ideology.* New York: Pelican, 1980.

Fisher, F. J. "London's Export Trade in the Early 17th Century." *Economic History Review,* 2nd series, 3(2), 1950.

Fisher, Joseph R. *The End of the Irish Parliament.* London: Edward Arnold, 1911.

Frazier, E. Franklin. *The Negro in the United States.* New York: Macmillan, 1949.

Freeman, T. W. *Ireland: Its Physical, Historical, Social and Economic Geography.* London: Methuen, 1950.

Pre-Famine Ireland. Manchester: Manchester University Press, 1957.

Froude, James A. *The English in Ireland in the Eighteenth Century.* 3 volumes. London: Longmans, 1872.

Galenson, David. *White Servitude in Colonial America: An Economic Analysis.* Cambridge: Cambridge University Presss, 1981.

Garvin, Tom. *The Evolution of Irish Nationalists Politics.* New York: Holmes and Meier, 1981.

Gates, Paul W. *The Economic History of the United States, Volume 3, The Farmer's Age: Agriculture, 1815–1860.* New York: Holt, Rinehart and Winston, 1960.

Gemery, Henry A. and Jan S. Hogendorn (eds). *The Uncommon Market: Essays in the Economic History of the Atlantic Slave Trade.* New York: Academic Press, 1979.

Geschwender, James. *Racial Stratification in America.* Dubuque, Iowa: William C. Brown, 1978.

Gibbon, Peter. "Colonialism and the Great Starvation in Ireland, 1845–1849." *Race and Class,* 17, Autumn, 1975.

Gitelman, Howard M. "The Waltham System and the Coming of the Irish." *Labor History,* 8(3), 1967.

Gill, Conrad. *The Rise of the Irish Linen Industry.* London: E. Arnold, 1968.

Glazer, Nathan. "Sociology of Ethnic Relations, 1945–1955." In Hans Zetterberg (ed.), *Sociology in the United States of America, 1945–1955.* Netherlands: UNESCO, 1956.

    and Daniel Moynihan. *Beyond the Melting Pot.* Cambridge: M.I.T. Press, 1970.

Goodrich, Carter and Sol Davidson. "The Wage Earner in the Westward Movement." *Political Science Quarterly,* 50(2), June, 1935.

Gordon, Milton. *Assimilation in American Life.* New York: Oxford University Press, 1971.

Gossett, Thomas F. *Race: The History of an Idea in America.* Dallas: Southern Methodist University Press, 1975.

Gould, J. D. "The Trade Depression of the Early 1620's." *The Economic History Review,* 2nd series, 7(1), 1954.

Gouldner, Alvin. *The Coming Crisis of Western Sociology.* New York: Basic Books, 1970.

Grada, Cormac. "The Investment Behavior of Irish Landlords, 1850–1875: Some Preliminary Findings." *Agricultural History Review,* 23(Part II), 1975.

Graf, John R. *Economic Development of the United States.* New York: McGraw-Hill, 1952.

Grant, Madison. *The Passing of the Great Race.* New York: Scribner, 1916.

    and Charles S. Davison (eds.). *The Alien in Our Midst.* New York: Galton, 1930.

Greeley, Andrew. *Why Can't They Be Like Us?* New York: Dutton, 1971.

Greene, Evarts B. *American Population Before the Federal Census of 1790.* Gloucester, Ma.: P. Smith, 1966.

Griffith, G. Tabbot. *Population Problems of the Age of Malthus.* Cambridge: At the University Press, 1926.

Hacker, Louis M. *The Triumph of American Capitalism.* New York: Columbia University Press, 1966.

Hakluyt, Richard. *A Discourse Concerning Western Planting.* Cambridge, Mass.: Press of J. Wilson, 1877.

Handley, James E. *The Irish in Scotland, 1798–1845.* London: Cork University Press, 1945.

Handlin, Oscar and Mary Handlin. "The Origins of the Southern Labor System," *William and Mary Quarterly,* 3rd Series, 7(2), 1950.

Hansard's Parliamentary Debates, 2nd series, Vol. 21, March 31 to June 24, 1829.

    Vol. 25, 1830.

Hansen, Marcus. *The Immigrant in American History.* Cambridge, Mass.: Harvard University Press, 1940.

Harper, Chancellor. *The Pro-Slavery Argument.* New York: Negro Universities Press, 1968.

Hartz, Louis. *The Founding of New Societies*. New York: Harcourt Brace and World, 1964.

Hegel, G. W. F. *Hegel's Philosophy of Right*. Oxford: Clarendon Press, 1945.

Helleiner, Karl. "The Population of Europe from the Black Death to the Eve of the Vital Revolution." *Cambridge Economic History of Europe*. Cambridge: At the University Press, 1967.

Hertz, Robert. "The Right Hand." In Rodney Needham (ed.), *Essays on Dual Symbolic Classification*. Chicago: University of Chicago Press, 1973.

Hidy, Muriel (ed.). *British Investments in American Railways, 1834–1898*. Charlottesville: University of Virginia Press, 1970.

Higginbotham, A. Leon. *In the Matter of Color: Race and the American Legal Process*. New York: Oxford University Press, 1978.

Hill, Christopher. *The Century of Revolution, 1603–1754*. Edinburgh: T. Nelson, 1961.

Hobsbawm, Eric and George Rudé. *Captain Swing*. New York: Norton, 1968.

Hollander, Barnett. *Slavery in America*. New York: Barnes and Noble, 1963.

Hopkins, A. G. *An Economic History of West Africa*. New York: Columbia University Press, 1973.

Hoy, Don R. (ed.). *Essentials of Geography and Development*. New York: Macmillan, 1980.

Hueckel, Glenn. "Relative Prices and Supply Response in English Agriculture during the Napoleonic Wars." *The Economic History Review*, 2nd series, 29(3), August, 1976.

Hurd, John C. *The Law of Freedom and Bondage in the United States, Vol. 1*. New York: Negro Universities Press, 1968.

Innes, A. D. *The Maritime and Colonial Expansion of England Under the Stuarts*. London: A.D. Innes, 1932.

Jencks, Christopher. *Who Gets Ahead? The Determination of Economic Success*. New York: Basic Books, 1979.

Johnson, James E. *The Irish in America*. Minneapolis: Learner, 1966.

Johnston, H. J. M. *British Emigration Policy, 1815–1830: Shoveling Out Paupers*. Oxford: Clarendon Press, 1972.

Jordan, Winthrop. *White Over Black: American Attitudes Toward the Negro, 1550–1812*. Chapel Hill: University of North Carolina Press, 1968.

July, Robert W. *Trade and Politics on the Gold Coast, 1600–1720*. New York: Scribner, 1975.

Kanter, Rosabeth. *Men and Women of the Corporation*. New York: Basic Books, 1977.

Kardnier, Abraham and Lionel Ovesey. *The Mark of Oppression*. Cleveland: World, 1962.

Kerr, Barbara. "Irish Seasonal Migration to Great Britain, 1804–1838." *Irish Historical Studies*, 3(9), 1968.

Kingsbury, Susan M. (ed.). *The Records of the Virginia Company of London*. Volumes 1 to 4. Washington, D.C.: U.S. Government Printing Office, 1933.

Klein, Martin A. and Wesley G. Johnson (eds.). *Perspectives on the African Past*. Boston: Little, Brown, 1972.

Knobel, Dale. *Paddy and the Republic*. Middletown, Ct.: Wesleyan University Press, 1986.

Krader, Lawrence (ed.). *The Ethnological Notebooks of Karl Marx*. Assen: Van Gorcum, 1972.

Kwamena-Poh, Michael, J. Tosh, R. Waller, M. Tidy. *African History in Maps.* London: Longmans, 1982.

Lacey, Robert, *Sir Walter Raleigh.* New York: Atheneum, 1979.

Large, D. "The Wealth of the Greater Irish Landowners, 1750–1815." *Irish Historical Studies,* 15(57), 1966.

Lees, Lynn Hollen. *Exiles of Erin.* Ithaca: Cornell University Press, 1979.

Leggett, John. *Class, Race and Labor: Working Class Consciousness in Detroit.* New York: Oxford University Press, 1968.

Levine, Edward. *The Irish and Irish Politicians.* Notre Dame, Indiana: University of Notre Dame Press, 1966.

Levi-Strauss, Claude. *The Savage Mind.* Chicago: University of Chicago Press, 1967.

Levitzion, Nehemia. *History of West Africa,* New York: Columbia University Press, 1971.

Ancient Ghana and Mali. New York: Holmes and Meier, 1980.

Lieberson, Stanley. *A Piece of the Pie.* Berkeley: University of California Press, 1980.

Light, Ivan. *Ethnic Enterprise in America.* Berkeley: University of California Press, 1972.

"Asian Enterprise in America." In S. Cummings (ed.), *Self-Help in Urban America.* Port Washington, N. Y.: National University Press, 1980.

Lindsey, Arnett. "The Economic Condition of the Negroes of New York Prior to 1861." *Journal of Negro History,* 6(2), 1921.

Lippincott, Isaac. *A History of Manufactures in the Ohio Valley to the Year 1860.* New York: Arno Press, 1973.

Lovejoy, Paul. "Indigenous African Slavery." In Michael Craton (ed.), *Historical Reflections* 6(1). Toronto: Pergamon Press, 1979.

Lukes, Stephen. *Power: A Radical View.* New York: Macmillan, 1974.

Emile Durkheim. Stanford: Stanford University Press, 1985.

MacCurtain, Margaret. *Tudor and Stuart Ireland.* Dublin: Gil and MacMillan, 1972.

MacDonald, William (ed.). *Selected Charters of American History, 1606–1775.* New York: Macmillan, 1899.

Madden, Richard Robert. *The United Irishmen: Their Lives and Times.* Volume 1. New York: Tandy, 1910.

Mahdi, Adamu. "The Delivery of Slaves from the Central Sudan to the Bight of Benin in the 18th and 19th Centuries." In H. Gemery and J. Hogendorn (eds.), *The Uncommon Market: Essays in the Economic History of the Atlantic Slave Trade.* New York: Academic Press, 1979.

Main, Gloria. *Tobacco Colony.* Princeton: Princeton University Press, 1982.

Malthus, R. T. *An Essay on the Principle of Population.* 7th ed. London: Reeves and Turner, 1872.

Manning, Patrick. "The Slave Trade in the Bight of Benin, 1640–1890." In H. Gemery and J. Hogendorn (eds.), *The Uncommon Market: Essays in the Economic History of the Atlantic Slave Trade.* New York: Academic Press, 1979.

Marx, Karl. *Pre-Capitalist Economic Formations.* New York: International Publishers, 1965.

Grundrisse. Translated by Martin Nicolas. New York: Vintage Books, 1973.

Capital. 3 volumes. New York: International Publishers, 1974.

and Engels, Friedrich. *Ireland and the Irish Question: A Collection of Writings.* New York: International Publishers, 1972.

McCaffrey, Lawrence. *The Irish Diaspora in America.* Bloomington: Indiana University Press, 1976.

McCusker, John and Russell Menard. *The Economics of British America, 1607–1789.* Chapel Hill: University of North Carolina Press, 1985.

McDowell, R. B. *Ireland in the Age of Imperialism and Revolution, 1760–1801.* Oxford: Clarendon Press, 1979.

McNeill, William. "The Influence of the Potato on Irish History." Unpublished Ph.D. dissertation. Ithaca: Cornell University, 1947.

Meillassoux, Claude (ed.). *The Development of Indigenous Trade and Markets in West Africa.* London: Oxford University Press for the International African Institute, 1971.

Merivale, Herman. *Lectures on Colonization and Colonies.* New York: A.M. Kelley, 1967.

Middleton, John. *The Effects of Economic Development on Traditional Political Systems in Africa South of the Sahara.* The Hague: Mouton, 1966.

Montero, D. *Vietnamese Americans: Patterns of Resettlement and Socioeconomic Adaptation in the U.S..* Boulder, Colo.: Westview Press, 1979.

Moody, T. William, F. X. Martin, F. S. Byrne. *A New History of Ireland, Volume III.* Oxford: Clarendon Press, 1976.

Morgan, Edmund. *American Slavery, American Freedom.* New York: Norton, 1975.

Morse, Samuel F. B. *Imminent Dangers to the Free Institutions of the United States Through Foreign Immigration.* New York: Arno Press, 1969.

Murray, Alice E. *A History of the Commercial and Financial Relations Between England and Ireland from the Period of the Restoration.* London: P.S. King and Son, 1907.

Myrdal, Gunnar. *The American Dilemma.* New York: Harper and Brothers, 1962.

Needham, Rodney. *Symbolic Classification.* Santa Monica, Calif.: Goodyear Publishing, 1979.

Neibor, H. J. *Slavery as an Industrial System.* The Hague: Martinus Nijhoff, 1910.

Neill, Edward. *History of the Virginia Company of London.* New York: B. Franklin, 1968.

Newby, I. A. (ed.). *The Development of Segregational Thought.* Homewood, Ill.: The Dorsey Press, 1968.

Nicholls, George. *The Irish Poor Law.* New York: A.M. Kelley. 1967.

Northrup, David. *Trade Without Rulers: Pre-Colonial Economic Development in South-Eastern Nigeria.* Oxford: Clarendon Press, 1978.

Nugent, Nell M. *Cavaliers and Pioneers: Abstracts of Virginia Land Patents and Grants, 1623–1800, Volume I, 1623–1666.* Baltimore: Genealogical Publishing, 1963.

O'Brien George. *The Economic History of Ireland in the 18th Century.* Dublin: Maunsel and Company, 1918.

and Augustine Thomas. *An Economic History of Ireland from the Union to the Famine.* New York: A.M. Kelley, 1972.

O'Connell, Daniel. *The Correspondence of Daniel O'Connell*. Maurice O'Connell. (ed.). New York: Barnes and Noble, 1973.

Odum, H. "The Education of Negroes." In I. A. Newby (ed.), *The Development of Segregational Thought*. Homewood, Ill.: The Dorsey Press, 1968.

Oliver, Ronald and Caroline Oliver (eds.). *Africa in the Days of Exploration*. Englewood Cliffs, N.J.: Prentice-Hall, 1965.

Omnedt, Gail. "The Political Economy of Starvation." *Race and Class*, 17(3), 1975.

Onwuejeogwu, M. Angulu. *The Social Anthropology of Africa: An Introduction*. London: Heinemann, 1975.

O'Rourke, Reverend John. *The History of the Great Irish Famine of 1847, With Notices of Earlier Irish Famines*. Dublin: M. Glashan and Gill, 1875.

Osgood, H. L. *The American Colonies in the 17th Century*. 3 volumes. Gloucester, Mass.: P. Smith, 1958.

Park, Robert E. *Race and Culture*. Glencoe, Ill. The Free Press, 1950.

Patterson, Orlando. *The Sociology of Slavery: An Analysis of the Origins, Development and Structure of Negro Slave Society in Jamaica*. London: MacGibbon and Kee, 1967.

Slavery and Social Death: A Comparative Study. Cambridge: Harvard University Press, 1982.

Pendergast, John. *The Cromwellian Settlement of Ireland*. Dublin: Mellifort Press, 1922.

Perkins, Edwin. *The Economy of Colonial America*. New York: Columbia University Press, 1980.

Phillips, Ulrich. *Life and Labor in the Old South*. Boston: Little, Brown, 1963.

Polanyi, Karl. *The Great Transformation*. Boston: Beacon Press, 1957.

Dahomey and the Slave Trade: An Analysis of an Archaic Economy. Seattle: University of Washington Press, 1966.

Conrad Arensberg, and Harry Pearson (eds.). *Trade and Market in the Early Empires: Economics in History and Theory*. Chicago: Henry Regnery, 1957.

Pomfret, John E. *The Struggle for Land in Ireland, 1800–1823*. Princeton: Princeton University Press, 1930.

Ramsay, George O. *English Overseas Trade During the Centuries of Emergence*. New York: St. Martin's Press, 1957.

Redford, A. *Labour Migration in England, 1800–1850*. Manchester: At the University Press, 1926.

Ridley, Mark. *Evolution and Classification*. New York: Longmans, 1986.

Robbins, L. *Robert Torrens and the Evolution of Classical Economics*. London: Macmillan, 1958.

Robinson, Olive. "The London Companies as Progressive Landlords in 19th Century Ireland." *Economic History Review*, 15(1), 1962.

Rodney, Walter. "Gold and Slaves on the Gold Coast." *Transactions of the Historical Society of Ghana*, 10(2), 1964.

A History of the Upper Guinea Coast, 1545–1800. Oxford: Clarendon Press, 1970.

Roper, H. R. Trevor. "The Decline of the Mere Gentry." In Lawrence Stone (ed.), *Social Change and Revolution in England, 1540–1640*. London: Longmans, 1965.

Rose, J. H., A. P. Newton, and E. A. Benians (eds.). *Cambridge History of the British Empire*. 8 volumes. Cambridge: The University Press, 1929.

Rubin, Jay. "Black Nativism: The European Immigrant in Negro Thought, 1830–1860." *Phylon,* 34(3), Fall, 1978.

Ruchames, Louis (ed.). *Racial Thought in America. Volume I, From the Puritans to Abraham Lincoln: A Documentary History.* Amherst: University of Massachusetts Press, 1969.

Schaler, N. S. "The Permanence of Racial Characteristics." In I. A. Newby (ed.), *The Development of Segregational Thought.* Homewood, Ill.: The Dorsey Press, 1968.

Schuman, Howard, Carlotte Steeh, and Lawrence Bobo. *Racial Attitudes in America: Trends and Interpretations.* Cambridge: Harvard University Press, 1985.

Schwartz, Barry. *Vertical Classification.* Chicago: University of Chicago Press, 1981.

Scisco, L. O. "The Plantation Type of Colony." *American History Review,* 8(2), 1903.

Scott, William R. *The Constitution and Finance of English, Scottish and Irish Joint Stock Companies to 1720.* 3 volumes. New York: Peter Smith, 1951.

Shils, Edward. "Color, The Universal Intellectual Community, and the Afro-Asian Intellectual." *Daedalus,* 96(2), Spring, 1967.

Smart, William. *Economic Annuals of the 19th Century.* Volume II. New York: A.M. Kelley, 1964.

Smith, Abbot E. "Indentured Servants and Land Speculation in 17th Century Maryland." *American Historical Review,* 40(3), 1934–1935.

  Colonists in Bondage: White Servitude and Convict Labor in America, 1607–1776. Gloucester, Mass.: P. Smith, 1965.

Smith, Adam. *An Inquiry into the Nature and Causes of the Wealth of Nations.* Oxford: Clarendon Press, 1976.

Smith, G. Elliott, B. Malinowski, H. Spinden, and A. Goldenweiser. *Culture: The Diffusion Controversy.* New York: Norton, 1927.

Smith, William. *History of the First Discovery and Settlement of Virginia.* New York: Johnson Reprint Corporation, 1969.

Smyth, George Lewis. *Ireland: Historical and Statistical.* Volume II. London: Whittaker, 1847.

Snowden, Frank, Jr. *Before Color Prejudice: The Ancient View of Blacks.* Cambridge, Mass.: Harvard University Press, 1983.

Sraffa, Piero (ed.). *The Words and Correspondence of David Ricardo. Volume VII, Letters, 1816–1818.* Cambridge: At the University Press, 1951.

Stein, Leon and Philip Taft (eds.). *Labor Politics: Collected Pamphlets.* Volume I. New York: Arno and The New York Times, 1971.

Steinberg, Stephen. *The Ethnic Myth.* Boston: Beacon Press, 1982.

Stinchcombe, Arthur. *Theoretical Methods in Social History.* New York: Academic Press, 1978.

Stith, William. *The History of the First Discovery and Settlement of Virginia.* New York: Johnson Reprint Corporation, 1969.

Stone, Lawrence. "The Nobility in Business." In B.E. Supple (ed.), *The Entrepreneur.* Cambridge: Harvard University Press, 1957.

  and Jeanne C. Stone. *An Open Elite? England 1540–1880.* Oxford: Clarendon Press, 1984.

Stride, G. T. and Caroline Ifeka (eds.). *Peoples and Empires of West Africa.* New York: Africana Publishing, 1971.

Supple, B.E. *Commercial Crisis and Change in England, 1600–1642*. Cambridge: At the University Press, 1959.

Tabb, William. *The Political Economy of the Black Ghetto*. New York: Norton, 1970.

"Race Relations Models and Social Change." *The Society for the Study of Social Problems,* 18(4), Spring, 1972.

Talpalar, Morris. *The Sociology of Colonial Virginia*. New York: Philosophical Library, 1960.

Tawney, Richard H. *Agrarian Problems in 16th Century England*. London: Longmans, Green, 1912.

Terray, Emmanuel. "Long-Distance Exchange and the Formation of the State." *Economy and Society,* 3(3), 1971.

Marxism and Primitive Societies: Two Studies. New York: Monthly Review Press, 1972.

Thomas, Brinley. *Migration and Economic Growth: A Study of Great Britain and the Atlantic Economy*. Cambridge: At the University Press, 1954.

Thomas, W. I. and Florian Znaniecki. *The Polish Peasant in Europe and America*. 2 volumes. New York: Dover, 1958.

Trevelyan, G. M. *History of England: The Tudors and the Stuart Era*. Volume II. New York: Doubleday Anchor Books, 1953.

Turner, F. J. *The Frontier in American History*. New York: Henry Holt, 1920.

U.S. National Advisory Commission on Civil Disorders. *Kerner Commission Report*. Washington, D.C.: United States Government Printing Office, 1968.

Unwin, G. *Industrial Organization in the Sixteenth and Seventeenth Centuries*. London: Cass, 1957.

Van den Berghe, Pierre. *Race and Racism*. New York: Wiley, 1967.

Race and Ethnicity. New York: Basic Books, 1970.

Wallerstein, Immanuel. *The Modern World-System,* Volume 1. New York: Academic Press, 1974.

Ware, Caroline. *The Early New England Cotton Manufacture*. New York: Russell and Russell, 1966.

Ware, Norman. *The Industrial Worker, 1840–1860*. New York: Quadrangle, 1974.

Warner, W. Lloyd and Paul Lunt. *The Social Life of a Modern Community*. New Haven: Yale University Press, 1941.

Weber, Max. *Economy and Society*. 2 volumes. Berkeley: University of California Press, 1978.

Wertenbaker, Thomas. *The Planters of Colonial Virginia*. New York: Russell and Russell, 1959.

Westie, Frank R. "Race and Ethnic Relations." In Robert E. L. Faris (ed.), *Handbook of Modern Sociology*. New York: Rand McNally, 1964.

Willcox, Walter (ed.). *International Migrations*. Volume II. New York: National Bureau of Economic Research, 1931.

Williams, Eric. *Capitalism and Slavery*. New York: Capricorn Books, 1966.

Williams, Robin, Jr. "Racial and Cultural Relations." In B. Gittler (ed.), *Review of Sociology: Analysis of a Decade*. New York: Wiley, 1957.

Williamson, J. A. *A Short History of British Expansion*. New York: St. Martin's Press, 1956.

Wilson, William. *The Declining Significance of Race*. Chicago: University of Chicago Press, 1978.

The Truly Disadvantaged: The Inner City, the Under Class and Public Policy. Chicago: University of Chicago Press, 1987.

Wirth, Louis. "Problems and Orientation of Research in Race Relations in the U.S." *The British Journal of Sociology,* 1(2), June, 1950.

Wittke, Carl. *We Who Built America.* Englewood Cliffs, N. J.: Prentice-Hall, 1964.

The Irish in America. New York: Teachers College Press, 1968.

Woodham-Smith, Cecil. *The Great Hunger: Ireland, 1845–1849.* New York: Harper & Row, 1962.

Wrighton, Keith. *English Society 1580–1680.* New Brunswick: Rutgers University Press, 1982.

Index

183